THE TRINIDAD AWAKENING

Recent Titles in
Contributions in Afro-American and African Studies
Series Advisers: John W. Blassingame and Henry Louis Gates, Jr.

THE TRINIDAD AWAKENING

West Indian Literature of the Nineteen-Thirties

REINHARD W. SANDER

Contributions in Afro-American and African Studies,
Number 114

GREENWOOD PRESS
NEW YORK · WESTPORT, CONNECTICUT · LONDON

Library of Congress Cataloging-in-Publication Data

Sander, Reinhard.
  The Trinidad awakening : West Indian literature of the nineteen-
thirties / Reinhard W. Sander.
     p. cm.—(Contributions in Afro-American and African
studies, ISSN 0069–9624 ; no. 114)
  Bibliography: p.
  Includes index.
  ISBN 0–313–24562–2 (lib. bdg. : alk. paper)
  1. Trinidad and Tobago literature (English)—20th century—History
and criticism.   2. West Indian literature (English)—20th century—
History and criticism.   I. Title.   II. Series.
PR9272.S24   1988
810′.9—dc19   87–31777

British Library Cataloguing in Publication Data is available.

Library of Congress Catalog Card Number: 87–31777
ISBN: 0–313–24562–2
ISSN: 0069–9624

First published in 1988

Greenwood Press, Inc.
88 Post Road West, Westport, Connecticut 06881

Printed in the United States of America

The paper used in this book complies with the
Permanent Paper Standard issued by the National
Information Standards Organization (Z39.48-1984).

10 9 8 7 6 5 4 3 2 1

For Rhonda and Petra

CONTENTS

PREFACE

When I began my research on early Trinidad literature, only the 1971 re-publication of C. L. R. James's *Minty Alley* was readily available to the general reader. In the meantime, almost all the literature produced by the *Beacon* group has reappeared: James's play was published in 1976; *The Beacon* was reprinted in its entirety in 1977; selections from both *The Beacon* and *Trinidad* gave rise to my anthology *From Trinidad* in 1978; Alfred H. Mendes's novels *Pitch Lake* and *Black Fauns* were republished in 1980 and 1984; and Ralph de Boissière's *Crown Jewel* and *Rum and Coca-Cola* appeared in revised form in 1981 and 1984. In view of the renewed interest in the creative writing produced by West Indians before the 1950s, this study is meant as a critical aid for the reader who wants to find out more about the times that produced this particular body of literature and about the lives and works of the writers. In addition, the book is meant as another piece in the critical patchwork which, it is to be hoped, will eventually make possible a comprehensive literary history of the West Indies.

Throughout my research, Alfred H. Mendes, C. L. R. James and Ralph de Boissière, as well as other members of the *Beacon* group, corresponded with me generously and provided me with a wealth of information about their work and about their experiences in Trinidad during the interwar years. I would like to express my deepest gratitude to them, and to the late Albert M. Gomes in whose home in England I spent many an hour drinking rum and listening to stories about the thirties. I would also like to thank my wife Rhonda Cobham for her assistance in revising the various drafts of this study; Bernth Lindfors of the University of Texas at Austin for his continuing encouragement; Pia Treutwein for typing the final manuscript; and Helga Schuster, Stella Ogunyemi, Günter Bielemeier, and David Ackley for their help with proofreading.

Bayreuth, W. Germany
July 1985

THE TRINIDAD
AWAKENING

INTRODUCTION

Until fairly recently it was not uncommon for West Indian writers and critics to speak of their culture in the following terms:

The history of the islands can never be satisfactorily told. . . . History is built around achievement and creation; and nothing was created in the West Indies.[1]

For nearly three centuries the West Indian thought nothing, created nothing, explored nothing. If at any time between Columbus and the Second World War the British Caribbean islands had sunk beneath the sea, the world would have lost little that enriches the imagination of mankind.[2]

Both statements implicitly dismiss the existence of a rich folk culture in all the Caribbean islands, created during the period of slavery and sustained until the present day. Afro-Caribbean forms of dance, music, religion, philosophy, art, and oral literature appeared in response to the demands of the new environment and were used as weapons of protest against the European colonial establishment. Under cultural pressure from their rulers, the slaves and their descendants modified their customs and beliefs, syncretized European and neo-African forms, but hardly ever surrendered the core of their cultural expression. It is commonplace now to cite the example of Haitian Voodoo, in which Catholic saints and West African gods were merged to create a religion and world view that became the rallying point of the first black republic in the New World. The slaves also modified the European languages they were forced to learn, a process which affected the speech of the European colonists themselves.

Since the focus of this study is restricted to one aspect of West Indian culture—the written literature—a discussion of West Indian folk culture *per se* is impossible. However, the emergence of West Indian literature is intimately linked with the interest which the early writers took in the folk culture, and a number of the cultural features which attracted them will be touched upon in the course of this study.

To return to the opening quotations, the second statement also implies that the West Indies have begun to "enrich the imagination of mankind" since the Second World War. The author of this statement, John Hearne, belongs to a group of writers which includes V. S. Naipaul, George Lamming, Wilson Harris, Samuel Selvon, Andrew Salkey, Edward Brathwaite, and Derek Walcott, all of whom contributed to the outpouring of West Indian creative writing in the 1950s. They were all born in the late 1920s or early 1930s and grew up during one of the most turbulent periods in West Indian history, when dramatic changes were taking place in the political and social structure of their region. George Lamming has drawn attention to the profound significance of these pre–World War II social upheavals for the writers of his generation:

I remember as a boy, a very young boy, Barbados being thought of as a very orderly, very conventional, very conservative society. But in July 1937 nobody could have had those illusions when those barefooted men marched on Government House with the demand to see the Governor. And in the town, whites fleeing, cars overturned into the harbour, stores being smashed.

In Trinidad there was the very sinister episode of the policeman who was actually soaked in paraffin and set alight by Butlerite sympathisers. These were very, very violent moments, but more important than the violence was the creation of a confidence in very ordinary people that they could and should be heard by those who were called authority. And I think there is a connection between the political character of many of the early novels which were then published in the fifties and the events of the late 1930s.[3]

Lamming goes on to comment on the emergence of three of the region's most important literary magazines, all of which were launched during the war years: Frank Collymore's *Bim* (1942–) in Barbados; Edna Manley's occasional *Focus*, which first appeared in Jamaica in 1943; and *Kyk-over-al*, edited in Guyana by A. J. Seymour between 1945 and 1961. Before they became established overseas, many aspiring writers used these magazines as outlets for their early creative writing. The regional approach of *Bim* and *Kyk-over-al* in particular, together with the BBC *Caribbean Voices Programme,* helped foster an awareness among the writers in different islands of creative developments taking place in neighboring territories, and encouraged them to see their work as part of a new regional phenomenon.

It is hardly surprising therefore that the writers and critics of the 1950s came to regard the Second World War as the watershed of West Indian creative writing. Apart from their increased awareness of what was taking place in other islands contemporaneously, they would have known very little of the region's literary past, as their Anglocentric education would hardly have encouraged them to ask whether any significant West Indian literature had appeared before their time. The years immediately preceding the Second World War had been particularly lean ones for West Indian fiction, and the fact that they were followed by a period of intense political activity tended to obscure the links between the young writers of the 1950s and those of the first three and a half decades of the twentieth century. In the last few years, West Indian literature has been given a place within the West Indian school syllabus and a pattern of continuity has begun to emerge. Future West Indian writers are likely to be aware of the significance of the creative writers of Lamming's generation and be influenced by their precedents.

To date, however, no comprehensive history of West Indian literature has been compiled, although certain groundwork has been covered. Louis James's early collection of critical essays, *The Islands in Between* (1968), was published before the appearance of many major West Indian literary works, at a time when it was still too early to predict or analyze regional trends. Bruce King's more recent collection, *West Indian Literature* (1979), devotes separate chapters to important decades in the development of West Indian literature, but lacks the scope and the space to develop this historical perspective. A genuinely comprehensive historical perspective depends on specialist studies of specific eras or genres or themes, and these have only recently begun to become available: Kenneth Ramchand's pioneering *The West Indian Novel and Its Background* (1970) was followed by Michael Gilkes' *The West Indian Novel* (1981). Poetry and drama have been treated in Lloyd W. Brown's survey of *West Indian Poetry* (1978), Kole Omotoso's *The Theatrical into Theatre: A Study of the Drama and Theatre of the English-Speaking Caribbean* (1982), and Ken Corsbie's *Theatre in the Caribbean* (1984). Thematic approaches to West Indian writing have been used in Gerald Moore's *The Chosen Tongue* (1969), Selwyn R. Cudjoe's *Resistance and the Caribbean Novel* (1979) and O. R. Dathorne's *Dark Ancestor* (1981). In the related field of cultural history, a start has been made in Jamaica with Ivy Baxter's *The Arts of an Island* (1970), which includes a history of Jamaican literature extending from historical times to the present day; and for Trinidad, with Keith Q. Warner's *The Trinidad Calypso: A Study of the Calypso as Oral Literature* (1983). Before a truly comprehensive study of West Indian literary history can be compiled, however, it would seem essential that the literary histories of each of the English-speaking territories be established. So far the emphasis has been on individual authors, especially those who first came into prominence after World War II. At the last count there were at least half a dozen full-length critical studies of V. S. Naipaul as well as several theses and major publications on George Lamming, Roger Mais, Wilson Harris, Jean Rhys, Derek Walcott, and Edgar Mittelholzer. In most cases the writers have done careful research on the individual backgrounds of each of these authors, but even their work remains incomplete without a fuller understanding of groups and creative writers who preceded the postwar generation and contributed directly or indirectly to the sociocultural milieu of the late 1940s and the 1950s.

Lloyd Brown traces half a dozen poets of the period 1760 to 1900 in his survey of *West Indian Poetry*. They include Francis Williams (1700-1770) whose "Ode to Governor Haldane," written in Latin, appeared in 1759; James Grainger (1723-1767), author of a pastoral epic on Caribbean plantation life, *The Sugar-Cane* (1764); M. J. Chapman, an antiabolitionist who in *Barbadoes and Other Poems* (1833) put forward in verse his arguments against the freeing of the slaves; and the Guyanese poet, Egbert Martin (1859-1887), who published two collections of poetry, *Poetical Works* (1883) and *Lyrics* (1886), under the pseudonym "Leo."[4] However, it was only at the beginning of the twentieth century that a recognizable West Indian literary genre began to take shape. In this respect Jamaica clearly emerges as the center of literary activity during the first three decades of the twentieth century. As early as 1929 the president of the Jamaica Poetry League, J. E. Clare McFarlane (1894-1966), was able to produce a wide-ranging anthology of local poetry, and some twenty years before that an attempt had been made by Thomas MacDermot (1870-1933) to establish an indigenous publishing house. The All Jamaica Library published four works of fiction: MacDermot's *Becka's Buckra Baby* (1904) and *One Brown Girl And—* (1909); E. A. Dodd's *Maroon Medicine* (1905); and W. A. Campbell's *Marguerite: A Story of the Earthquake* (1907). In the foreword to *Becka's Buckra Baby*, MacDermot explained the rationale behind the enterprise:

In "The All Jamaica Library" we are presenting, to a Jamaican public at a price so small as to make each publication generally purchasable, a literary embodiment of Jamaican subjects. Poetry, Fiction, History and Essays, will be included, all dealing directly with Jamaica and Jamaicans, and written by Jamaicans.[5]

Like many subsequent attempts to set up a West Indian publishing house, the All Jamaica Library did not survive for very long, but as editor of *The Jamaica Times* MacDermot continued to give sincere support and encouragement to local writers until the end of his active life. Had he lived longer or been born later, he might have become the Jamaican equivalent of Barbados's Frank Collymore, whose contribution to the development of West Indian writing as liberal editor of *Bim*, and friend and mentor of many aspiring creative writers has become a symbol of all the selfless dedication which went into the nurture and development of creative writing after World War II. MacDermot was posthumously declared Jamaica's first poet laureate.

Overshadowing all other Jamaican writers and dominating the cultural scene well into the thirties was H. G. de Lisser (1878-1944). As secretary of the Jamaica Imperial Association, Chairman of the Board at the Institute of Jamaica, and the influential opinion-making editor of *The Daily Gleaner*, de Lisser consistently defended the position of the colonial ruling class and was opposed to any moves to give political rights to the black majority. He was a talented and intelligent individual, fully aware of the new ideas and aspirations which challenged the *status quo* after the First World War, but determined not to relinquish any of the power he had acquired under the old colonial system. De Lisser put forward his reactionary views in novels which made clever use of familiar features of Jamaican life. His first novel, *Jane's Career* (1914), is an early precursor of the barrack-yard story and is as entertaining and realistic as anything the *Beacon* group in Trinidad ever produced. Although later works such as *Triumphant Squalitone* (1917), *Revenge* (1919), and *Under the Sun* (1937) were more overtly reactionary, they are thematically the natural ancestors of the West Indian historical novel and the social and political satire. V. S. Reid's *New Day* (1949), in which Reid attempts to reinterpret the Morant Bay rebellion of 1865, may even have been conceived as an attempt to counter de Lisser's unfavorable interpretation of the rebellion in *Revenge*.

De Lisser and MacDermot were both men of some standing in the Jamaican community. It is not surprising therefore that on the whole Jamaican writers were generally accorded a degree of respect in their own country and were often patronized by the ruling class.[6] This was certainly not the case in Trinidad, where the pioneering writers of the late 1920s were ostracized socially. One of the Trinidad writers, Ralph de Boissière, has suggested that the difference between the attitudes to local talent in the two islands was the result of their different social and political histories:

[Trinidadian] whites and near-whites were doing their best to purge themselves of any taint of local culture, the folk arts, which survived despite suppression by law. They rejected these links with the people, regarding them as "niggers' amusements." They attached themselves to British culture without becoming cultured. British education was designed to black out Negro culture and inculcate a deep sense of one's inferiority to foreign whites, with whom culture was supposed to originate. But did the middle class really absorb this British culture? Is it possible to absorb completely the culture of a country in which you have never lived? Dickens, Galsworthy, Fielding; snow, fog, springtime, white Christmases; Parliament, public school ethics, the nobility—do you *absorb* all that? It lies on you like an ill-fitting, oversize coat, a ridiculous disguise, a cast-off garment given a poor orphan. A coloured man, Ralph Vignale, used to write novels which were serialised in the *Port-of-Spain Gazette* in the 20's—all about the English upper class, riding to hounds and all that. How pathetic! What a commentary on British rule! The slow emergence of literature arose from this one-sided British education and the barriers of colour set up between us for . . . historical reasons. . . . If it was not the same in Jamaica this was because that island had had its own House of Assembly and controlled its affairs until 1865. They had time to feel that Jamaica was their country. But in Trinidad we did not feel this, we felt we were owned and controlled.[7]

The difference between the two islands, however, was merely one of degree. The Jamaican upper class may certainly have felt more equal to the British ruling class than the white creoles of Trinidad: They were more powerful as a class and had deeper roots in Jamaica and stronger links with the mother country. De Lisser may have had the cultural assurance to give his novels Jamaican settings, but the lifestyle he describes in many of them bears more resemblance to Vignale's fantasies on the English upper class riding to hounds than the reality of Jamaican life outside of the privileged plantocracy. While MacDermot was prepared to encourage writing in creole, there were nevertheless limits beyond which it was impossible for Jamaican writers of the early twentieth century to take their interest in local culture and still remain acceptable in polite society. For every Jamaican writer who stayed in the island and established a modest reputation as a man of letters, there was one who became frustrated with the cultural restrictions of colonial society and stopped writing, or went abroad.

The Trinidad writers of the 1930s have more in common with the Jamaicans Claude McKay (1889-1948) and Walter Adolphe Roberts (1886-1962), both of whom left Jamaica when they were in their early twenties. Claude McKay's poetry collections *Songs of Jamaica* and *Constab Ballads*, both published in 1912, represent a completely different line of development to that encouraged by the Jamaican literary establishment. McKay never returned to Jamaica and became instead one of the foremost writers associated with the Harlem Renaissance in the United States. Walter Adolphe Roberts, a near-white Jamaican creole, had a background and intellectual stature comparable to that of de Lisser, but he was firmly opposed to Crown Colony government and was unable to get the opportunities in his journalistic career in Jamaica that de Lisser obtained. He left Jamaica to work as a journalist in New York and Paris during the First World War and developed a life-long interest in French culture and republican ideals. His best known novels are a trilogy dealing nostalgically with the decline of French culture in Louisiana after the American Civil War. He joined the bohemian set of Greenwich Village in the 1920s and, though his work is uneven in quality, he produced some fine individual poems and a number of historical and political treatises on Jamaica. His only novel with a Caribbean setting is *The Single Star*, a romance dealing with the involvement of an idealistic young Jamaican creole in the Cuban War of Independence at the end of the nineteenth century. In 1936 Roberts formed the Jamaica Progressive

League in New York to fight for Jamaican self-government and he returned to Jamaica in the 1940s to participate in the political and cultural changes that followed the Second World War.

Until the late 1920s the literary scene in Trinidad, by contrast, seems to have produced nothing very remarkable. In a first survey of Trinidad writing entitled *Self-Discovery Through Literature* (1972), Anson Gonzalez mentions two plays by L. O. Inniss written in the late 1890s; a book of poems called *Legends of the Bocas* (1922) by A. D. Russell; and the occasional work of fiction: Michel Maxwell Philip's *Emmanuel Appadocca or Blighted Life: A Tale of Buccaneers* (1854), George H. Masson's *Her Nurse's Vengeance* (1898), and S. N. Cobham's *Rupert Gray: A Tale of Black and White* (1907). In addition, two important nonfictional works by the black Trinidadian schoolteacher J. J. Thomas should be noted: *The Theory and Practice of Creole Grammar* (1869), the first attempt to examine the French creole spoken in Trinidad at the time as a legitimate linguistic development, and *Froudacity* (1889), in which Thomas makes a spirited defence of West Indian society against the scathing remarks of the negrophobe James Anthony Froude's assessment of the region in *The English in the West Indies or the Bow of Ulysses* (1888). The sporadic nature of literary output in the island before the late 1920s can partly be explained as the consequence of the island's linguistic diversity and its rapidly changing patterns of settlement. Trinidad had been a Spanish colony until 1797 with a large proportion of French-speaking inhabitants. It was not until the end of the nineteenth century that English replaced French and Spanish as the *lingua franca*. One of the island's earliest historians under British rule, P. G. Borde, wrote *Histoire de l'île de la Trinidad sous le gouvernement espagnol* in French, and had it published in Paris in 1876. It is possible that such poetry and fiction as was written or published has now passed into the annals of France and Spain and bears little relationship to twentieth–century writing in English. Among the lower classes the situation was further complicated by the widespread use of French creole and the influx of indentured laborers from China, India, and Madeira to work on the sugar plantations after the abolition of slavery in 1838. Unlike most of the English colonies of the region, Trinidad was underpopulated, which made it attractive for migrants from other, more crowded areas. The flood of linguistically and culturally diverse immigrants into the colony tended to retard the spread of the English language and undermine the patterns of social and racial stratification which in Barbados and Jamaica had led to the creation of a powerful and self-assured indigenous leisured class. By the beginning of the twentieth century, however, the tide had begun to turn, and though there was still a massive movement of immigrants into the island, they were mostly workers from the English-speaking West Indies who flocked to the country to work in the oil fields and on the prosperous wharves as other outlets of migration to Panama, Cuba, Brazil, and North America began to fail. Their presence helped stabilize the island's social and linguistic character though Trinidad for a long time remained a society in a state of flux.

The burst of creative activity in the late 1920s was in a sense related to this new ascendancy of English and the fact that the society had begun to resolve itself into well-defined racial and social groupings, based on a series of shared assumptions which the new intellectuals could discuss, support, analyze or attack in their work. Chapter 1 of this study deals with the development of Trinidad society during the interwar years and the spread of antiestablishment ideas during this period. By the end of the 1920s, the middle classes (black, colored, and creole elements)[8] were clamoring for a greater say in the country's administration and for constitutional reforms to the Crown Colony system. The working class, based in Trinidad's oil fields and docks, had also begun to agitate for labor representation within industry and a greater share in the country's wealth. The approach of the middle class was reformist and nationalist; the approach of the working class was militant and socialist. However, most of the pioneering Trinidad writers were middle-class intellectuals who, to a greater or lesser degree, sympathized with the aspirations of the working class. As Daniel Guérin has observed in *The West Indies and Their Future*:

A Caribbean culture only started to come into being when . . . a minority split away from the middle classes and made contact with the people, turned its attentions to their problems, studied their customs, their beliefs, what of the African inheritance the people have kept alive, and voiced the people's aspirations and anger.[9]

Frantz Fanon and Amilcar Cabral have both attempted to elucidate this process, which was triggered off in the Third World after the First World War. Cabral, from the outset, debunks the elitist notion implicit in Guérin's evaluation by reminding us that "when . . . the pre-independence movement is launched, the masses have no need to assert or reassert their [cultural] identity, which they have never confused nor would have known how to confuse with that of the colonial power. This need is felt only by the indigenous petite bourgeoisie which finds itself obliged to take up a position in the struggle which opposes the masses to the colonial power."[10] Although Cabral's assessment is based on the African experience of cultural nationalism, it seems relevant to the Caribbean experience and should help guard against the confusion of the cultural efforts of the middle class, with which this study is concerned, and the birth of culture implied in Guérin's analysis. Throughout the history of the Caribbean it has been the masses of the people who created an indigenous culture and successfully defended it against the inroads of imperialist hegemony. As Cabral affirms, they are "the repository of culture and at the same time the only social sector who can preserve and build it up and *make history.*"[11] Within the educated middle class, where the values of the European colonizers had been most emulated, cultural suppression and assimilation had combined to alienate the individual from the rest of his community. As a result of these processes the "rebel" fraction of the middle class had first to question its own cultural assumptions before it could begin to rediscover its cultural roots. This process of cultural resistance has often preceded the struggle for national liberation. Frantz Fanon in *The Wretched of the Earth* has described it as the phase during which the educated native begins to set "a high value on the customs, traditions and the appearances of his people." It usually follows a period during which the native has done his best to show that he can beat his superiors at their own game, by perfecting his knowledge of the language, culture and manners of the colonizer. Finally, Fanon adds:

In the third phase, which is called the fighting phase, the native, after having tried to lose himself in the people and with the people, will on the contrary shake the people. Instead of according the people's lethargy an honoured place in his esteem, he turns himself into an awakener of the people; hence comes a fighting literature, a revolutionary literature, and a national literature.[12]

Most of the literature produced by the Trinidad writers of the early 1930s did not reach Fanon's third phase. This was partly because that nationalist struggle was interrupted by the outbreak of the Second World War and subsequently it never developed into an armed liberation struggle.

The early Trinidad writers published their work in two magazines, *Trinidad* (1929-1930) and *The Beacon* (1931-1933, 1939). Chapters 2 and 3 of this study discuss a selected number of the nonfictional contributions in the magazines as well as the poetry and short stories produced by the group. The poetry is only of historical interest, but the short stories are generally of a very high standard. In choosing the subjects for their short fiction, the writers put into practice their theoretical demands that West Indian writing should utilize West Indian settings, speech, characters, and conflicts. Their stories cover all aspects of Trinidad life, though a significant proportion of these were concerned exclusively with the lifestyle and culture of the lower classes, especially the urban proletariat living in the slums or barrack-yards of the city. The writers laid great stress on the independence and vitality of the women who lived in these yards and tried to reproduce their creole speech.

The piquancy of some of the political articles and editorials in *The Beacon* are reminiscent of the satiric thrust of the calypso songs of the period. At times the "eavesdropping" narrator of the short stories also seems to borrow his narrative stance from the calypsonian:

The calypsonian would usually adopt the pose of a disinterested listener, or of a newspaper reporter who is always on the spot, or of one who had been told hot news by a reliable source or a barrack-room dweller who cannot help but overhear what is going on in bed next door.[13]

In addition, both the calypsos and the short stories of the 1930s frequently have the same element of ironic reversal in their surprise endings. Unfortunately, at the time when the research for this study was carried out, it was not possible to gain access to a sufficient number of early calypsos to provide further support for the relationship which seems to exist between the two genres. It is, however, intriguing to speculate on the extent to which Trinidad fiction over the years has been influenced by this vital art form. Anson Gonzalez implies the existence of just such a link when he remarks in *Trinidad and Tobago Literature on Air:* "It is only to be expected that in the land of 'ole talk,' Polycar, robbertalk, grandcharge, mamaguy, nancy stories and half a million politicians that short fiction should be one of the more popular modes of creative writing."[14]

In chapters 4, 5, and 6, three of the most important literary figures to have emerged from the *Beacon* group are singled out for special attention. Alfred H. Mendes, C. L. R. James and Ralph de Boissière were the only members of the group who went on to write full-length novels. Although they wrote on similar themes, their work reflects the different perspectives from which they viewed colonial society. Two of their novels, James's *Minty Alley* (1936) and Mendes's *Black Fauns* (1935), are set in barrack-yards. They indicate some of the strengths and limitations of early Trinidad writing. The writers' self-conscious approach to the lower class produced a perspective which emphasized rather than bridged the social gap between the classes. The middle-class protagonist who controls the narrative perspective in *Minty Alley* observes and records events with sympathy but at the same time feels separate from and superior to the yard-dwellers. James later became aware of the fundamental alienation of the educated black members of the colonial middle class from the masses. In his play *Toussaint L'Ouverture* (1936) he tried to correct the perspective of the earlier novel by taking a more critical view of the relationship between the educated Haitian leader and his followers. Mendes's *Black Fauns* makes no attempt to examine the relationship between the middle-class writer and his proletarian subjects. Instead he tries to interpret the barrack-yard for his reader by reproducing the creole conversations of his lower-class characters and exploring the economic and emotional tensions of the yard community. Conversely, in *Pitch Lake* (1934) Mendes succeeds in making the reader inhabit the consciousness of his protagonist, who is a member of the Portuguese middle class in Trinidad, so that we begin to understand the deep-rooted feelings of insecurity which make the prejudices of this class against the black masses so virulent.

Unlike Mendes and James, Ralph de Boissière remained in Trinidad throughout the 1930s and early 1940s and witnessed the development of the working class from a vulnerable and dependent sector of the society to a class with a definite political voice of its own. His novels, *Crown Jewel* (1952) and *Rum and Coca-Cola* (1956), record this development and present members of the working class as the moral and intellectual equals of the middle-class characters. His novels are committed to a radical analysis of Trinidad society between 1935 and 1945, and they explore the limitations and achievements of the political alliance between the classes which brought an end to the more overt forms of colonial domination in the English-speaking Caribbean.

In conclusion, this study attempts to put the work produced by these early writers into perspective in relation to the post–World War II Trinidad novelists and short-story writers. The group may be regarded as the direct literary ancestors of Samuel Selvon and V. S. Naipaul, both of whom take up the Trinidad story at the point in the Second World War where de Boissière's second novel leaves off. The polished narrative technique of both of the later authors lives up to the precedent set by the early short-story writers, and there is even a line of physical continuity between the younger writers and some members of the *Beacon* group who continued to meet and discuss their writing within other informal gatherings well into the 1940s.

NOTES

1. V. S. Naipaul, *The Middle Passage* (Harmondsworth: Penguin, 1969), p. 29.

2. John Hearne, "Foreword" in *The Artist in West Indian Society: A Symposium*, ed. Errol Hill (Trinidad: University of the West Indies, Dept. of Extra-Mural Studies [1963]), p. 5.

3. George Lamming, "Caribbean Politics from 1930s to Tense 70s," *Caribbean Contact*, 5, 11 (March, 1978), 10.

4. See chapter 1, "The Beginning: 1760-1940," in Lloyd Brown, *West Indian Poetry* (Boston: Twayne Publishers, 1978), pp. 19–38. See also Anthony Boxill, "The Beginnings to 1929," in *West Indian Literature*, ed. Bruce King (London: Macmillan, 1979), pp. 30-44.

5. Quoted in Mervyn Morris, "The All Jamaica Library," *Jamaica Journal*, 6, 1 (March, 1972), 47-49.

6. See Rhonda Cobham-Sander, *The Creative Writer and West Indian Society: Jamaica 1900-1950* (Ann Arbor: University Microfilms International, 1982).

7. Ralph de Boissière, personal communication, January 2, 1979.

8. Trinidadian writers are inconsistent in the usage of the terms "black," "colored," and "creole." In this study, these terms have been used as follows: "black" signifies a person of predominantly African descent; "colored" signifies a person who is a mixture of any of the major races—a mulatto (Afro-European), but also a "dougla" (Afro-Indian); "creole" means a person born in the Caribbean (usually used to describe locals of predominantly European descent, e.g., French creole,

Portuguese creole). The term "creole" also refers to the languages which developed in the Caribbean as a result of the contact between African and European languages. In Trinidad, two creoles coexist—a French-based creole (on the wane) and an English-based creole.

9. Daniel Guérin, *The West Indies and Their Future* (London: Dennis Dobson, 1961), p. 80.

10. Amilcar Cabral, "Identity and Dignity in the Context of the National Liberation Struggle," in *Return to the Source: Selected Speeches of Amilcar Cabral,* ed. Africa Information Service (New York and London: Monthly Review Press, 1973), p. 67.

11. Ibid., p. 61.

12. Frantz Fanon, "On National Culture," in *The Wretched of the Earth* (Harmondsworth: Penguin, 1971), pp. 178 and 179.

13. See Gordon Rohlehr, "The Development of the Calypso: 1900-1940" (Unpublished cyclostyled paper, 1972), p. 33.

14. Anson Gonzalez, *Trinidad and Tobago Literature on Air* (Port of Spain: The National Cultural Council, 1974), p. 61.

CHAPTER 1

THE BACKGROUND: TRINIDAD 1919-1938

The literary awakening in Trinidad came as a response to specific political and cultural developments that had their parallels throughout the colonial world and in black America. Not the least of these was the global extent of involvement in the First World War and the political and social upheavals that came in its aftermath. Trinidadians of all social classes were strongly influenced by their wartime experiences. The writer Alfred H. Mendes, who served with a British regiment, remembers:

I went through the First World War from almost start to finish in France. . . . As you may well imagine it stirred up a revolutionary change in my whole outlook on life. Even before that I was tending towards the left, very much to the left, and the War sort of crystallised the changes that were taking place inside of me. I emerged from all its horror . . . a very different human being. However, that experience, placed against the background of Imperialism, the Crown Colony form of government that we were working under here in Trinidad, *and* the Bolshevik Revolution, completely opened our eyes to the evils inherent in the imperialist concept of domination.[1]

Mendes, as a white West Indian, was allowed to serve in a British regiment, but most of the 15,000 black West Indians who volunteered to fight for King and Empire were excluded from enlisting in the regular British Army because of their color. Unlike the French, the British were reluctant to use black troops against white forces. One battalion of the permanent West India Regiment which had been used in the Ashanti wars of 1873-1874 remained in Jamaica throughout the war, while the other battalion was sent to East Africa where it was engaged in very limited action against the Germans. It was only in mid-1915 that the British Colonial Office, which was concerned that the continued rejection of black West Indians would have an adverse effect on their loyalty to the Crown, was able to persuade the War Office to change its policy. As a result of this change, the British West Indies Regiment was formed under the command of white West Indian officers. However, the regiment was seldom allowed to function as a body. Sections of it were deployed to provide work units for white battalions. The nearest that these West Indians came to participation in active combat was when they were used as ammunition carriers in France and Egypt—a job that entailed heavy casualties but little honor. Instances of personal discrimination were often encountered and matters reached a head in Italy after the war, when Allied troops were assembled to await demobilization. C. L. Joseph in an article on "The British West Indies Regiment: 1914-1918" describes how the 15,000 West Indians assembled at Taranto were given all the menial duties including cleaning the latrines of prisoners of war.[2] When the South African general in charge of the camp was reminded of an earlier promise made to the West Indians by the War Office that they would be given the same privileges as British troops, he replied "that he was perfectly aware of the promise and intended to take no notice of it; that the men were only niggers, and that no such treatment should ever have been promised to them; that they were better fed and treated than any nigger had a right to expect."[3]

Black West Indians returned from the war with the slogan, "If we can die for the white man against his German brother, we can die better for ourselves."[4] While awaiting demobilization in Italy in December 1918, the sergeants of the British West Indies Regiment met secretly and formed an organization called the Caribbean League for the promotion of closer union among the West Indian islands after the war. In meetings of the league, many of the political issues which would be taken up during the interwar years were raised and discussed. Among these was "the demand that the black man should have freedom to govern himself and that force should be used if necessary to attain that object."[5] All West Indian governors were informed of the formation of the Caribbean League and a warship was kept ready in the vicinity of Jamaica should any major trouble arise on the regiment's return.[6] As it turned out, the expected social explosions were relatively mild. Many of the ex-servicemen were unable to find jobs in their home territories, consequently they joined the exodus of workers to Cuba, the United States, and Latin America. It was only in the late 1920s when these outlets were closed as a result of the Great Depression that these migrant workers were forced to return.

The war brought West Indians into contact with new ideas. In Egypt especially, West Indians came into contact with troops from Australia and New Zealand, countries which had achieved a degree of self-government within the British Empire. To many West Indians, their inferior status as soldiers became associated with their inferior status as colonies. Many of the soldiers stationed in Egypt had worked on the Panama Canal before the war. In the Canal Zone they had come to appreciate the necessity and value of organized industrial action. The war experience added a note of militancy to this stance. It is not surprising therefore that one of the most prominent labor leaders of the interwar years, Captain Arthur Cipriani, was a member of the British West Indies Regiment. Cipriani, a white Trinidadian of French descent, had been instrumental in organizing the Trinidad contingent within the regiment. During the war he was often called upon to defend the rights of soldiers charged with various military offences. After the war he led the criticism of the failure of both the colonial and British governments to honor their promises of payment of arrears, war allowances, and pensions.

The labor movement of the 1930s was part of the expression of the new nationalist sentiments which emerged after the war. It had become clear that in matters relating to their own labor and government the majority of West Indians had no representation. This was particularly true of Trinidad, which, since its capture from the Spanish in 1797, had been administered as a Crown Colony. Under Crown Colony rule all power was vested in the governor who was responsible only to the Colonial Office in Britain. In Trinidad the governor was assisted by a Legislative Council which consisted of equal numbers of official and nominated unofficial members. The Legislative Council was little more than an advisory body. Matters of government policy were put to a vote but the governor held a casting vote and the official members were required by law to vote with the government. Unlike Jamaica which occasionally attracted well-known British administrators, Trinidad often found itself saddled with incompetent or mediocre governors. As C. L. R. James has remarked, "Now and then among the officials one finds a really brilliant man, although not often, because brilliant men would stay at home, and even if they do come out, quickly pass on elsewhere to occupy the highest positions in more important colonies."[7] Before the discovery of oil, Trinidad was certainly not considered an important colony.

Historically the group which resented the imposition of Crown Colony government in Trinidad most was the French planter class. In 1783, in an effort to boost the population of the island, the Spanish had encouraged French planters, French free people of color, and their slaves to settle in the island. It was this group which established the island's prosperous cocoa industry. However, with the British occupation of the island, the plantation system of sugar production was expanded, and for a whole century French cocoa interests clashed with British sugar interests. By the beginning of the twentieth century the French creoles had lost much of their land to the large, new sugar combines. On the cultural level it was a battle between two religions, two languages (and their related creole variants), and two ways of life. C. L. R. James has suggested that the French creoles were the early pioneers of the cultural resistance to British Crown Colony government:

They were, some of them, men of great culture, and fully able to stand up against the domination of sugar planters and colonial officials. They had a language of their own, in addition to their economic independence. . . . They were Roman Catholic and therefore were able to feel a differentiation between their religion and the Protestant religion of the British domination. Therefore, while they shared to some degree the superior status and opportunities that all local whites had, they were constantly aware of themselves as a body of people distinct from, and even opposed at times to the British colonial caste.[8]

During the interwar years, some of the younger generation of French creoles whose families had declined began to gravitate toward the opposition movements of the day: Captain Cipriani, whose championship of West Indian soldiers has already been noted, was one of the most outspoken members of the French creole community. Other French creoles chose to express their dissatisfaction with Trinidad society by patronizing the much despised calypso tents which were organized for the first time during the 1920s. Gordon Rohlehr comments on this form of protest within the French creole community in an article on the calypso:

Early in the [twentieth] century, the Calypso had provided French Creole young men with something to defend against the inroads which a Puritan and Anglo-Saxon administrative elite were making into the waning French Creole culture in Trinidad. By the 1920's frustrated young colonials of various backgrounds were realising that in order to liberate themselves, they would have to liberate the barefoot man, and that in order to find themselves they would have to come to terms with the so-called "Jamette" class.[9]

Another group of young French creoles turned to literature and journalism. The two best known of this group were Jean de Boissière, a notoriously eccentric bohemian who was considered the *enfant terrible* of the *Beacon* group, and Ralph de Boissière, a near-white creole who was distantly related to the well-known de Boissière clan of which Jean was a part. Jean, or Tony as he was called by his friends, published two magazines, *Picong* and *Callaloo,* in the late thirties and forties, in which he inveighed against the establishment in a mixture of invective and ridicule. Ralph de Boissière published short stories in *The Beacon* and later developed into one of the group's most militant writers in his novel *Crown Jewel.*

Other elements within Trinidad society also found themselves at odds with the establishment. Trinidad had been underpopulated in the nineteenth century and the abolition of the Atlantic Slave Trade in 1807 had limited the increase of the black population by direct importation. After emancipation in 1838, Trinidad more than most of the other English islands was faced with a labor shortage, as those freed slaves who wanted to leave the plantations had little difficulty in finding unoccupied Crown land on which to start small farms. Other ex-slaves drifted into the towns to join the already substantial free colored population there. The gap created by this exodus of labor was filled by a new supply of indentured laborers from India, Madeira, and China. The Indian workers came in the largest numbers. In *From Columbus to Castro: The History of the Caribbean 1492-1969*, Eric Williams estimates that of the 145,000 East Indians introduced into the colony between 1838 and 1917, only about one in every six took up their contractual option of returning to India at the end of their indenture.[10] Of those who remained, some continued to work on the sugar estates. Others accepted grants of Crown land in lieu of their return passage to India and became small cane farmers themselves or grew cash crops or vegetables for local consumption. After oil was discovered in commercial quantities in the island in 1910, many of these farmers were cheated out of their land by local and English companies who bought up the leaseholdings at exploitative prices and proceeded to make fortunes in oil. Those who had the presence of mind not to sell, were able to collect oil royalties from the wells drilled on their property, and overnight found themselves catapulted into the ranks of the middle classes. After a wild period of indiscriminate spending, members of this new class found themselves up against the harsh realities of maintaining their position in a society where commerce and government were monopolized by British companies and French creole families. They found difficulties put in their way when they tried to obtain credit from the foreign-owned banks; they were excluded from the higher circles of government where policies relating to commerce were framed. During the 1930s however, the first wave of Indian businessmen began to move into politics using as the base of their support the large mass of East Indian peasants whom they were able to rally on the basis of mutual cultural and religious interests. Their antiestablishment position was heightened by the growing opposition to colonialism in India itself. In 1932, five issues of *The Beacon* were devoted to cultural and political topics of importance to the local East Indian community. Some of the articles were contributed by leaders of the Muslim and Hindu communities in the island. Others were produced by liberal British expatriates residing in Trinidad who had formerly lived in India. One of *The Beacon*'s younger East Indian contributors, Adrian Cola Rienzi, went on to become a leading figure in the trade union movement in Trinidad after the social upheavals of 1937.

The notion of a group identity (however superficial) which transcended class barriers was a characteristic that was seldom encountered within other sectors of the Trinidad middle class, who were for the most part anxious to put as much distance as possible between their present status and their humble origins. The Portuguese middle class in particular was extremely sensitive to issues which threatened its racial or social prestige. The Portuguese had come to Trinidad as indentured laborers in two small waves of immigration in 1840 and at the end of the nineteenth century. They were quick to grasp the advantages which a white skin bestowed in colonies such as Trinidad and moved rapidly through the social ranks from indentured laborers to petty merchants and rumshop keepers and ultimately into commerce. Socially however, they were never fully accepted in local British or French creole society. Like the Indian middle class, they also turned inward and made a virtue of their exclusion by forming a self-contained clique, but they still aspired to the social heights occupied by other Europeans in Trinidad. Some of the descendants of the first group of Portuguese immigrants eventually managed to enter this upper circle. Though the Portuguese, like the French creoles, resented the superior status of the British administrative caste, they were too small as a group and culturally too insecure to challenge its position effectively. By the 1920s, however, the more progressive young creoles had become impatient with the limited social ambitions of their group. Some of the rebels were prominent members of the *Beacon* group: Mendes, whose commentary on the war experience has been quoted above, was one of the best and most controversial writers in *Trinidad* and *The Beacon;* Albert Gomes, editor of *The Beacon*, was also of Portuguese descent though he did not come from as privileged a background as Mendes.

Similar patterns of protest and sycophancy were also typical of the colored middle class, within which distinctions of shade and social status were rigidly enforced. The end result of this development was that socially and economically it was almost impossible for black Trinidadians to reach middle-class status. The world of commerce was virtually closed to them. The color of their skin made it impossible for them to shed their association with slavery with the same ease with which the Portuguese middle class dispensed with their early history of indentured labor, and they lacked the shared memory of an earlier culture which sustained and unified the Indian community. The only means by which they could achieve a measure of economic independence and social respectabililty within the colonial system was through education. Black parents who had worked their way up in the system to the position of clerks or primary school teachers made great sacrifices to prepare their children for entry into secondary school. C. L. R. James recalls:

This was the battleground. The Trinidad Government offered yearly free exhibitions from the elementary schools of the island to either of the two secondary schools, the Government Queen's Royal College and the Catholic College, St. Mary's. The number today is over four hundred, but in those days it was only four. Through this narrow gate boys, poor but bright, could get a secondary education and in the end a Cambridge Senior Certificate, a useful passport to a good job. There were even more glittering prizes. Every year the two schools competed for three island scholarships worth £600 each. With one of these a boy could study law or medicine and return to the island with a profession and therefore independence.[11]

Both C. L. R. James and Eric Williams, who grew up in the interwar years, have written about their parents' relentless efforts to secure a better future for them. James's father was a schoolmaster himself, and could coach young C. L. R. for the exhibition exams. Eric Williams's father, a junior civil servant, had to hire a private tutor:

The third step which my father thought necessary for the attainment of the goal he had marked out for me involved only his purse and not his soul. It was the "private lessons," one of the principal articles of the educational faith of the Trinidad parent, then as now. It was a system of cramming, designed to supplement the formal training given in the school. A financial sacrifice was involved; private tuition in the primary school cost a dollar a month. But my father paid cheerfully.[12]

A formidable collection of hurdles, financial and otherwise, ensured that only the fittest survived. Those who made it to secondary school under these conditions were usually more gifted than the average child from a privileged background whose parents could afford to pay fees, but in any academic year only one of them could win the coveted scholarship to university which alone provided a passport to privilege. Many who missed this chance spent years trying to save enough to further their education. Others settled for jobs which may have paid more than those held by their parents, but which were just as intellectually frustrating and seemed at the time to hold as few prospects of advancement. It was from backgrounds such as these that the black members of the *Beacon* group were drawn. C. L. R. James, C. A. Thomasos, and Ernest A. Carr were schoolteachers. Joseph Belgrave was a lawyer's clerk. Ralph Mentor was a reporter and James Cummings was a printer's apprentice. In the years to come, James and Cummings would emigrate, and James would become a leading left-wing intellectual of international stature. Thomasos was to become a politician, Carr a senior civil servant, and Mentor a leading trade unionist. In Trinidad in the late 1920s such careers would have been inconceivable for individuals with their backgrounds, however, and their prospects must have seemed relatively grim. Young men such as these would have had every reason to attack a system which for them was very limiting. Within the protection of the *Beacon* group they did so with impunity.

By the beginning of the twentieth century, Port of Spain had become a major trans-shipment port and was attracting laborers from the interior of Trinidad and from smaller islands further north. These laborers formed the nucleus of a modern urban working class. During the late 1920s when the oil industry began to develop, a second concentration of workers began to build up in the south of the island. There was no legislation at the time to protect the rights of workers: They were ill-paid, badly housed, and could be dismissed at random. Moreover, there were no provisions for workers' representation in industrial matters. Once the workers began to appreciate the importance of their skills to the efficient running of these major commercial enterprises, it was only a matter of time before they took action to improve their lot. The first confrontations occurred on the Port of Spain waterfront in November 1919, only months after the ex-servicemen had returned from the war. Stevedores, lightermen, warehouse workers, and bargemen went on strike and demanded increased wages, pay for overtime, and shorter working hours. Similar strikes occurred in British Honduras, St. Lucia, British Guiana, St. Kitts, and Anguilla. In Trinidad the waterfront strike developed into an island-wide general strike and a British warship was called in to restore order.

The working class seems to have acted spontaneously in 1919: There was little organization and no leadership to speak of. After the strike, however, the Trinidad Workingmen's Association (TWA) emerged as the organization in control of the new antiestablishment mass movement. It was neither a trade union nor a political party. Under Captain Cipriani's middle-class leadership it initially combined two broad aims: constitutional reform and new measures to improve the standard of living of Trinidad's working class. The TWA achieved a number of important reforms during the 1920s, among them the introduction of the eight-hour working day and the Workmen's Compensation Law. On the constitutional side its agitation resulted in the introduction of an elective element within the Legislative Council following the recommendations of the Wood Commission of 1921. As of 1925 the number of unofficial members in the Legislative Council was increased to thirteen by the introduction of seven new elected positions. The number of official members was also increased to twelve, however, so that the old balance between the government side and the unofficial side was maintained. As Arthur Calder-Marshall, the English novelist and journalist who visited Trinidad shortly after the disturbances in 1937, points out:

The fact that there are twelve official members apart from the Governor, and thirteen unofficial members, does not mean that the unofficial members have a majority. The Governor has an original and casting vote which gives the Government a final majority of one. This means that the business of the Legislative Council is in fact a farce since Government is able to carry any measure that it wants. It is an elaborate game in which the opposition is allowed from time to time to win a point or two so that they may not feel too sore.[13]

It is hard to believe that Captain Cipriani and several other TWA leaders, who were among the first elected members, did not realize that they were merely being co-opted by a system that had hardly changed at all. The Great Depression of 1929 and his decision in 1932 to turn the TWA into the Trinidad Labour Party (TLP) marked the end of Cipriani's career as Trinidad's first mass leader. He would remain an elected member of the Legislative Council and continue "to propose and oppose legislation" until 1945, but the Trinidad working class began to bypass him and his organization in their fight for better conditions. In fact, Cipriani and the middle-class TLP leadership became more and more identified with the *status quo*.

During the late 1920s and early 1930s the *Beacon* group led the criticism of Cipriani's brand of socialism within the middle class. Within the working class a number of organizations sprang up to replace the gap in leadership that Cipriani's defection had created. This was the period of Garvey's greatest influence in America and the Caribbean, and a strong chapter of the U.N.I.A. was established in Trinidad. In the tents the calypsos became increasingly concerned with political satire. In the political field the two most important new organizations were the Negro Welfare Cultural and Social Association in the north and the British Empire Workers and Citizens Home Rule Party in the south. The Negro Welfare Association (NWA) began as the National Unemployment Movement in Port of Spain. It was led by militant working-class people such as Jim Barrette, Elma François, Clement Payne, Bertie Percival, and Jim Headley. In his *History of the Working Class*, Bukka Rennie decribes the NWA as a "revolutionary" organization. It combined a strong ethnic position with radical socialist ideas and sought to link its struggle for the Trinidad working class with the worldwide socialist movement of that period. The NWA attacked Cipriani for his betrayal of the working class, advocated the formation of trade unions, led hunger marches, and held regular political rallies. Its members also became members of other working-class organizations where they attempted to disseminate their ideas and encourage the discussion of international issues which they felt were relevant for the future of the Trinidad working class. Like the U.N.I.A. they drew attention to the implications of the Italian invasion of Abyssinia for the future of black people throughout the world. The failure of the League of Nations to go to Selassie's aid was widely criticized by common people throughout the West Indies and added to their cynicism about the concept of Empire.

By 1937 the NWA had virtually destroyed Cipriani's credibility within the working class, but the organization was too small and its sphere of influence too limited outside of Port of Spain to gain the leadership of the national labor movement. Cipriani's place was therefore taken by Uriah Butler, whose British Empire Workers and Citizens Home Rule Party had its base in the oil belt of South Trinidad. Butler was a flamboyant, charismatic figure, sincerely devoted to the interests of the workers, but though he was able to articulate the discontent of the masses he had only vague ideas of how their situation could be remedied. The name of his party reflected this limitation of his vision: For him the most radical solution was home rule within the British Empire. He failed to identify the problems of the workers as the predictable consequences of an imperial system which concentrated power in the hands of a few remote groups. His failure to understand the nature of imperialism would later enable opportunist, middle-class leaders to step in and take control of the mass movement, turning it away from its earlier militancy and back to the path of compromise it had rejected during the latter part of Cipriani's leadership. One result of this development was that much of the work accomplished by the NWA was forgotten or reversed. As Bukka Rennie has pointed out:

The inability of the NWA, a serious organisation with an extraordinarily capable working-class leadership, by far the most capable leadership seen so far in our history, to foresee this drastic shift in the objective conditions, together with the inability of Butler to provide capable keen leadership and build an efficient organisation, especially in light of the increased middle-class manoeuvrings and intrigue, was the tragedy of the period 1935-47. Sad, because as the years went by, NWA was forgotten and Butler revered despite the fact that the history of Trinidad and Tobago remains incomplete, loses its continuity, and is almost meaningless without the history of the NWA.[14]

One of the earliest attempts to provide this continuity was made at a literary level by Ralph de Boissière, one of the only members of the *Beacon* group who remained in Trinidad and continued to write after the magazine ceased publication. His novels *Crown Jewel* (1952) and *Rum and Coca-Cola* (1956) reconstruct the events of the period 1935-1947 as they affected the lives of a group of representative characters, drawn from all walks of Trinidad life. Though most of his major characters are fictitious, the novels capture the spirit of the period accurately. Indeed, it is easy to forget that they were written years before any serious attempt at historical reconstruction of the period had been made.

On June 19, 1937, an attempt was made by the Trinidad authorities to arrest Butler on charges of sedition. The oil belt exploded: Within days the whole island was engulfed in a general strike. Once more, in the absence of any clear leadership, the Trinidad masses acted spontaneously and rioted until the upheaval was suppressed by British intervention. Similar events had occurred in St. Kitts, Jamaica, British Guiana and St. Vincent in 1935, and the Trinidad upheavals sparked off another wave of unrest in Barbados, Jamaica, and British Guiana. The British Government reacted in its usual manner and appointed a Royal Commission, chaired by Lord Moyne, but "such was the ugliness of [the Commission's] exposures about the British Colonial record in the British West Indies that the War Cabinet decided against publication of its contents until the war had ended."[15] In the interim, Butler and most of the leaders of the NWA were interned for the duration of the war, and the government made every effort to see that the newly established trade unions developed along lines which were acceptable to the establishment. It was into this vacuum of leadership that the middle class stepped to take control of the labor movement. It is one of the ultimate ironies of this period that many of the very people who had criticized Cipriani so fiercely in the pages of *The Beacon* were the first to adopt his style of politics when they entered the political arena. In his autobiography *Through a Maze of Colour,* Albert Gomes, editor of *The Beacon*, dismissed the protest politics of Captain Cipriani in the following terms:

Although in the personal sense loud and angry, [his opposition] was in reality no more than a medium of ritual protest in that club-gathering of smug bureaucrats and gaudy sycophants.[16]

Gomes's comments on Cipriani provide a fitting epitaph to his own political career, which began shortly after the disturbances in 1937 and ended when he left Trinidad in 1962 on the eve of the island's independence from Britain. During this period he moved through all the same stages of promises, protest, compromise, and co-option into the ranks of the ruling class which distinguished Cipriani's career. Gomes has left us his own comment on his career in the words of Ernesto Montales, one of the autobiographical figures in his only published novel to date, *All Papa's Children*. Ernesto, like Gomes, is Portuguese, and enters politics as a "stowaway" when the winds of change take Trinidad out of the "political doldrums" in 1937. Looking back on his career, Ernesto muses:

Think of all the impossible things I promised them to get their votes. And I really believed, at the time, that I would be able to do everything as promised. It's like that with ideals before they're tested.

Think of the times I told them I stood for "the people," carried away by my own eloquence and sense of mission. I ask myself now, what the hell did it mean? And all those other woolly abstractions like "freedom from want" etc., borrowed from Roosevelt's Atlantic Charter-what did they mean? I suppose they rolled well on the tongue and made good rhetoric. And they did bring in the votes. Mine was a pretty impressive win.[17]

Gomes was not the only member of the *Beacon* group to betray earlier ideals. Adrian Cola Rienzi's career as a trade unionist has left him open to similar criticism; Mendes, though he never really forsook his socialist ideals was ultimately forced to abandon his attempts at becoming a novelist in order to support his family. He joined the Civil Service and rose to the position of General Manager of the Port Services Department, a position which placed him repeatedly on the receiving end of attacks on the establishment by militant dock workers. With the two notable exceptions of C. L. R. James and Ralph de Boissière, few of the original *Beacon* group were able to sustain their early radicalism. In this respect the literary movement in Trinidad during the thirties differs little from contemporaneous intellectual movements thoughout the Western world. The success of the Russian Revolution in 1917 and the disillusionment with Western democracy which followed the First World War propelled a whole generation of Western intellectuals toward radical politics. The thirties have become known as the Red Decade, but of the intellectuals who became Marxists, socialists, and fellow travellers during this period, only the most committed survived the wave of disillusionment with the new ideology that followed the advent of Stalinism, the fiasco of the Spanish Civil War, and the creation of the Stalin-Hitler pact.

The Trinidad intellectuals of the 1930s were no exception to the rule, but the idealism with which they responded to the social upheavals and political changes which characterized their era has left us with a body of literature which marks an important turning point in the cultural history of the West Indies.

NOTES

1. "The Turbulent Thirties in Trinidad: An Interview with Alfred H. Mendes," ed. R. W. Sander, *World Literature Written in English*, 12, 1 (April, 1973), 67-68.

2. See C. L. Joseph, "The British West Indies Regiment: 1914-1918," *The Journal of Caribbean History*, 2 (May, 1971), 94-124.

3. C. L. R. James, *The Life of Captain Cipriani: An Account of British Government in the West Indies* (Nelson, Lancs.: The author, 1932), pp. 33-34.

4. See Bukka Rennie, *The History of the Working Class in the 20th Century (1919-1956): The Trinidad and Tobago Experience* (Toronto and Trinidad: New Beginning Movement, 1973), p. 19.

5. Joseph, "The British West Indies Regiment," 120.

6. Social unrest was expected everywhere in the West Indies. Fitz A. Baptiste opens his pamphlet *The United States and West Indian Unrest: 1918-1939*, Working Paper No. 18 (Jamaica: U.W.I., Institute of Social and Economic Research, 1978) with a quotation from a report by the Acting American Consul in Port of Spain in late 1919: "There are serious indications from many directions that Trinidad, and perhaps the British West Indies, are on a social volcano . . . liable to burst into eruption at any time."

7. James, *Life of Cipriani*, p. 54.

8. C. L. R. James, *The Making of the Caribbean Peoples* (London: Bogle L'Ouverture Publications, 1968), p. 16.

9. Gordon Rohlehr, "The Development of the Calypso: 1900-1940" (Unpublished cyclostyled paper, 1972), pp. 27-28.

10. See Eric Williams, *From Columbus to Castro: The History of the Caribbean 1492-1969* (London: André Deutsch, 1970), pp. 348 and 352.

11. C. L. R. James, *Beyond a Boundary* (London: Hutchinson, 1969), p. 31.

12. Eric Williams, *Inward Hunger: The Education of a Prime Minister* (London: André Deutsch, 1969), p. 31.

13. Arthur Calder-Marshall, *Glory Dead* (London: Michael Joseph, 1939), p. 277.

14. Rennie, *History of the Working Class*, pp. 60-61.

15. Baptiste, *The United States and West Indian Unrest*, p. 45.

16. Albert Gomes, *Through a Maze of Colour* (Port of Spain: Key Caribbean Publications, 1974), p. 16.

17. Albert Gomes, *All Papa's Children* (Surrey: Cairi Publishing House, 1978), p. 99.

CHAPTER 2

THE MAGAZINES: *TRINIDAD* AND *THE BEACON*

Soon after his return from Europe at the end of the First World War, Alfred Mendes met C. L. R. James, who was then a junior master at Queen's Royal College in Port of Spain. They discovered that they shared a common interest in literature, art, music, and creative writing. James has described the friendship which ensued:

We were as close as possible, considering he was a white man and I was a colored man. We didn't meet in a social way, but I was always at his place, his study; he was regularly at mine. We exchanged books and talked two or three times a week. . . . He was interested in literature, *The New Statesman* and *The Spectator* and various books and reviews and so on. Mendes and I lived as close together in a literary way as two brothers.[1]

In time, other young Trinidadian intellectuals of various ethnic backgrounds and a number of liberal British expatriates were drawn into these meetings and discussions.[2] Eventually a group of about twenty people emerged who "met regularly and informally at Mendes's home where they listened to recorded music, argued way into the night, and read excerpts from each other's writings."[3] Mendes and James remained at the center of this group: Mendes provided the others with books from his "collective library" of about five or six thousand volumes, and James became their literary doyen after the British *Saturday Review of Literature* published his short story "La Divina Pastora" in 1927. James's success—Mendes has referred to it as "a sensation in Trinidad amongst those of us who were really interested in the arts"—gave a tremendous boost to the group's creative endeavors.[4] In 1929 James and Mendes decided to create a local outlet for the group's writing, and the literary magazine *Trinidad* was launched. It appeared twice: at Christmas 1929 and at Easter 1930.

Albert Gomes, another young Trinidadian who was in New York at the time, received a copy of the second issue of *Trinidad*. Gomes had developed an interest in history, philosophy, and literature during his two-year stay in the United States, where he attended courses at New York's City College. In his autobiography *Through a Maze of Colour* he recalls his excitement on receiving a literary magazine from home:

It was elegantly put together, its form suggesting the influence of *The London Mercury*, J. C. Squire's English monthly of the time. I was very excited by Mendes's publication. Did this really mean that a cultural breakthrough was imminent in Trinidad? At 17 or 18 one desires passionately that events should bear witness to one's dreams and hopes.[5]

On his return to Trinidad, Gomes was introduced to the group. Although he shared their enthusiastic interest in literature and the arts, he felt that the time had come to launch a magazine with a broader perspective. In March 1931 he published the first issue of *The Beacon*, and over the next three years, 28 issues of the magazine appeared. *The Beacon* magazine became the rallying point of the original literary group, and as its reputation as an antiestablishment journal became known, other Trinidadians who were "at odds with a lot of what was happening around them" made contact with the editor and his friends.[6] The constant supply of material for publication from aspiring writers and budding politicians soon transformed the magazine from being the "mouthpiece of a clique" to what Gomes has described as "the focus of a movement of enlightenment."[7]

One of the significant features of the movement was the multiracial background of its members. Gomes has suggested that this feature was one of the sources of the movement's strength:

The great thing about our little *Beacon* society was the way it cocked a snook at the larger society mocking its stratified conventions in deed as well as in word. . . . Racial and colour barriers certainly weren't reproduced there. The only criterion was a common bond of shared convictions—and, of course, identification with the magazine and its general approach. In what other social crucible would it have been possible to bring together Ralph Mentor, C. A. Thomasos, Beatrice Greig, Adrian Cola Rienzi, Ernest A. Carr, James Cummings, Alfred H. Mendes, Jean de Boissière, R. A. C. de Boissière, Alice Pashley, Hugh Stollmeyer. . . . *Beacon*-ism signified a distaste for the divisive humbug which was the worst feature of the outer society.[8]

Romanticizing the past leads Gomes to underestimate the extent to which pressures from the outer society must have affected the group. Outside their cosy private democracy, members were constantly exposed to the frustrations and restrictions of the wider society—restrictions which eventually contributed to the breakup of the group. A talented writer such as Mendes, for example, was liable to be ostracized by members of his family and social class when he wrote about the lower classes. In order to extend his readership beyond the confines of the group, he was ultimately forced to leave Trinidad and take his work to foreign publishers. On the social side, there seems to have been a dichotomy within the group, already implied in the opening quotation from James: Outside of their literary meetings there were few social events at which group members of different races were likely to meet, and in their private lives many found themselves ranged on opposing sides when it came to the day-to-day business of earning a living. The black members of the group, for example, were not likely to find their chances for getting responsible or rewarding jobs increased because they were the intellectual equals and colleagues of a few liberal whites who held responsible positions. James has emhasized these harsher realities in commenting on his reasons for leaving Trinidad, and in comparing his options to those of Gomes and Mendes:

Albert Gomes told me the other day: "You know the difference between all of you and me? You all went away; I stayed." I didn't tell him what I could have told him: "You stayed . . . because your skin was white; there was a chance for you, but for us there wasn't—except to be a civil servant and hand papers, take them from the men downstairs and hand them to the man upstairs." We *had* to go, whereas Mendes could go to the United States and learn to practise his writing, because he was white and had money.[9]

The Beacon ceased publication not long after James and Mendes left for careers abroad. Mendes has suggested that "this trend must have discouraged Gomes and he began to lose interest in his magazine."[10] Four years later, in 1937, Gomes and a few of the remaining members of the group published an anthology entitled *From Trinidad: A Selection from the Fiction and Verse of Trinidad, British West Indies.* By then the social upheavals within the island had created a new intellectual climate in the island and politics had replaced literature as the medium of protest. In 1939 Gomes made an attempt to resurrect *The Beacon*, but only one issue appeared.

From a purely literary point of view, *Trinidad* is perhaps more noteworthy than *The Beacon*. The first magazine contains some of the best short stories by early Trinidad writers. These include James's "Triumph" and "Her Chinaman's Way" by Mendes. There are also two excellent impressionistic pieces by F. V. S. Evans and practically all of Ralph de Boissière's short fiction. The short stories in *The Beacon* were rarely of as high a standard as those in *Trinidad*. Mendes in comparing the two magazines has stressed this qualitative difference:

The creative work in Gomes's *The Beacon* was not related in any sense to the creative work that was published in *Trinidad*. . . . The fiction appearing in *The Beacon* were [sic] largely traditionally composed stories—derivatively made stories. The stories in *Trinidad* were much more serious.[11]

While it is hardly accurate to describe the creative writing in the two magazines as totally unrelated (after all, Mendes himself was a major contributor of "serious" writing to both) there is a sense in which the *Beacon* writing was derivative. Talented writers such as Percival Maynard, C. A. Thomasos and Olga Yaatoff contributed stories to *The Beacon* which were closely patterned on those in the earlier magazine. In this context one might even speak of a literary school, initiated by Mendes and James, whose style is apparent in the fiction published in *The Beacon* as well as in the 1937 *From Trinidad* anthology. *The Beacon* helped transform the brilliant but isolated achievement of *Trinidad* into an accepted and recognizable trend.

The first issue of *The Beacon*, however, was a peculiarly esoteric affair. Mendes's short story "Pablo's Fandango" was the only contribution which had any specific bearing on Trinidad. In the rest of the magazine, James discussed "The Problem of Knowledge," Gomes explored "Reason, Intuition and Instinct," and the Reverend James Glen dealt with "The Meaning and Aim of Philosophy." A fourth article was even more ambitious and debated "Einstein's Place in Science." There were a couple of poems by Americans and a review of the American literary scene by Nathan Schneider, the American associate editor of *The Beacon* for its first issue.[12] Apart from Gomes, Mendes and James, all the contributions were by white Americans, young people on the left whom Gomes had met during his stay in New York. Later *The Beacon* would occasionally feature articles by its American contacts, but from the second issue on the bulk of its contributions came from Trinidadians. Remembering the magazine's staid beginnings, Gomes has commented wryly that "it read more like *The Hibbert Journal* than the debunker of bourgeois morality, obscurantist religion and primitive capitalism it soon became."[13]

By the second and third issues the philosophical flood had abated. Apart from an article on the philosopher Robert Bridges and a discussion "On Taking One's Life," there were a number of short stories written by Trinidadians. There was also an article on the Soviet Union by Schneider, in which he describes Russian Communism as "a great and highly progressive experiment . . . worthy of a trial at a time when democracy is beginning to lose favour in the eyes of the world."[14] A number of Trinidadians associated with *The Beacon* shared Schneider's view, and this must certainly have caused the colonial establishment some anxiety. However, it was the fourth issue of the magazine in July 1931 which brought the police to the editor's door. The lead article was a short piece entitled "Black Man," in which Gomes described and attacked in shrill tones incidents of discrimination in the United States, urging black men everywhere "to fight the white man's fury . . . put aside the law-abiding tradition . . . [and] show a little resistance."[15] It was hardly surprising that the government interpreted the article as a direct attack on colonialism. This first brush with the law was exactly the kind of publicity that *The Beacon* needed in order to attract the attention of a wider audience. Thereafter sales sometimes reached a peak of 5,000 copies per issue. The group celebrated the occasion as "proof indeed that its impact was being felt."[16]

In addition to Gomes's controversial article, the July 1931 issue carried the first editorial notes and announced a new correspondence column. Commenting on the changes the editor explained:

Too many things of importance were happening, or not happening, about us to go unnoticed. A point of view was essential . . . our expression of opinion will be honest in purpose and unflinching.[17]

Another sensitive issue was raised in an article by Dr. Sydney Harland of the Imperial College of Tropical Agriculture, which put forward the view that the black man was genetically inferior to the white man. His article drew angry responses as well as some support, and a controversy on the subject raged in the pages of *The Beacon* for several months. Most members of the *Beacon* group rejected Harland's position but, as Gomes has been eager to point out, the magazine aimed at providing a liberal forum in which opinions on both sides of any debate would be aired:

The policy of the magazine was really the absence of one, for although the editorial notes reflected more or less my own views, in all other sections contributors of most riotously conflicting views coexisted. If we wrote something attacking some aspect of church policy and a defender appeared who was prepared to state his views in writing, these views were published. The same privilege was granted to any other person, from whatever section of vested interest in the community, who wished to do likewise. Thus controversies, always the best boost to circulation, were frequent. When they did not occur spontaneously we deliberately engineered them.[18]

In spite of the wide range of positions taken up by its contributors, there is a clearly discernible pattern of interests reflected in the subjects and views raised in *The Beacon*. The magazine was, for instance, deeply engrossed in the exploration of what constitutes a Trinidadian or West Indian identity. An attempt was made to provide information about other cultures which were important to Trinidadians. Articles on Africa were meant to create pride in the ancestral past among the black readers, and a special "India Section" catered to the local East Indian community. *The Beacon* also encouraged reading and an interest in the arts through its reviews of books, films, musical performances, and art exhibitions. Gomes has suggested that "*The Beacon* assisted in no small measure in providing the improved cultural infrastructure in preparation for the stirring events of 1937," and that "the magazine's pages . . . show the gathering storm, in a sort of preview . . . they tell, in most explicit language, of the deep-seated dissatisfaction in the community."[19]

Both *Trinidad* and *The Beacon* had a mixed reception in the island. Apart from the group of intellectuals around Mendes, Gomes and James, many people seem to have read the magazines for their scandal value. In his "Commentary" on the reception of the first issue of *Trinidad*, Mendes records how one of the magazine's contributors, who was ostracized as "obscene" by women in the office where he worked, overheard some of them later "giggling over the spicy portions of the stories."[20] Both publications encountered open hostility from the official newspapers and the Catholic press, and were also censured by individual planters and merchants. Their uninhibited approach to sexual matters was often criticized: When *The Beacon* published "Boodhoo," a short story that explored the themes of miscegenation and racial prejudice, it provoked such an outcry that the editor was forced to come to its defence. In response to the charge made in one of Trinidad's newspapers by a correspondent signing himself "Planter" that the story was "in the very worst of taste," the editor commented:

We assume that the Planter considers it bad to have an English woman seduced by an East Indian. Let us assure the Planter that it has happened more often than once, not only in this island, but in other parts of the world.[21]

The editorial goes on to contrast the "Planter's" sense of moral outrage with the reception given to some of the most controversial stories outside of Trinidad:

"Faux Pas" appeared in *The Manchester Guardian*, that doyen of conservative dailies, and "Triumph" and "Her Chinaman's Way" were listed in the *Best Short Stories of 1930*. Also, Aldous Huxley wrote a personal letter to the author of the two longer stories . . . as we have more faith in the literary judgement of *The Manchester Guardian*, Mr. R. B. Cunninghame Graham, Mr. Aldous Huxley and the Editor of the Annual volume of *Best Short Stories* we can only conclude that the Planter is wrong . . . e as were those others who two years ago thought it fit to bring down the wrath of many on the heads of the writers of "Triumph," "Her Chinaman's Way" and "Faux Pas."[22]

The artists who joined the *Beacon* group and whose pen drawings were reproduced in the magazine were the victims of similar attacks in the local press. Carlisle Chang in an essay on "Painting in Trinidad" has linked the formation of a local school of painting with the general awakening spear-headed by *Trinidad* and *The Beacon*. The four major artists who were iden-tified with the group were Alice Pashley, an Englishwoman; Hugh Stoll-meyer, a creole of Anglo-German descent, whose poetry was also featured in the magazine; and two Chinese-Trinidadians, Amy Leong Pang and Ivy Achoy. Their work was influenced by Matisse and Gauguin but they fre-quently also made use of motifs from West Indian folklore. *The Beacon* reviewed their exhibitions and called for the creation of an art school and gallery, but their work was considered indecent and the press exhorted parents: "Don't let your children cross their doors lest what they see will shock and demoralise them." One of *The Beacon's* foreign connections, a Russian painter known as Vassilieff, was refused permission to bring his paintings into the island for an exhibition because they included a number of studies of nudes.[23]

The Trinidad establishment was even more disturbed by the articles and editorials in *The Beacon* that expressed anticapitalist, anticolonial or anti-Catholic views. The Catholic Church frequently brought pressure to bear on small businessmen who advertised in the paper, and parents of the more privileged members of the group were privately warned by the govern-ment that their rebellious offspring were running the risk of legal prose-cution. Gomes has admitted that the magazine would hardly have survived beyond the first four issues had it not been for his mother, who shared his contempt for the ruling class and joined him each month in the struggle to coax more money out of the pockets of his father, a cautious Portuguese shopkeeper.

The Beacon's notoriety attracted the attention of intellectuals in other parts of the West Indies. Mendes recalls that they had the occasional visi-tor "who told us that he or she belonged to a group in that island or the other island and was interested in our group, which had become the only well-known group in the Caribbean because of the noise which had been made about our activities."[24] Outside of Trinidad, the magazine was best known in Barbados where it had received the usual hostile attention from the official press. *The Beacon* established links with two progressive Bar-badian magazines: *The Outlook*, edited by Clennell Wickham, and *The Forum Quarterly*, edited by Gordon O. Bell. In reviewing the first issues of these magazines that they received, Gomes wrote enthusiastically that they proved Barbados was not as English as was usually made out and exploded "the myth of isolation which travel writers are always so eager to apply to these islands. Good landscape, sugar and cocoa are not our only products."[25] Copies of *The Beacon* were sold in Barbados, and in June 1932 *The Forum Quarterly* carried a number of contributions written by members of the *Beacon* group. The work of a few Barbadians likewise appeared in the pages of the Trinidad magazine. Within Trinidad, *The Beacon* also shared some of its contributors with *The Royalian*, a magazine put out by the Literary Society of Queen's Royal College, and *The Quarterly Magazine* edited by Austin M. Nolte.[26]

One of the charges most often levelled at the *Beacon* group by its critics was that it was a communist organization. The pages of *The Beacon* do, in fact, reflect the group's sympathy with the Soviet experiment and with socialism in various ways. Since a number of Marxist publications were banned in Trinidad, the magazine frequently republished important speeches and documents by Russian political personalities and writers, which Trinidadians were unable to obtain directly. According to Gomes, this material "found its way to the editor's home . . . via European seamen who were under instruction from the Communist International and who visited [him] whenever their ship called at Port of Spain."[27] It would seem that the *Beacon* group hoped by publishing this material to encourage the magazine's readers to assess for themselves the claims that the Soviet Union was making about her progress in the economic and cultural field. The reprints included excerpts from a speech by Stalin on "The Five Year Plan and the Future" and a long interview with him by the German Marxist Emil Ludwig. Other articles present Russia's perspective on the First World War as an imperialist struggle, and explain the rationale behind the Soviet Union's policy of nonaggression and peaceful coexistence. The reprints were complemented by original articles written for *The Beacon* by members of the group who had some special knowledge of the Soviet Union.[28] W. V. Tothill's article on "Russia: A Great Experiment" is of particular significance as it attempts to relate certain precepts of socialism to problems within Trinidad society. Pointing to the Soviet Union's progress in the creation of an indigenous culture which was both national and proletarian, he deplores the eagerness of Trinidadians "to import tripe music, tripe cinemas, tripe books, from the world's greatest tripe market—America." He calls on Trinidadians to emulate the Soviet Union's efforts to eliminate illiteracy and praises the Soviet Union for its strong line on religion.[29]

Most members of the group adopted the posture of freethinkers and enjoyed any opportunity to attack the powerful Catholic Church. Their most serious clash with the Church occurred in the debate over the Divorce Bill. The colonial government had attempted to introduce the bill, but encountered stiff opposition from the Church and the Catholic labor leader Cipriani, whose Trinidad Labour Party held most of the unofficial seats in the Legislative Council. This was probably the one time that the *Beacon* group sided with the colonial government, but they felt that there could be no doubt about the order of priorities, and several lengthy essays were published in *The Beacon* in support of the proposed legislation. They attacked the Catholic Church as "the largest Capitalist organization in the world," and challenged Cipriani to show how he could "reconcile his Socialist ideals with his rigorous allegiance to the Catholic ethic."[30] The successful passage of the Divorce Bill was seen as a personal victory by the group and as a vindication of their views on the Catholic Church. It also heightened their antagonism to Cipriani who thereafter became a favorite butt of criticism.

Though it was true that Cipriani had compromised himself in the eyes of the labor movement by his religious and political vacillation, he was at the time one of the few West Indian politicians with a clear vision of what the island's political future should be. He was at the forefront of the regional demand for a self-governing West Indian Federation with dominion status. When he outlined his proposals in an article in *The Beacon*, emphasizing that a full measure of representation based on universal adult suffrage was the prerequisite for such a federation, the editor countered with arguments which exposed the underlying elitist notions of the intellectual movement. Gomes made it clear that in criticizing the Crown Colony system of government the magazine did not wish to be interpreted as supporting the view that every Trinidadian should be given the vote. His socialist rhetoric suddenly gave way to the assertion that "the average member of the working class is on an intellectual parity with any ape and is, consequently, incapable of distinguishing a counterfeit from a genuine coin."[31] Gomes went on to state that he considered it a "very dubious premise that West Indians are best fitted for the administration of their own affairs."[32] Mendes has tried to account for the group's wavering between radical iconoclasm and conservative elitism by pointing to the class origins of its members:

There was this dichotomy. We were contradictions in terms. Our background was too deeply embedded in us to overcome the growth of our intellect from adolescence onwards, so that we still unconsciously hankered after what was behind us. . . . Most of us in that group were intellectuals, and intellectuals are usually by-products of the bourgeoisie.[33]

It was again in respect of Cipriani that underlying divisions within the group became apparent. Soon after his departure from Trinidad in 1932, James published a biography of the labor leader entitled *The Life of Captain Cipriani: An Account of British Government in the West Indies*. James presented a positive appraisal of Cipriani's activities during World War I and in Trinidad's political life, even glossing over his stance on the Divorce Bill as a mere trifle. The book was reviewed in *The Beacon* by Ralph Mentor, Joshua Ward and Gomes, all of whom attacked James for his "senseless hero worship." While Mentor in his review was content to deal mainly with the book's inaccuracies and shortcomings as a biographical study, Ward in "One Negro to Another" attacked James personally, accusing him of unfairness to the colonial government and ingratitude to the Englishmen who had helped him to emigrate to England. Dismissing James's claims for Cipriani as the first truly popular labor leader, he goes on to assert that "every negro and every civil servant of any class in this colony will say they prefer to work under the Colonial Englishman rather than under a creole of any type."[34]

In spite of the ideological confusion which occasionally surfaced within the *Beacon* group, and which foreshadowed the group's eventual disintegration and identification with conservative political trends in the period after 1937, the magazine did gain a deserved reputation for championing a number of causes which affected the day-to-day life of the underprivileged Trinidad masses. They campaigned against the persecution of the African-derived spiritual Baptist cult—known locally as "Shouters." An editorial in *The Beacon* demanded: "Why may not we be allowed to Shout in peace? There are no longer persecutions of any one professing even the remotest forms of Christianity; 'Infidels' go unguarded; Mormons daily infest Hyde Park; the Salvation Army strikes up at every corner."[35] *The Beacon* advocated the creation of trade unions and the introduction of national unemployment insurance to safeguard the rights and well-being of working people. The magazine campaigned relentlessly to ameliorate the working conditions of shop girls, who they claimed were ill-paid and overworked. The Trinidad oil industry was fiercely attacked because of its discriminatory hiring policy. *The Beacon* pointed out that much of the capital for the industry came from South Africa and that South African methods of discrimination were operated to keep local people out of white-collar jobs.

On at least one occasion *The Beacon* published an article by a member of Trinidad's proletariat. The article entitled "Barrack Rooms" was written by James Cummings. It gives an inside view of conditions within the slums which contrasts sharply with the more romanticized treatment the middle-class writers gave to the yard environment in their short stories. Gomes has recalled his first encounter with Cummings:

When I received his first manuscript he lived, with his mother, who did laundry work, in a barrack-room then owned by the Archbishop of Port of Spain. He was thin and underfed and, so I felt at the time, destined to follow his mother in the disease (tuberculosis) from which she died shortly afterwards. . . . I dropped in to see him one morning . . . and saw the awful one-room hovel in which he and his mother lived. He was writing about what he had experienced and in protest against the frustration and cruelty an iniquitous social system imposed upon him.[36]

In his article Cummings refers to the barrack rooms as "the boxes horses are shipped in. A long line of ten by twelve feet boxes, nailed together with a window and a door allotted to each."[37] He draws attention to the filthy and insanitary conditions which prevailed in the yard and to the collapse in moral standards which was often the result of the inevitable lack

of privacy. He shows particular concern for the effect of these conditions
on the children who grew up in the yards:

Here prostitution is born and here, too, prostitution flourishes. In some of the
yards many sleepless nights are passed through the gaming, liquor-drinking and
prostitution of some of the neighbours. The little children are shown the regrettable
step to degradation. Many an ambitious one's posterity has been hampered through
the reputation of some of these barrack-room tenants.[38]

Cummings also makes an implicit attack on the colonial government which
allowed such conditions to flourish unchecked. Ernest Carr in "The Negro
Child and Its Environment," an article published in the same issue as
Cummings's account of the barrack-yard, takes up some of these points in
his analysis of the way in which social conditions within the poorer classes
often led to feelings of racial inferiority among black children. He emphasizes the complicity of many black parents in fostering such attitudes by
unfavorably comparing the children's physical appearance and performance
at school with that of the more privileged white children.

The first ten issues of *The Beacon* were dominated by articles related to
issues concerning the status of Afro-West Indians and, with one exception,
the East Indian presence in Trinidad was virtually ignored. The exception
was a review by James of C. F. Andrews's *Mahatma Ghandhi: His Own
Story*. In his review James puts forward his own assessment of Gandhi as
"the greatest figure in world affairs today" and praises the Indian nationalist
for his theory and practice of nonviolence in South Africa and India. James
was quick to relate the implications of Gandhi's spiritual strength and per-
severance in the struggle for India's independence to the situation in Trinidad. Under the influence of Andrews's account of Gandhi's life, James
apparently changed his perspectives on the underprivileged East Indians
in Trinidad.

The book leaves me with . . . impressions which are likely to remain with me for
a long time. . . . [Now], when I meet the average unwashed scantily-clad East
Indian crouching by the side of the street, I see in him much more than I did
formerly, for I realise that in that frail and unkempt body move spiritual powers far
beyond me.[39]

It was possibly with the intention of extending this understanding of East
Indians and the Indian political scene that *The Beacon* launched its "India
Section" in May 1932. The official press was hostile to the nationalist struggle in India, and though between 1919 and 1928 at least three East Indian
journals published locally had provided the reading public with information
about the East Indian community, there seem to have been no equivalent

publications during the early thirties.[40] *The Beacon* took it upon itself to fill this gap. Its eleventh issue dealt almost exclusively with India and five subsequent issues contained special "India Sections." Beatrice Greig, an Englishwoman living in Trinidad, seems to have initiated the magazine's coverage of Indian affairs. She had lived in India for several years before moving to Trinidad and had become deeply involved in Hindu philosophy. As associate editor of *The Beacon* during this period, she took charge of the "India Section." Her interest in India seems to have irritated several members of the *Beacon* group who, though they were sympathetic to India's nationalist struggle, had little patience with a religious mysticism which they themselves had eschewed. Mendes is quite harsh in his criticism of Gomes for allowing Mrs. Greig such a free rein:

At one stage in *The Beacon* [Gomes] went off into some vague esoteric area because of an Englishwoman who was living here and who was a very rabid follower of Indian philosophy. This aberration put us off him completely, because we couldn't reconcile what we were trying to tell the Trinidad public with this kind of opaque mysticism that covered a field of human thinking that was absolutely of no interest to us at all.[41]

Mendes's criticism is in some ways justified, as few of the articles in the "India Section" dealt with issues related to the social conditions of the local Indian community. The India which was presented was an India of poets and philosophers. Even Gandhi was celebrated almost exclusively as a spiritual leader rather than a political activist. Mendes, however, underestimated the real need among East Indian immigrants and creoles to maintain contact with their former country and to protect their cultural identity from the neutralizing effects of imperial hegemony. Beatrice Greig took the view that Trinidad's Indians would have to reassert the culture of their mother country before they could "in time develop a culture of their own based on the best of East and West."[42]

An investigation of the past is inevitably a central concern of colonial peoples in the process of forging a national identity, and the *Beacon* group was no exception to the rule. Henry Alexis' article on "The Water Riots of 1903" was the first attempt in the pages of the magazine to historically assess the potential of the West Indian masses to act together in their mutual interest. His account of the confrontation which resulted in 1903 when the government tried to introduce water meters in order to finance their plans for extending the island's reservoirs, reveals a number of important features which were to reemerge in the 1937 confrontations. He points out that the people were united in their conviction that the proposed tax would ultimately be of no benefit to them. They saw the measure as another indication of the goverment's policy "to oppress the poor for the benefit of the rich." They also were united in the belief that their point of view would never receive a fair hearing within the Legislative Council. Consequently, when the council met at the Red House for the final reading of the bill, they stormed the building and set it on fire.[43] A historical article by James assesses the quality of local leadership by examining the life of Michel Maxwell Philip, a colored Trinidadian lawyer, who in the nineteenth century had risen to the position of Solicitor General of the island. James describes Maxwell Philip as "the most brilliant native of his time and within memory."[44] Maxwell Philip had been trained in England and, according to James, could have stayed there and had a brilliant legal career, but had chosen to return to Trinidad and work among his people. He had served as an unofficial member of the Legislative Council and had been Mayor of Port of Spain. The article on Maxwell Philip also contains a brief appraisal of Sir Conrad Reeves, the colored Chief Justice of Barbados who had refused to collaborate with Governor John Pope-Hennessy's attempts to impose Crown Colony government in Barbados. James describes Maxwell Philip's speech on the occasion of Reeves's visit to Trinidad in the 1880s in which the Trinidadian lawyer alluded to the difference in status accorded to native Barbadians, who had their own constitution, and natives of Trinidad like himself, who were forced to depend for promotion on the whim of the all-powerful governor. James's article is the first of his publications on important Caribbean personalities. In years to come, it was followed by his study of Cipriani referred to above and his major work on Toussaint L'Ouverture and the Haitian revolution, *The Black Jacobins*.

Historical articles on the development of the Trinidad Carnival were contributed by Joseph Belgrave and Lewis O. Inniss. They include vivid descriptions of the stickfights which were an important feature of Carnival during the nineteenth century. A series of articles on "Trinidad Then and Now" were contributed to *The Beacon* by Eleanor Waby, an 85-year-old Englishwoman, whose accounts of the Trinidad society she had had to grapple with when she first arrived in the island in the early 1870s, provide a fascinating contemporaneous account of nineteenth-century Trinidad. Another Englishwoman, Mary Milne-Home, contributed an article which traces the history of the Lopinot family, French creoles who had fled the Haitian revolution and come to settle in the foothills of the Northern range where they established a cocoa plantation.

The Beacon also contains a number of contemporaneous accounts of major events of the day which make it a valuable source for modern-day historians. Perhaps the most important of these is Tothill's article "With the West India Regiment in East Africa." As a medical officer attached to the West India Regiment during World War I, Tothill had recorded his impressions of the African war theater. Jean de Boissière's travelogues describing the impressions he gained of Germany and Italy during a tour of Europe in the early thirties, provide an interesting outside perspective on Fascism in prewar Europe. Of more relevance to the Caribbean is his article on "Cuba's New Deal," which analyzes the 1933 coup in Cuba within the context of American imperialism. De Boissière's scepticism about America's role in Cuba's internal affairs foreshadows later criticism of American attempts at hegemony in the Caribbean. His article ends on a prophetic note:

Perhaps some day when all the existing absurd political divisions that split mankind into highly antagonistic national groups have passed away and ridiculous boundaries no longer exist, Cuba will get a "Real deal" and take the place she is entitled to geographically, and ever-increasingly racially as the natural head of a unified Caribbean Archipelago.[45]

Trinidad, The Beacon, and Gomes's 1937 anthology contain between them nearly 200 poems, most of which are written by Trinidadians. Unlike the short stories and historical articles, few of the poems make any attempt to come to terms with the Caribbean environment. Mendes, for example, whose short stories more than any others announce the beginning of an indigenous literary tradition, published in the first issue of *Trinidad* this unashamedly Keatsian piece entitled "Inferno":

> Endymion came
> Like a flame
> To her sleep
> There to keep
> Tryst with her.
> 'Neath the stir
> Of the night
> He pressed her tight.
> Now, ah me!
> Sad to see
> She is dust.
> So all must
> Be the same
> Who touch flame.[46]

Apart from its clever use of extended metaphor, this poem has practically nothing to recommend it by any criteria. Like Mendes, most of the early Trinidad poets merely produced bloodless imitations of Romantic and Victorian poetry, dealing mostly with the themes of their models: death, despair and world-weariness, but lacking the genuine concern which the earlier age had shown for such issues. Gomes in retrospect has tried to explain the limitations of most of this early poetry:

What I found, in the days of *The Beacon,* was that the verse I received, for the most part, suffered because of the incrustations of a culture not its own, in both form and content. But cultural illegitimacy apart, it also was anachronistic in the sense that Yeats, Pound and Eliot had already written, but Trinidad was still with the English Romantics and their thee's and thou's and other overblown gestures.[47]

There is no reason to suppose that the *Beacon* group was unaware of postwar developments in English poetry, but while they emulated to varying degrees most of the *avant-garde* trends in art, politics, sociology, and morality, they seem to have viewed the "New Poetry" with suspicion. In an article in *The Beacon* on "Art and Tradition," Ernest Carr lists what he considers the crimes of modern poetry: its formlessness, its bitter, and often abusive tone, its attempts to be scientific, and its jettisoning of traditional emotional and aesthetic values. He concludes by observing that "these experimentalists are in ill-health and will not be made whole until they are welcomed into the fold dedicated to the service of tradition."[48] Part of the unwillingness of the *Beacon* group to explore or even imitate progressive trends in poetry may have stemmed from their conservative notions on the nature and function of poetry. For example, the group seems never to have considered creole as a proper form of poetic diction, although they frequently used it in their short fiction. Indeed, the archaic language of their poetry is not even related to the Standard English of their articles. They also seem to have rejected the events of everyday life as proper material for poetry. Their attitude is epitomized in another of Mendes's poems:

> The day is up: up rides the sun and we
> must out into the sun at sound of horn.
> The day is up and some of us must be
> dungeoned in offices where webs are born.
> For me another task: to stand and see
> a maenad wind dancing through a field of corn![49]

The poet is presented here, in jerky iambics, as a dreaming seer, an unworldly prophet, whose immersion in universal beauty does not even permit him to replace his cornfields with cane fields.

In spite of the limitations of this attitude to poetry, a few of the poems published do deal with issues of immediate relevance to the *Beacon* group and the wider Trinidad society. At times the universal themes they considered legitimate happened to overlap with their personal interests: Gomes, for instance, was notorious as a young man for his morbid obsession with death and the transience of life. His poems on these themes are among the better poems published by the group. Another notable example is Alfred Cruickshank's anti-Christian "When I am Dead," which, though heavily influenced by eighteenth-century models, manages through its traditional rhyme scheme and archaic diction to communicate some of the satiric wit and anti-Catholic fervor of the *Beacon* articles and editorials:

When I am dead, let not the canting tongue
Of hireling Churchman desecrate my bones,
Mocking his God and me, as he intones
His dreary service—brief, or loud and long,
As suits the fee.[50]

On other occasions the insistence on a formal structure weakens the poems. This weakness is perhaps most evident in attempts at protest poetry. Most of the verses on the race question, for instance, read like poor imitations of abolitionist tracts. The self-imposed limitations on the language considered suitable for poetry are perhaps the greatest contributing factor to the failure of the poems on racial themes. The high-sounding rhetoric of Hugh Stollmeyer's "The Time Has Come" seems almost to parody the appeal for racial dignity and the reaffirmation of indigenous cultures made in the poem:

Be not deceived! The time has surely come!
Arise! Rise up and learn to love
Yourselves. Yourselves and others
Of your race—to love them more,
Not less, than those who seem above you,
And who, you know well, crush you underfoot![51]

Like Percival Maynard's poem, "An African's Exhortation to His Country,"[52] which opens with the lines "Raise high thy head, O my land, raise it proudly!/Shake off thy sadness, look up, smile apace!," Stollmeyer's poem has a didactic tone which seems to suggest a certain superiority of the poet over those he addresses—as if the writer himself had no need for the advice he offers. Apart from asserting the need for action, neither poem appears to make any attempt to apply the advice it offers by raising the various features of the despised cultures it names to the status of a poetic theme. This omission becomes apparent when these poems are compared to another poem on the racial theme contributed by Gordon O. Bell, editor of the Barbadian magazine *The Forum Quarterly*. Bell and the Barbadian group had strong links with the black writers of the Harlem Renaissance. In his "Portrait of a Dark Virgin," Bell affirms the beauty of a black woman instead of exhorting others to do so. The form of the poem suggests an artist's notes to himself. The reader is left with the impression that the poem is meant to assist the writer's understanding of the subject rather than to educate his audience:

Eyes
The enigma of dark pools
Found under forest trees.

> Lips
> The fullness of an over-ripened cherry
> Ravaged by the seductive sun. . . .
>   Complexion
> Dark orchid of the Tropic Night
> Putting to shame the bloodless petals
>   of the fairer flowers.[53]

The West Indian landscape provides the material for another handful of poems on local themes in the Trinidad magazines. However, few of these ever really come to life because the poets approach their material through alien conventions and models. Olga Yaatoff's "Rainy Weather," for example, self-consciously strains for effect in its juxtaposition of local color and classical references:

> A month ago and cooks, hot from their kitchens
> Were cooling warm policemen on their beats
> And washerwomen comfortably suckling
> Their babes from large and jovial-nippled teats.
> Despite the chill, swans move upon lush rivers
> Begetting Castor and Pollux again
> And Apollo's golden bolt like lightning quivers
> To wreck Ossa and Olympus and Pelion.[54]

Not all the nature poems published in the magazines were as abstruse as this one. Alastair Scott's warmly nostalgic "Lines on Leaving Trinidad" contain sharply realized images of familiar details such as "Bird eaten mangoes lying,/Like torn soldiers, among the dead leaves? The crying/Of frogs in the short misery of twilight?"[55] The poem as a whole, however, is not particularly successful. The best of the nature poems is probably Mendes's "Tropic Night." Here Mendes, quite inexplicably, abandons his usual poetic diction and uses the indigenous image of the spider to suggest the sudden tropical change from day to night:

> Over this city from the outside
> crawls the tarantula of night:
> long hairy legs and two bright eyes
> and no light, no light.[56]

This "monster of an ancient mud-birth" carries on its back shadows of aboriginal Indians, and together "in wrath burning" they seem to punish the present-day population of the island by inflicting total darkness.

In an essay on the *Beacon* group, Peter Ayers has suggested that the poetry published by the group failed because of the "cultural isolation" of the West Indies during the late 1920s and the 1930s.[57] Such an explanation hardly takes into account how well-informed the group was, through their

reading and travels, about worldwide cultural trends, political developments and ideological changes. The articles and editorials in *The Beacon*
bear witness to the fact that, although they lived in a remote English colony, the Trinidad writers were quite up to date on most of the major issues
of their day.Their problem seems to have been one of cultural alienation
from their local environment rather than isolation from the outside world.
For ideas to be expressed through poetry, the creative writer must have at
his disposal a language and imagery with which he is totally familiar and
completely at ease. The colonial education of most of the *Beacon* writers
had taught them to function within the well-documented framework of the
English Romantic and Victorian traditions. Their own experiences put them
intellectually closer to the New Poetry of their age, but this poetry took its
images from a radically transformed postwar Europe, and even there the
new imagery was only partially defined and understood. To write convincingly on their own age, the *Beacon* poets had first to become aware of the
distinctive language and imagery of their immediate environment and to
utilize these new rhythms and images in exploring themselves and their
society. They took the first step in this direction when they attempted in
their short stories, essays, and historical articles to describe and account
for the anomalies within their society. Perhaps on account of that unconscious elitism which sometimes surfaced in their writing, they were unable
to conceive of themselves as an integral part of the society they described.
This made it difficult for them to express their highest personal ideals and
aspirations in poems which made use of local language and imagery.

Today, the *Beacon* group's poetic efforts are only of historical interest.
Through their prose writing, however, they helped create the new social
and cultural climate in which the poets of the 1940s and 1950s were able
to initiate a strong, indigenous tradition.

NOTES

1. "Interview with C. L. R. James," in *Kas-Kas: Interviews with Three Caribbean Writers in Texas*, ed. Ian Munro and Reinhard Sander (Austin: University of
Texas, African and Afro-American Research Institute, 1972), p. 33.

2. For details on members of the group and their ethnic background, see "The
Turbulent Thirties in Trinidad: An Interview with Alfred H. Mendes," ed. R. W.
Sander, *World Literature Written in English*, 12, 1 (April, 1973), 66-79.

3. Albert Gomes, *Through a Maze of Colour* (Port of Spain: Key Caribbean
Publications, 1974), p. 16.

4. Mendes interview, *WLWE*, p. 78.

5. Gomes, *Maze of Colour*, p. 16.

6. See Albert Gomes, *"The Beacon," Kraus Bibliographical Bulletin*, 21 (August,1977), 158-159.

7. Gomes, *Maze of Colour*, p. 18.

8. Gomes, *"The Beacon,"* p. 158.

9. C. L. R. James, "Discovering Literature in Trinidad: The Nineteen-Thirties," *Savacou*, 2 (September, 1970), 56.

10. Mendes interview, *WLWE*, p. 77.

11. Ibid, p. 78.

12. From the second to the seventh issue, Nathan Schneider, who became a prominent member of the American left in the 1930s, was *The Beacon's* "American agent."

13. Gomes, *Maze of Colour*, p. 20.

14. *The Beacon*, 1, 2 (May, 1931), 10.

15. *The Beacon*, 1, 4 (July, 1931), 2.

16. Gomes, *Maze of Colour*, p. 22.

17. *The Beacon*, 1, 4 (July, 1931), 18.

18. Gomes, *Maze of Color*, p. 23.

19. Gomes, "*The Beacon*," p. 159.

20. See Alfred Mendes, "A Commentary," *Trinidad*, 1, 2 (Easter, 1930), 68.

21. *The Beacon*, 1, 12 (April, 1932), 3.

22. Ibid.

23. See Carlisle Chang, "Painting in Trinidad," in *The Artist in West Indian Society: A Symposium*, ed. Errol Hill (Trinidad: U.W.I., Extra-Mural Studies, [1963]), pp. 25-37.

24. Mendes interview, *WLWE*, p. 77.

25. *The Beacon*, 1, 10 (Jan.-Feb., 1932), 24-25.

26. Most copies of both *The Royalian* and *The Quarterly Magazine* seem to have vanished. *The Royalian* first appeared in 1932 and lasted for about five issues. We were only able to locate the Christmas 1930 issue of *The Quarterly Magazine*, which is the ninth issue of the magazine.

27. See Brinsley Samaroo's introduction to the 1977 Kraus reprint of *The Beacon*, p. iv.

28. For example, Joy Carson,"Russia and the Coming War," *The Beacon*, 2, 1 (May, 1932), 18-21; and Adrian Cola Rienzi, "Communism and Chaos," *The Beacon*, 2, 3 (July, 1932), 9-10.

29. *The Beacon*, 2, 2 (June, 1932), 26-27.

30. *The Beacon*, 1, 11 (March, 1932), 8.

31. *The Beacon*, 1, 10 (Jan.-Feb., 1932), 3.

32. *The Beacon*, 2, 3 (July, 1932), 7.

33. Mendes interview, *WLWE*, p. 76.

34. *The Beacon*, 2, 5 (September, 1932), 17.

35. *The Beacon*, 1, 5 (August, 1931), 2.

36. Gomes, *Maze of Colour*, pp. 23-24.

37. *The Beacon*, 1, 7 (October, 1931), 21.

38. Ibid., p. 22.

39. *The Beacon*, 1, 5 (August, 1931), 19.

40. See Brinsley Samaroo's introduction to the 1977 Kraus reprint of *The Beacon*, p. viii. The three East Indian journals he mentions are: *East Indian Herald*, *East Indian Patriot*, and *East Indian Weekly*.

41. Mendes interview, *WLWE*, p. 73.

42. *The Beacon*, 2, 2 (June, 1932), 35.

43. See *The Beacon*, 1, 4 (July, 1931), 3-7.

44. *The Beacon*, 1, 6 (September, 1931), 17.

45. *The Beacon*, 3, 4 (November, 1933), 92.

46. *Trinidad*, 1, 1 (Christmas, 1929), 53.

47. Gomes, "*The Beacon*," p. 159.

48. *The Beacon*, 3, 4 (November, 1933), 80-81.

49. *The Beacon*, 2, 3 (July, 1932), 22.

50. *The Beacon*, 3, 4 (November, 1933), 86.

51. *The Beacon*, 3, 4 (November, 1933), 85-86.

52. *The Beacon*, 1, 10 (Jan.-Feb., 1932), 18.

53. *The Beacon*, 2, 3 (July, 1932), 25.

54. *The Beacon*, 2, 1 (May, 1932), 31.

55. *The Beacon*, 2, 7 (December, 1932), 7.

56. *The Beacon*, 1, 10 (Jan.-Feb., 1932), 17.

57. Peter K. Ayers, "Introduction: 2," in *From Trinidad: An Anthology of Early West Indian Writing*, ed. R. W. Sander (London: Hodder and Stoughton, 1978), p. 18.

CHAPTER 3

THE SHORT FICTION

The *Beacon* group set out its theoretical demands for an indigenous literature in two major statements published in *Trinidad* and *The Beacon*. The
first of the two "manifestos," Mendes's "Commentary," appeared in the second issue of *Trinidad*, in response to the furor created by the short stories
in the magazine's first number. In defending these short stories against the
charge of obscenity, Mendes declared:

The creative artist . . . who is sincere about his literary work (or any other art-
work for that matter) cannot stop to consider how much ugliness there is in the
matter that comes his way. It would be silly to tell the architect not to build in
stone because stone is rough and amorphous; to warn the sculptor to leave bronze
alone because bronze is brown and blatant is like warning the priest and parson
against heathens because they have no regard for *our* anthropomorphic god; even
so it is futile and puerile to ask the writer of fiction to leave bodies and barrack-
yards alone because they are obscene in the popular sense. It all depends on what
literary treatment they receive, though it does not necessarily mean that, so treated,
they shall be no longer obscenities; it simply means that they shall be obscenities
presented for reasons other than raising the disgust or sexual desires of the reader.[1]

Mendes's choice of metaphors seems to indicate that the group saw the
writer as an inspired individual, whose task it was to discover Truth and
Beauty. However, these qualities were to be found in features of form and
style rather than content. The obscene could become art if the creative
artist found the perfect form and images through which to express it. Thus
Mendes goes on to point out that some popular songs of the time could be
considered obscene "not because of the words, which are banal enough to

mean nothing, but because of the *tunes.*"[2] Such fine distinctions were probably meant to exasperate his critics more than anything else, but they do highlight the basic demand for aesthetic integrity that was part of the group's approach to short fiction. The "Commentary" also stresses the role of the writer as the moral conscience of his community:

The literature of fiction brings to the doors of people who otherwise would have known little or nothing of these things, the burden of this truth: our social organization is not what it ought to be; it is diseased . . . there are a few who think it their duty to present to their readers the other side of the coin of Life in all its stark realism of vermin and vice, especially when it is remembered that sex is the spring-board from which leap most of our desires. That way lies a readjustment (or should we say adjustment?) of the disordered condition of present-day society, for most of the literary artists, instead of acquiescing in the taken-for-granted expediency of a divinely revealed decalogue, are endeavouring to discover a more apt decalogue from the experience of human life, in short, they are looking within themselves for salvation instead of waiting for it to fall from heaven.[3]

The second "manifesto" was written by Albert Gomes in connection with a short-story competition announced in one of the early issues of *The Beacon.* In an editorial, which appeared while the competition was still in progress, Gomes indicated the kind of stories the judges were looking for and applied the general tenets of the group's literary theory directly to the specific problems of creative writing within the context of colonial Trinidad. He pointed out that the judges were not interested in "advertisements for the enhancement of [the] tourist trade," "anecdotes from the Good Book," or "extracts from *True Story.*" The stories should deal with aspects of Trinidad life and be peopled with Trinidadian characters. Emphasis was placed on a realistic treatment of language and a "natural" approach to sex. "We fail utterly to understand," wrote Gomes, "why anyone should want to see Trinidad as a miniature *Paradiso,* where grave-diggers speak like English M.P.'s and *vice versa.*"[4] Gomes felt that the strongest admonitions were necessary in dealing with the deeply engrained habits of imitation and self-deprecation, which he and his fellow countrymen had had instilled in them by their colonial education. As he remembers:

I never really ceased being shocked when the mail brought a manuscript from some remote corner of the island, written by a person who clearly had lived all his life in Trinidad, with fictional characters drawn from cinema types set in an ambiguous Anglo-American limbo, all complete with the occasional snowfall. It didn't help my understanding of this kind of literary heresy that I had myself, at the age of eleven, been asked by my first examination paper to write an essay about "A Snowfall."[5]

The winning stories did adequate justice to the group's theoretical demands. All four, to use Mendes's phrase, "smell" of Trinidad, but they do so to varying degrees.[6] The first prize went to a barrack-yard story, "His Right of Possession," which is included in the discussion of barrack-yard literature at the end of this chapter. The second prize went to an impressionistic piece by Olga Yaatoff called "Gasoline Station," which attempts to follow the stipulations in the "Commentary" on the necessity of finding the most apt form for a particular concept. The movement of the piece is swift and jerky as it follows the rhythm of the cars that pull in and out of the station during one long night, revealing their cargo of human happiness, lust, and misery to the lone station attendant. There is no plot as such but the piece is framed by the departure of the cars at the beginning of the evening's spree and their return during the early morning hours with their tired occupants. The third prize in the short story competition went to the expatriate doctor, W. V. Tothill, whose "Queer Story" was an account of the strange behavior of two rhinoceros beetles, told to a group of old school friends by an entomologist (who once lived in Trinidad) after a reunion dinner in Devon. The last of the prize-winning stories was a humorous piece by Fred E. Farrell called "The Other Side of the Picture," about a young member of Trinidad's upper middle class, who is persecuted with good wishes, sales propositions, and insurance policies when he wins a sweepstake. Each of the four winning stories makes use of aspects of Trinidad life which their authors knew well or had observed closely. The fact that one of the winning stories was written by a non-Trinidadian does not seem to have influenced the judges, though it is clear that they set greater store by the barrack-yard setting and the late night vigil at the gasoline pumps than by the more genteel after-dinner settings of the other two stories.

On the whole, the short fiction which appeared in *Trinidad* and *The Beacon* follows the same pattern of diversity within a common local setting established in the winning stories. Most of the stories make use of Trinidad settings. Several do so by describing typical local situations in stories that are conventional in form. One group, for example, makes use of the traditional short-story plot about a person who pursues one course of action relentlessly, only to discover that it has the opposite effect of what was intended, or was unnecessary in the first place. This plot is used to present features of middle-class greed and materialism in what at times amounts to a cautionary tale. In C. L. R. James's "Turner's Prosperity," a clerk who lives beyond his means and is chronically in debt is offered a reprieve by his manager who agrees to pay all his debts and then deduct repayment from Turner's salary in easy installments on condition that he avoid further indebtedness in the future. Turner and his wife scheme to turn his offer into a loan to surpass all previous loans by doubling the amount they actually owe in the figures they compile for the manager. On being confronted with the exorbitant figure, the manager fires Turner with one week's pay in lieu of notice and explains to him: "You owe too much money on too small a salary. I might have been able to help you had it been about half the amount, but not four hundred and fifty dollars. I am sorry."[7]

Joseph da Silva's story "The Pipe" is set along similar lines and concerns a young clerk who is tempted to steal one of the stylish pipes stocked by his company. He goes through with the theft on Saturday and is tortured with guilt all through the weekend. On Monday morning as he hangs around the pipe-stand trying to replace the stolen object, his boss mentions to him that the pipes are samples from one of the firms with which the company deals and that he can distribute them as he wishes. Da Silva sets up the simple plot effectively by describing the clerk's background and the social pressures on him to keep up with the round of parties and social events that are part of the lifestyle of the upper-middle-class circles to which he aspires. Mendes's "Faux Pas" is characteristically more direct and cutting. Unlike the stories by James and da Silva, in which the race of the protagonist is implied by his job, his speech, and the types of things on which he spends money, Mendes's story makes a point of stating the races of its three protagonists. Two are clerks, one white, one colored, and the third is a white commission agent. Their manner and conversation are crude (the colored clerk spends most of the time picking his nose) and their insensitivity about the poverty they see around them is matched by their lack of interest in matters of national importance and their lewd remarks on the women who pass before them on the street. The commission agent curses the poverty of the "coolies" he does business with because it deprives him of additional income. Their responses to the sight of a ragged street urchin scooping up a pigeon that has been run over by a cart and making off to eat it are, "That's a good joke. . . . Pigeon-pelau to-night," and "Helps to brighten up this God-forsaken job." The short sketch includes no overtly dogmatic moralizing, but simply ends when two good-looking women "both dressed up to the nines, in bright colours and nicely rouged" turn the corner and one of the clerks is about to start the usual train of coarse and suggestive remarks, when the commission agent snaps: "For God's sake . . . shut your damn mouth. That's my wife and daughter."[8]

Apart from exposing the weaknesses of the middle class, the short stories in the two magazines also picked up topical issues. Anti-Catholic stories with Trinidad settings and stories on the question of divorce appeared in *The Beacon*, when these issues were being hotly debated in the pages of the magazine. Kathleen Archibald's "Beyond the Horizon," for example, describes the loneliness and lack of fulfillment of a Trinidad woman, struggling to give her teenage daughters the means to enjoy a happy social life but resenting the way in which her marriage has thwarted her own earlier dreams of travelling "beyond the horizon." When the *Beacon* group began to take an interest in Trinidad's East Indian community and started the "India Section" of the magazine, Mendes's notorious story "Boodhoo" was serialized in three successive issues. "Boodhoo" describes the gradual seduction of a young Englishwoman, Minnie, by the enigmatic, half-caste houseboy, Boodhoo, who is her planter husband's natural child. Minnie dies as she gives birth to a child whose "blue eyes, pink skin, and fair hair" make it impossible for the reader to be sure whether it is the child or grandchild of Minnie's husband. The length of the story gives the author time to shade in the subtle nuances of emotion and the stages of discovery that lead to the story's climax, so that the story is able to address a number of different issues. In the first place we are given time to appreciate the social situation which leads first to Boodhoo's conception and then to Minnie's unfaithfulness. The isolation and futility of plantation life for the planters and their wives, shut off from society with their own kind and unwilling to establish real links with the dark-skinned workers who surround them and at times seem to encroach on their domain, is brought out in the opening scene of the story, when a large menacing cockroach interrupts Minnie's first, very correct, English-style tea party. Mrs. Hornby screams and smashes her ornate china cup, Minnie calls her maid to try and brush the bug away, and the stern, pragmatic Mrs. O'Halleran finally settles the matter smartly cracking the insect on the back, spreading its abdominal contents over the tea table, and then adding: "How silly of me not to have foreseen this!" The women's reactions reflect to a certain extent their attitudes to the "native question," especially to the effect which the native women have on their men. Mrs. Hornby sees the climate and the natives as evil and responsible for the failings of the men, while Mrs. O'Halleran declares that the behavior of the men is merely more noticeable in the restricted island community where it cannot be hidden. Her firm, no-nonsense views on natives, men, and cockroaches leave Minnie, who has hardly conceived of the possibility of miscegenation, bewildered and ill at ease.

Minnie's unease is amplified and sustained by the presence of Boodhoo in the house. She is first struck by his beauty, then, on realizing that he is of mixed blood, disgusted by the idea "that white men, men of our blood, should be so filthy as to take to themselves these Indian women. And to have children by them!" Her disgust gradually turns to consuming curiosity about Boodhoo's parentage and then to subtle sexual attraction to his strange, dark looks. The moment of first physical contact comes when he places his hand on her knee to brush away a scorpion that is crawling up her muslin dress. Soon after this, Boodhoo's mother suddenly turns up at the house like an evil omen and is hustled out of the yard by her son. As a result of this threat to his newfound happiness with Minnie, Henry sends Boodhoo away from the estate as well. Unknown to him, Henry's attempts to shield her from his past change Minnie's attraction to his son to one of longing and passion. The relationship between Boodhoo and Minnie is consummated one night when he comes back to the house, in conditions which a few months ago would have made Minnie recoil in horror.

Together, never saying a word, they stealthily trod the soft path, clasping each other. They passed under the shade of spreading trees that thickened as they advanced until they came to the little wood that hid them from the sight of the passionate moon. The ground, with a layer of rotting leaves from which rose a dull musky odour, was stippled with blots of lights of all shapes. An owl, startled by their presence, hooted, and they listened to the heavy flap of its wings as it bore its passage through the opaque dusk. Then all was quiet. Only the breeze made a rustling sound as it threaded its way through the maze of leaves overhead. . . . He sat on the broad root of an old immortelle tree and drew her down to him.[9]

After she becomes pregnant, Minnie discovers that this is the same spot on which Boodhoo was conceived. She learns of his true parentage from his mother, who finally finds a way to the new wife of her former lover and tells her the truth about Boodhoo in order to spite Henry. Minnie's old disgust at the thought of miscegenation is now matched by a double sense of guilt at the knowledge of her own act and its incestuousness. Though in making love to Boodhoo she overcomes her physical prejudices about Indians, her mental prejudices remain, and it is these, coupled with her sense of guilt and fear of discovery, that bring about her death. The sterility of the contact between whites and the alien peoples and cultures they encounter in the Caribbean is a recurring theme in the *Beacon* stories.

Ernest Carr's most important short fiction contribution to *The Beacon* was "Black Mother," a story which attempts to give mythical significance to the eruption of Mont Pelée in Martinique in 1902, in which all the inhabitants of the town at its base perished except for a condemned man in an underground dungeon. Like Mendes in "Boodhoo," Carr turns the event into a classic confrontation of opposing cultures, but in this case it is done by presenting the volcanic eruption as the fulfillment of the curse of the convict's mother who had sworn that she would not allow him to be killed by the agency of the white men's laws. As she warns the village, "Judge and jury is strong, eh? You just watch, Ma Mamba is sure stronger, mes petits." The story is one of the few in *The Beacon* in which Africa itself is invoked as the source of the folk culture of the West Indies which challenges the supremacy of the white colonizer. The description of Ma Mamba, at once compelling and disturbing, anticipates the dreaming, all-seeing ancestral figures in the novels of the Guyanese writer, Wilson Harris:

At this hour of the first bat and ghostly dusk, she looked as though carved whole out of a substantial block of Africa, the land of the weird and incomprehensible, the home of her ancestors. And with this evidence of an impregnable solidity there was also something ethereal and illusive about Ma Mamba. One felt, at certain moments, an eerie element, like a nimbus, streaming out from that black body, converting it into a symbol of the all-pervasive and all-knowable. But it was chiefly the face of this woman which made one so uncomfortably conscious of the oracular in her. It was of the strong, impressive, indomitable mould sometimes seen in her race, the face of a people who have suffered and know no surcease from suffering, no refuge except that they somehow find beyond our known reality; and the eyes, concentrated as they now were on some far-off thing, visible only to herself, stirred the beholder as some cosmic vista. They were incredibly old eyes, eyes which might have known the agony of the first created man. Awesome they were now with vision and a static calm, and in them there seemed no notion of the thing called Time.[10]

The village priest, Father O'Dowd, crosses himself as he comes upon Ma Mamba staring at the volcanic peak with an intensity that "seemed to be at one with some related force up there." He can only offer her words of comfort and alternative ways of resigning herself to the decree of the courts. Ma Mamba has no time for his kindly ineffectual suggestions and brushes aside his offer of prayer for the ultimate release of her son's soul from purgatory with scornful impatience: "Masses for his soul, par Dieu! I will hold masses for his body. That I will save." The dance by which she invokes the assistance of the mountain is a long, wild thing that evokes wonder as well as revulsion. The same emotions are aroused by the description of the figure of the mountain god that she fashions in anticipation of the success of her petition. At the end of the story, Ma Mamba's son Jean, wandering in the ruins of his mother's house where she has perished, along with the village, in the volcano's eruption, comes across his mother's image of the mountain god. He disappears into the forests with it, and it is at this point that Carr locates the beginning of his myth of a mountain shrine to the god Pel "held sacred to the slayer, to the man who, having slain, flees before the vengeance he has aroused."

One other attempt at exploiting legend deserves attention: Michael J. Deeble's "Yacua: A West Indian Romance" is one of the most conventional stories published in the magazines. It is a historical romance, dealing with the love of a dashing, handsome English adventurer for the beautiful daughter of a Carib chieftain. Though it is based on the actual history of the colonization of Grenada by the French, its characters are the stock heroes, villains, and damsels in distress of the romantic genre, and it ends with the marriage of the adventurer and the native princess. Beneath the pleasant but trivial trappings of the story, however, Deeble offers us an unusually critical insight into the methods and activities of the colonizers in their "pacification" of the natives. Though the European camp is divided into "heroes" and "villains," even the most attractive of their number are shown to be involved to a greater or lesser degree in the exploitation of the native population. It is the gracious M. Du Parquet, and not the venial Baron le Compte, who forces Canagundo to sign the deed of sale transferring the ownership of the island to the King of France in exchange for a few trumpery articles of barter. The story includes a description of the last stand of the Carib warriors who are caught in an ambush through the treachery of the Carib interpreter guiding the French. When the braves realize that there can be no alternative to defeat, they hurl themselves over the edge of a cliff in a heroic act of mass suicide. This particular incident forms part of the legend of the resistance of the region's original inhabitants to European colonization throughout the Caribbean. By incorporating it into the historical account of Grenada's settlement, Deeble helps establish it as a Caribbean legend which represents the other side of the story of colonization to that usually highlighted in the European romances of swashbuckling privateers and brave explorers.

Though most of the stories published by the *Beacon* group in their magazines and the 1937 anthology deal with serious, "adult" social issues, here and there among the stories one is pleasantly surprised by a refreshing, light piece which demonstrates the imaginative range of the contributors and the liberal tolerance of the editors. James's anecdote about the fat boy who refuses to play the part of Fatty Arbuckle in the movies is one example, while Ralph de Boissière's "Booze and the Goberdaw" displays the comic features and delicate fantasy of a real fairy tale. Other stories of fancy include T. M. Kelshall's "When Ignorance Was Bliss: An Extravaganza" about the ass's revenge on man, and E. G. Benson's "René de Malmatre" about a young French nobleman who inherits his uncle's estates but because of his weakness for pretty girls, is haunted by the old man in the shape of a pig until in desperation he takes holy orders. Some of these stories, like "Booze and the Goberdaw," are set in Trinidad as a matter of course, while others take place in dream settings. Many display a high standard of originality and ingenuity.

The magazines, however, contain few stories which make use of children as central characters. The one notable exception is Ralph de Boissière's story, "The Old Year Passes," which appeared in the 1937 anthology. It describes the growing awareness of a small boy of the disturbing complexity of adult life, as his hero worship of his gay, debonair bachelor uncle changes to a hurt realization that his uncle's charms are first of all for the amusement of pretty women rather than the humoring of little boys. De Boissière takes a craftsman's pains over the reproduction of the child's perspective on nature and the adult world in passages such as this recollection of the boy's impressions of the old cocoa estate, where he spends his vacations:

He remembered, too, waking with a sensation of strangeness in the early mornings. Where was he? Whose bed was this? What sounds were those? But the next minute such a feeling of joy would take hold of him that he would jump out of bed, convinced that something important was going to happen to-day. . . . One morning when the sun had only touched the tops of the tall nutmeg trees, he heard the voices of Uncle Harry and Uncle Willie in the dining-room. Heavens! They were eating before starting off somewhere. Was he in time? Would they wait for him. . . .

In the dining-room Uncle Harry, spreading his strong hairy arms on the table and greedily buttering his bread on both sides did not notice when Dickie came in. His expressive black eyes were dancing as he said: "She's a mighty fine girl. Boy, what a figure! But what the hell . . . women are a damn ruination." He suddenly gave his brother a defiant look.

"I shouldn't wonder," growled Uncle Willie through a mouthful. "Look at the expensive presents you make them." . . .

Their tones of voice made the room seem so still and tense with anger that Dickie was oppressed, and went into the yard. By the stable door two saddled horses were tethered, and his hopes sank like lead in his heart. Nevertheless he hung around till his uncles came out. Still too busy talking to notice him, they mounted the horses (which kept shaking their flanks in order to drive off the flies) and rode down the hill. Their bodies swayed clumsily in the saddle to the careful steps of the horses; they shaded their eyes from the rising sun.

How sad and lifeless everything seemed now! The fowls throwing themselves forward after the chipped coconut which cook threw for them while she wailed: "Tee-te-te"; the cows stretching their necks and tongues to bite mangoes off the trees; Joseph, the stableman, spreading hay for the horses—all became repulsive to him in a moment. He was assailed by self-consciousness and a sense of desolation. How he disliked this old place! He wandered away under the cocoa trees.[11]

The child's swiftly changing moods; the lack of comprehension with which he registers each detail of his uncle's appearances and manner without being able to discern what it is about a particular remark besides its tone which makes him feel uneasy; and the extreme egotism with which he enjoys or rejects the fantasy world of the old estate are all accurately captured. De Boissière's story, and Kathleen Archibald's "Clipped Wings," which also appeared in the 1937 anthology, seem to anticipate the Trinidadian "novels of childhood" of more recent years such as Ian McDonald's *The Humming-Bird Tree* (1969) and Michael Anthony's *The Year in San Fernando* (1965), both of which use techniques similar to those of the two short stories to suggest the child's intense but limited perceptions of the adult world.

To turn now to the barrack-yard stories, it should be stated from the outset that these stories are not as numerous or as uniform in approach to their material as is sometimes assumed. Of the 80-odd short stories which appeared in *Trinidad, The Beacon* and the 1937 anthology, *From Trinidad*, only a dozen of them could accurately be described as "barrack-yard" type stories. Apart from James's "Triumph," they are all written by Alfred Mendes, Percival Maynard and C. A. Thomasos. In addition, there are two related pieces by Kathleen Archibald and her brother Charles. The attention which has been given to this comparatively small group of stories derives from the fact that they were the most original, in terms of theme, of the stories which appeared in the group's publications. Even the other topical indigenous theme of racial prejudice and miscegenation was one that had already been well worked by European writers of tropical romances. One has also to bear in mind that a number of the barrack-yard stories written by members of the group were not published in their anthology or the two magazines. Several of Mendes's better-known barrack-yard stories were first published abroad or in other local magazines. The barrack-yard stories which were reprinted or appeared for the first time outside of the pages of *Trinidad* and *The Beacon* tended to reach a wider and more diverse audience than the local literary magazines could command; the stories circulated in this manner became the group's best-known work. One of the short stories written around the time that *Trinidad* was started but not published until after the collapse of *The Beacon* is Mendes's "Afternoon in Trinidad." It is discussed in this chapter because it is one of the earliest authentic barrack-yard stories and it illustrates clearly the most distinctive features of the genre.

Mendes's "Afternoon in Trinidad" contains all the major features of plot, setting, and characterization which we have come to consider typical of the barrack-yard story. The plot revolves around the attempts of one kept woman in the barrack-yard, Queenie, to steal the keeper of her neighbor, Corinne, and ends in a free-for-all battle between the yard's inhabitants. All the stock characters are present: Ma Nenine is the name given to the elderly black woman versed in the arts of obeah, which she uses to help the younger women find new keepers. She acts as everybody's *confidante*, and in this story is also the gossip who carries tales of Queenie's intrigues to her jealous keeper. Corinne, whose affairs occupy our attention throughout the story and for whom the author attempts to elicit our sympathies, is the typical barrack-yard heroine—pretty, indolent, fat ("there's nothing your creole admires more in a woman than ample proportions," the author explains), and not particularly clever or aggressive. She is aware of Queenie's attempts to seduce her keeper, "but did not in the least mind them in spite of the fire her friend, Georgie, was pushing. Nothing ever upset her, nothing could ever stir her into excitement and she did her washing quietly, with the greatest economy of movement, and when she didn't have any washing work to do . . . she sat on her doorstep gazing out into the yard and putting in a word only now and again."[12] Georgie, her fiery bosom companion, who protects her from the more predatory members of the yard and lectures her when necessary on her lack of initiative and her naivety about men, is another stock character. Mendes does not mention the details of complexion and physical appearance of the women, but usually in a barrack-yard story the placid pretty woman who is having trouble with her man is of mixed race with dark skin, but "good" (European-type) hair, while her stronger, more assertive friend is a black woman. At times the older *confidante* figure and the supportive friend are combined into one for greater economy of characterization. The trouble-making "other woman" is often a mulatress, who feels she is superior to her neighbors because of her fairer skin.

Apart from these four major female characters Mendes also introduces two keepers in this story who are typical of the two types of male providers we encounter in the barrack-yard. About Napoleon, Corinne's keeper, we are told: "besides being a Beau Brummel, a stickfighter and what not, [he] was certainly not a one-woman man. All the women in Port of Spain knew him and he was perpetually in trouble with their keepers." He resembles the typical "sweetman" of the barrack-yard stories, and like the sweetmen he spends most of his time gambling. Mendes implies that he is something of a card shark, which is why he can afford to keep women rather than be a sweetman and be kept by them. The other keeper in the story is the hardworking cabdriver, Dodo, whose name suggests one of his typical characteristics—he is easily duped. Dodo provides adequately for his woman, Queenie, but lacks the resources that Napoleon has to provide her with glamor and excitement as well. He works long, unsociable hours as a cab-driver, which leave Queenie free to entertain other men. He is jealous by nature but too much in awe of Queenie to cause trouble unless he is pushed. This kind of keeper is usually portrayed in the stories as having a fairly stable relationship with his mistress and being a respectable man of high principles. The crisis in the story comes when both the long-suffering Corinne and the timid Dodo are pushed beyond endurance by Queenie's behavior and a fight breaks out.

The setting of "Afternoon in Trinidad" includes all the familiar props of the barrack-yard story: There are the bleaching stones in the center of the yard, on which the women spread the clothes they wash to supplement their incomes from their keepers, and the communal latrine with its characteristic stench near the mango tree at the bottom of the yard. The women all cook their meals on coal pots just outside their doors, and the smell of meat cooking on a Sunday is the acknowledged symbol that all is well financially with each of them. Ma Nenine gives Corinne the mandatory bush bath, which for some reason is practically the only form of obeah ever described in a barrack-yard story. In this story we are also given a sample of the women's views on obeah, which range from the credulous to the frankly skeptical. The story is full of well-captured exchanges between the women in which they show their skill at repartee and express their views on life in a mixture of biblical rhetoric and pithy folk adages. Most of the better barrack-yard stories manage to suggest the distinctive idiom and ethics of the Trinidad lower classes in their reproduction of dialogue, and this is one of the major achievements of the genre. The fact that the women are unmarried and move freely from one keeper to another is never raised as a moral issue, just as there is no attempt to judge Ma Nenine's use of obeah. Even Queenie's advances to Napoleon are played down as harmless, and trouble only breaks out in the yard when Queenie becomes deliberately provocative and tries to place Dodo in a bad light in the presence of her neighbors, implying he has hit the old woman, Ma Nenine. It is this malicious action that stirs the lethargic Corinne into action:

"Wutless bitch," Corinne said quietly, not looking at anyone.

"Who you callin' bitch, enh? Who you callin' wutless, enh?" Queenie demanded.

"Why for some people does go to church, I ain' know," Corinne said, addressing nobody in particular.

"Hol' you' noise, all you," Napoleon shouted, his arms raised authoritatively, "Ole lady, you get strike?"

For answer, Ma Nenine, still with her hands over her face, rocked and screamed and wailed.

"Is me you was calling bitch?" Queenie demanded, belligerently approaching Corinne.

Corinne smiled sarcastically, while Dodo, refusing to believe his ears, refusing to accept her treachery, stood gazing at his woman. Suddenly the significance of her attitude dawned on him and, losing his temper, he sprang at her and struck her full on the mouth with clenched fist.[13]

By limiting external commentary and allowing the characters to pass judgement on each other, Mendes is able to place the moral issues which arise in his stories squarely within the ethical framework of the yard and present the barrack-yarders as whole individuals capable of both good and evil.

Other writers found alternative methods of dealing with the inescapably sordid nature of life in the barrack-yard when judged by middle-class standards of respectability. James in "Triumph" uses a technique associated with the writer Henry Fielding of ironically distancing himself from both his subject and his audience and making use of the epic devices to ennoble his humble protagonists. "Triumph" opens with a leisurely, urbane guided tour of the physical and cultural peculiarities of the barrack-yard and its inhabitants. The tongue-in-cheek manner of the eighteenth-century novelist is aptly reproduced in James's wry comment on the function of the bleaching stones in the yard:

In the centre of the yard is a heap of stones. On these the half-laundered clothes are bleached before being finally spread out to dry on the wire lines which in every yard cross and recross each other in all directions. Not only to Minerva have these stones been dedicated. Time was when they would have had an honoured shrine in a local temple to Mars, for they were the major source of ammunition for the homicidal strife which in times past so often flared up in barrack-yards.[14]

James links his opening discourse with the reader to the body of the story by making use of something approaching an epic simile:

On a Sunday morning in one of the rooms of a barrack in Abercromby Street sat Mamitz. Accustomed as is squalid adversity to reign unchallenged in these quarters, yet in this room it was more than usually triumphant, sitting, as it were, high on a throne of royal state, so depressed was the woman and so depressing her surroundings.[15]

"Triumph" is probably the most entertaining of the barrack-yard stories. Its plot is similar to that of "Afternoon in Trinidad," except that both the flashy and expansive keeper and the hard-working jealous one are after the affections of the placid and long-suffering character, Mamitz. The story does not end with a fight. Mamitz, with the aid of her shrewish friend and supporter, Celestine, is able to confound the attempts of their jealous neighbor to arouse the suspicions of the hard-working butcher who is paying Mamitz's rent. Instead of starting a fight, he apologizes and gives Mamitz all the money he has made over the Easter weekend. Celestine and Mamitz convert the money into small bills and pin them all over Mamitz's door into the yard, which they then swing open so that the whole yard can see how Mamitz has triumphed over her jealous neighbor. "Triumph" is a truly comic story which sticks to the spirit of the yard, but plays down the misery and violence that were part of the real-life situation. James goes as far as implying in his opening remarks that real barrack-yard violence was a thing of the past, but there seems to have been little justification for this statement.

Laughter was one way in which the author of the barrack-yard story could elicit sympathy for his characters without identifying himself too closely with their morals or way of life. The black middle-class writers who came after James and Mendes and contributed barrack-yard stories to *The Beacon* seem to have been particularly self-conscious about being associated with their characters. C. A. Thomasos manages to retain a degree of objectivity in his stories, but he writes under a pseudonym, Norman Collingwood, a practice which was usually frowned upon by members of the *Beacon* circle. Percival Maynard follows Mendes's pattern of plot and setting closely, but in his first two barrack-yard stories he goes out of his way to distance himself from his characters. In "Francisco" for example, which is set in a small agricultural town, he introduces a first-person narrator who seems to occupy a privileged position in the community and can patronize the lower-class people he writes about—he addresses Francisco, the central character in the story, as "My dear man." With gentle ridicule, the narrator records Francisco's attempts to wear shoes and spend money in order to impress a smart newcomer to the community and makes little effort to reproduce the creole speech of his lower-class characters. In another of Maynard's stories, "His Right of Possession," which won the first prize in *The Beacon*'s short story competition, he gives a comic description of a calypso tent which verges on the derogatory:

Cliff piloted them through the crowd and into the "tent," and got seats for them on a bench not far from the musicians. These last named, three in number, were a tough looking set. The light from a gas lamp lit up their features which were of the kind that any Rogues' Gallery would be proud to treasure and hand down to posterity. A red-faced, red-eyed, bloated individual glared savagely at a bass-viol which he was trying to tune, and whose appearance warranted the presumption that it had existed long and suffered much. A guitar, whose antiquity and fortunes seemed on a par with those of the viol, rested on the lap of a long-necked, squint-eyed creature who was engaged in mending a broken string. And a thick-set, shifty-looking youth toyed idly with a cuatro, whose newness struck one in the eye, the while he grinned, or rather, grimaced terrorisingly, at some young female who had caught his fancy.[16]

Maynard's poor imitation of Dickens here dehumanizes the musicians and makes them appear the vicious, perverted creatures many members of the middle class seem to have considered them. His description, though quite legitimate within the context of social realism, makes it difficult for the reader to believe that he wishes to elicit sympathy for his characters, and consequently the reader also becomes distanced from the people and events he describes.

Maynard bases "His Right of Possession" on the importance of the traditional value of faithfulness within a sexual relationship. His heroine Vera, though she is incensed by her brutal treatment at the hands of her keeper, seems to lack the highly developed instinct for survival of the kept women in the other barrack-yard stories and is unable to retaliate effectively. At first Vera intends to report Pedro to the police, then she decides to go off with another man, but she ends up crawling back to the room of her friend and *confidante* Olive, unable to go through with either resolve. In a thinly disguised Hollywood confession, she explains to Olive:

"I suppose yo' dyin' to know why I here instead of being wid Donal'? Well, I couldn' go and live wid him—like dat. I said yes at fus' because I did want to make Pedro see dat I coulda get some body else if 'e didn' want me again. But I cahn' go t'rough wid it. I fin' dat out w'en Donal' kiss me. I nearly scream. . . . I feel so funny—and cheap. Yo' see, I don' love 'im, and to live wid 'im would be cuttin' off me nose to spite me face. Besides"—and here her eyes grew moist with tears—"I still love Pedro—in spite of everyt'ing—an' I feel I belong to 'im. And—I couldn' give somebody else—w'at was his."[17]

Vera's delicately phrased periphrasis and refined sentiments seem quite out of character for the kept woman of a barrack-yard story, who would hardly have shrunk from calling a spade a spade or considered a chaste kiss a betrayal of her honor. Vera tries to decide between living with Olive, going back to Pedro, or going back home to her parents. For most of the barrack-yard women in the stories, the choice is usually between staying with their keeper, starving, or working on the streets as a prostitute. Somehow Maynard's story seems to miss this brutal but realistic connection between the moral priorities of the kept women and survival. Even in James's comic portrayal of the barrack-yard in "Triumph" we do not lose sight of this reality. Often in the stories, the protagonist's dilemma is that she must choose between the man to whom she feels emotionally and sexually drawn and the one who can provide her with an adequate source of income. The pain and frustration which usually accompany the decision to opt for food rather than love or sexual excitement are often the root cause of the outbreaks of violence described in the yard.

Perhaps the best example of this dilemma is given in Mendes's story, "Her Chinaman's Way." Here Mendes dispenses with the human and physical trappings of the barrak-yard and concentrates instead on the plight of a particular woman who realizes that she no longer loves her keeper but is afraid to abandon him for a new one because of his possible claims on their child. Maria's keeper is a Chinese shopkeeper, Hong Wing, from whom she feels culturally and emotionally isolated. She had gone to live with him after a period of severe financial distress during which she had resorted to the traditional bush bath prescribed by her friend and *confidante*, Philogen. She finds herself committed to Hong Wing within a stable and dependent relationship quite unlike her former experiences with keepers. She bears his child, works in his shop, and remains faithful to him for over a year. As the author explains:

Maria had taken Hong Wing, wondering if she was doing the right thing, for she had felt that she would never get to understand him; and though she had been living with him for such a long time, she had never been able to understand him. He cowed her with his sleek, mysterious manner so much that she had grown to fear him. That had disturbed her. She had been accustomed to dictate, control; now she had to beg timidly, and since she had met Adolphus, the lithe black carterman, she had realized that life with Hong Wing could never be anything but annoying and uninteresting.[18]

She turns to her friend for advice, and Philogen in assessing her dilemma states one of the basic precepts of the barrack-yarders' moral code:

Gerl, you likes too much man. You carn' stick to one foo longer dan you can help. But, perhaps you right. Man does go all about; I don' see why woman carn' go all about, too. Maria, chil', you good foo dem. An' I don' blame you, for is time dey see dat us women got rights too.[19]

This insistence that the Trinidad woman had as much of a right to sexual freedom as a man, and was not to be considered more immoral than a man if she chose to assert it, was one of the more overt ways in which the barrack-yard genre attacked the double standards of the local community. While it was accepted that men at all levels of the society were entitled to sexual freedom, a woman who joined the middle classes was expected to be chaste. Couples who had lived together for years often married when they acquired means and wished to appear respectable. Increasingly, the fact that a woman was legally married, whatever forms of promiscuity her husband chose to indulge, was the one factor which distinguished a member of the lower class from a member of the lower middle class.

Maria is trapped in the beginning of this syndrome because Hong Wing, as a shopkeeper, is a potential member of the petty bourgeoisie. Maria is attracted to Hong Wing because of his superior status, having previously been kept "for periods ranging from three months to one year . . . [by] men of her own class . . . whom she understood, and whom she could always manage to get rid of when she grew tired of them without causing much trouble." However, she has not considered the consequences of her middle-class aspirations. By leaving her room in the barrack-yard for Hong Wing's shop and then a shared home, she gives up the comparative freedom of her life in the yard and is more effectively "owned" by Hong Wing than she has been by any of her previous keepers. Not only will she lose the roof over her head if she leaves him, but he also has a greater claim on their child. Had she remained in the barrack-yard and received Hong Wing there occasionally, no one could have taken away her child in any situation, even if it was she who deserted Hong Wing and not vice versa. As Hong Wing's common-law wife she has already forfeited some of her rights as a single woman, but she only begins to realize the full implications of her actions when her attraction to Adolphus becomes urgent and she realizes her hands are tied. The irony is that Hong Wing hates their child, whom he considers his rival for Maria's affections and a drain on his resources, another form of materialism which is alien to Maria's lower-class code of ethics.

Philogen advises Maria to protect her luck by repeating a series of obeah "praises," waiting until Hong Wing next goes to collect smuggled opium, and then betraying him to the police. Maria's devious method of eliminating her keeper transgresses two more important tenets of barrack-yard life. In the first place, though some of the women were sometimes kept by policemen, the police as a body were usually considered the natural enemies of the barrack-yarders, and to involve them in the betrayal of one's keeper would have been an unnatural and hypocritical act. Moreover, by getting Hong Wing arrested, Maria is in a position to keep his child as well as his property, and it is an unwritten rule of the yard that the sweetman or kept woman never takes the spoils of a former relationship when he or she moves on to a new keeper. In the barrack-yard story, the relationship between two parties in such a situation has well-defined limitations, and there is seldom any confusion between moral responsibility and contractual obligation as might have arisen within a middle-class marriage. Fathers could be sued to provide support for their children, but no one expected a keeper to continue to support a man or a woman merely on the basis that they had formerly shared a prolonged sexual relationship. Each step Maria takes carries her deeper into the contradiction between her former status and her present aspirations. She even pretends to Hong Wing that she loves him more than ever after she has tipped off the police, thus arousing his suspicions. The story ends when Hong Wing escapes temporarily from the police search party and returns to murder his child before going into hiding and leaving Maria free to go to Adolphus. Hong Wing strangles the baby with a new dress Maria has been making while she is occupied in the second room of their comparatively spacious home making coffee for her reputed husband.

"Her Chinaman's Way" is a very effective, suspenseful horror story. Mendes builds up each detail of the final scene in advance. We are told of the division between the kitchen and the "drawing-room" as Maria proudly refers to it early in the story as an example of her middle-class aspirations, and of the pleasure she takes in the new dress she is making. Her concern for the baby is constantly reiterated, and Hong Wing's dislike for the child is suggested by a flashback in which Maria remembers an occasion on which he had accidentally or deliberately stepped on the child one busy Saturday night at the shop, when Maria had come with the baby to help out behind the counter. For most of the story we follow her mental anguish as she tries to hide her relationship with Adolphus, arrange her escape from Hong Wing, and look after her child. Throughout, we are aware of a vague threat hanging over her that could result in her new lover being hurt or she herself being killed or losing the custody of her child, but Mendes delays the bizarre denouement until the very last sentence of the story:

When she re-entered the drawing-room Hong Wing was standing in front of the sofa. There was nothing in his attitude to suggest anything to her, but his face had undergone a complete change. His eyes were almost closed, his thin lips were pressed tightly together, the skin on his cheeks puckered up. Her flesh tingled as though pins were pricking her all over her body. She would have rushed to her baby, snatched it up and taken pot-luck with a race to the back-door, through the yard, into the street, but he barred the way. She waited, the coffee spilling onto the floor. He held his hand out for it and drank it off with one gulp. A cock in the yard crew.

"Who tell police I go las' nigh' for op'um, enh?" he hissed at her through two rows of black mouselike teeth. She cowered before him, though he had not moved. She heard the empty cup smash against the partition, and then his voice, thin, steady:

"I no vex, love. You give me op'um. I go give flien' some," and he limped out of the room into the windy street.

Maria gazed at the closed door, wondering what he had gone out to get. To await his return would be folly. She would go straightway to Philogen. She could walk the distance quite comfortably with her baby. Going up to it, she withdrew the shawl. She couldn't believe her eyes. Her new dress was on the baby, around its neck, drawn tight—tight.[20]

From the stories which have been discussed it can be seen that the barrack-yard story could be used to present horror, comedy or social intrigue. If one examines the barrack-yard stories in *Trinidad, The Beacon,* and the 1937 anthology in order of their chronological appearance, a certain line of development can be traced. The earliest stories—James's "Triumph"; and "Sweetman," "Her Chinaman's Way," and "Five Dollars' Worth of Flesh" by Mendes—all place great emphasis on the physical and social context of their stories. There are descriptions of the barrack-yard and explanations of all of the special features of lower-class life which are introduced. In Mendes's "Sweetman," for example, the dance at which the altercation between Seppy and his keeper takes place is described in great detail and there is a full explanation of the role of the sweetman and his relationship to his keeper. We are given similar background information about kept women in "Her Chinaman's Way." In "Five Dollars' Worth of Flesh," the names of specific districts of Port of Spain, such as St. James, St. Clair, Belmont and Four Roads are mentioned, as well as particular streets such as Tragarete Road, Queen Street and George Street, along which the protagonist Isadora walks in search of work. Each area is associated with a particular lifestyle or class or person.

After the *Beacon*'s short-story competition in 1932, when Thomasos and Maynard began to write barrack-yard stories in imitation of Mendes and James, there was less emphasis on recreating the entire social milieu. The stories tend to concentrate on individuals within the yard and take the details of the inhabitants' way of life for granted. In Thomasos's "Daughter of Jezebel" for instance, there is no attempt to describe the physical layout of the yard. All we are told is that "there were eight rooms in the barrack and Rosita occupied the one at the end." The heroines of the stories written in this second phase tend to look and think a lot more like the heroines of a conventional romance. In another barrack-yard story, "The Dougla," Thomasos describes his "dougla" (Afro-Indian) woman as "elegant" with a body of "perfect symmetry," while Maynard's heroine in "His Right of Possession" is referred to as "pretty little Vera." This seems a far cry from the buxom creole favorites Mendes and James had observed in the yard. Their ways of dealing with wayward keepers also have an effeminate edge which is absent in the brawling, heckling Amazons of the early stories. Maynard's Vera in "His Right of Possession" threatens to report her keeper to the police, Rosita in "Daughter of Jezebel" attempts to poison her keeper rather than stabbing him in a public brawl, and the dougla in Thomasos's story entices her keeper back by turning up with another man. Even the ways in which the keepers are shown supporting their women are less basic. Whereas Mamitz in James's "Triumph" is rewarded with hard cash and chunks of meat from her butcher, the second generation of keepers concentrate on shoes and dresses. None of these variations are less likely or even less authentic, but they make the later stories less distinctive than the earlier ones.

On the other hand, both groups of stories concentrate on features of barrack-yard life which would have been considered exotic in middle-class circles. Their emphasis is on sexual intrigue, violence, obeah, colorful names and speech, and exotic women. Both invariably feature heroines who are racially mixed. Thomasos's Elaine and James's Mamitz are "douglas;" Maria in "Her Chinaman's Way" is described as "handsome in an exotic way with . . . full lips, large nose, and small eyes that told you there was Chinese blood in her veins," with a "voluptuous figure, inherited from her half-breed Venezuelan mother." Isadora in "Five Dollars' Worth of Flesh" outbids them all and has "five bloods in her veins: Spanish, Negro, East Indian, Red Indian and Chinese." It is clear that the middle-class writers who came from rigidly stratified racial cliques were intrigued by the exciting mixtures they observed within the barrack-yard and shared the taste for voluptuous exotic women that Mendes attributes to the creole in "Afternoon in Trinidad." In both the first and second phases of writing within the barrack-yard genre the emphasis is on the attractive or exciting elements of lower-class life.

In the third phase of barrack-yard writing, a new element of protest or social consciousness begins to surface in the stories. This had already been anticipated in Mendes's "Five Dollars' Worth of Flesh," in which the descent of a lower-class woman selling her body in order to feed her two young children introduces the well-known theme of proverty leading to prostitution. In spite of its exotic touches, the story strikes a more sombre note than other early barrack-yard stories and suggests something of the unrelieved misery and degradation of barrack-yard life which James Cummings emphasizes in his factual account of life as he had experienced it there. The three last of the barrack-yard stories to appear in *The Beacon* and Gomes's 1937 anthology, *From Trinidad,* by Percival Maynard, Charles Archibald and Kathleen Archibald, all turned their attention to this aspect of barrack-yard life. Each of their contributions highlights the plight of the children of the yards.

Charles Archibald's sketch "Rupert" is short and direct with hardly any pretensions to the traditional techniques of the barrack-yard genre. It describes the life of "a little black boy" who lives with his mother in a room in a barrack-yard. It is written in the present tense and addresses the reader directly in an effort to touch his social conscience. It gives a completely new perspective on the washing jobs that the women in the other barrack-yard stories are often described as taking in order to supplement their incomes from their keepers.

> If it rains she still has to have the clothes she washes dry and ironed by a certain day, each week.
>
> When it rains her life is a hell of worry and anxiety.
>
> She has nails on the inside of her room's partitions. She put knotted lengths of twine across the rooms [sic]. She hangs the clothes on these.
>
> They drip all night.
>
> She always abandons her bed on such nights. She sleeps under it.
>
> Sometimes a little runlet of water finds its way to her. She puts a bundle of rags to protect her.
>
> Rupert fends for himself.[21]

Archibald goes on to describe "the most wearying part of her work," the ironing, which was done with heavy irons heated over a coal pot: strenuous and monotonous work which, as he points out, could often go on until midnight or after. Instead of a fun-loving, high-spirited, exotic beauty, Archibald's barrack-yard woman is a brooding, foul-tempered, overworked creature who batters her son out of sheer frustration. The sketch ends on a particularly grisly note, when Rupert's mother takes to beating him with a stick studded with nails. Rupert exhibits his scars and becomes a celebrity at the primary school he attends intermittently, until one day another boy remarks, "If I had a bottom like that I'd be shame to show it," and Rupert ceases to be the only type of celebrity he has ever had a chance of becoming. Archibald's sketch may have been written in reaction to the frivolity and exotism of the earlier barrack-yard stories, but it swings to the opposite extreme and presents the barrack-yarders purely as the victims of social injustice. He misses out on the vitality and resourcefulness which Trinidad writers before and after him portrayed in their description of the culture and lifestyle through which the barrack-yarders defied their fate and tried to maintain their humanity. In the hands of his sister Kathleen Archibald, for example, a similar incident of bizarre exhibitionism in "Clipped Wings" is converted by a barrack-yard boy into a source of income from those who wish to stand and stare.

In "His Last Fling," Percival Maynard attempts to achieve some form of synthesis between the two extremes. The story opens with Harry Wilkinson Vanroy, better known as Snakey, "sweetman and inveterate gambler," running through large sums of money at the Saturday night fair preceding the Siparia fête. Snakey has exhausted his finances and is trying half-heartedly to flirt with a pretty girl when he remembers Kezia, his conquest of the Siparia fête a year previously. He decides to look her up for old times' sake, only to discover that she has had his child and is now living in disgrace away from her family in a ramshackle room with the baby. Moved to contrition, Snakey suddenly decides to take on his responsibilities as a father and returns to the fair to try and win some money gambling with Kezia's last few pence. When he loses even these he attacks the banker at the gambling booth and has to be pried off him by "two officers of the law." He is led away still shouting "Kezia, Kezia!" Apart from Maynard's disappointing handling of creole speech, his story suffers from its poorly executed plot. Snakey's transition from sweetman to desperate father is far too sudden and hardly seems motivated. It is difficult to imagine that a sweetman of his experience has never before been confronted with this type of situation. Even if he is genuinely disturbed and shocked by Kezia's plight, it seems slightly ludicrous for an expert con man, who not a moment ago had cheerfully frittered away twenty dollars, suddenly to be driven to despair over the loss of an initial investment of twelve cents. However, the story does show a new awareness on the part of one regular writer of barrack-yard stories of the other side of the sweetman's way of life, which until then had been played down.

The most effective of the serious stories about the barrack-yard, however, did not appear until the publication in 1937 of Gomes's anthology, *From Trinidad*. Written by Kathleen Archibald, "Clipped Wings" departs somewhat from the earlier stories' emphasis on plot and dialogue and makes greater use of impressionistic descriptive passages and symbolism to communicate the atmosphere and reality of barrack-yard life. The central image, as indicated in the title, is the symbol of a bird that is unable to fly. Miss Archibald describes the grace and beauty with which the ungainly scavenger birds, known locally as corbeaux, soar high above the dirt and squalor of the Labasse or city dump, where they rummage for food:

Once one of these birds separates from the rest and wings its way up, until it is a black speck against the blue sky, all but lost in the distance. Space—Wondrous! Limitless! The bird may fly where it wishes.[22]

The story is divided into four sections of unequal length, each of which presents an aspect of life related to the barrack-yard or its occupants. The first and longest section describes the way in which a group of youngsters from a barrack-yard pass their day on the streets of Port of Spain. Their natural children's curiosity constantly transforms their hunger and restlessness into exciting flights of fancy about the unattainable objects they see around them. Their rough game of football in the rain and their excited bets for kicks as to who can reach the goalpost first, or whose inch of wood can sail fastest down the city's swollen gutters, are interspersed with deeper longings:

They gaze at the motor cars lined up on one side and give free criticism. They run their fingers along the fenders and venture boldly to blow the horns.

Willy has seen a leather belt displayed in a glass case.

"Next time A go an' bet," he says, "A going to bet for something like dat. Den A'll bet wid a dressed up man."

They come to the wharf and the muddy sea and wish they could get a boat to row about. Just then the Island steamer moves off. Harold is inspired with ambition and says seriously, "A shall be de captain, or de purser or something."

"Den it will be like going to New Yark, or to England like dem cricketers," says Willy. "De islands come fust. It rough out dere you know." [23]

Their games, fantasies, and aimless wanderings take the place of school and food and home, for they know that if they return to the yard "they may be beaten for being out so long, instead of being there to take messages for their mothers. The risk is too great; kicks are sure, but never the food."

The next section of the story looks at the home of one of the boys, Willy. He sleeps under the spring cot in the room which he shares with his mother and sister, and his night is disturbed by the sounds of other members of the yard community making love, quarreling, and fighting. The author makes an attempt to account for the seeming callousness with which Willy is beaten by his mother:

The food that the children eat is the breakfast given her where she is employed. All day she has thought of them. The day before they went hungry, to-day it is her turn. Willy thinks that his mother is unfair, cruel, and she that the child is stubborn. [24]

Willy comforts himself after his beating with pleasant fantasies: "To-night he sees before him food, clean clothes, beautiful things, a leather belt instead of a string to hold up his pants. Pennies arrange themselves before his eyes and also little threepenny bits." Willy gets a chance to realize part of his fantasy briefly when a fight breaks out in the yard and one of the women, Coxi, stabs a man to death. A feud develops between the rival groups in the yard and one enterprising member of the yard "place[s] himself at the gate and asks sixcents per head for admission into the yard." As the battle continues night after night, Willy joins him to help round up the stragglers and before the spectacle is halted by the police he has built up a small cache of pennies and three-penny bits: "He looks at the money and thinks what a good thing it is that Coxi killed Eddy."

Violence as a form of sublimation is the idea explored in the third section of the story: To compensate for the fact that he has no clothes presentable enough to go to school in, and therefore misses out on the presents which each child receives at the end of the Christmas term, Willy begs a penny of someone on the street and goes to the cinema:

There he loses himself and for one hour and a half lives the life of a strong man in a gold rush. He jumps up and shouts every now and then and when he sees the men slogging at each other he screams out "Go it," and then "Ay, Ay, all you making love." He comes out refreshed and goes to bed thinking of gold, no longer envying the Christmas presents of those lucky ones, nor pacifying himself with the thought that on Christmas day he will take a little rum."[25]

The story ends with a brief impression of the drivers of the city's refuse carts as they wend their way to the Labasse. It is one of these drivers who stops and observes the flight of the corbeau before he is rudely jolted out of his reverie by the other drivers who are waiting for him to move so that they can deposit their loads of garbage on the dump. In comparing the barrack-yarders' flights of fancy to the corbeau's flight, the writer emphasizes the hope and resilience that enables the barrack-yarders to rise even momentarily above the squalor and deprivation of their lives. At the same time, however, she points out the real limitations which their clipped wings impose on their freedom to soar.

In considering the barrack-yard genre as a whole, a pattern begins to emerge in its presentation of lower-class life. The descriptions of the life and people of the yard at times appear overpredictable or stereotyped. Chinese shopkeepers are invariably caricatured as miserly, inscrutable, opium-smoking orientals, obeah women are always black, and mulatresses are invariably unfaithful; stones are used to bleach clothes and knives are used to cut people. However, it must be borne in mind that in the history of Trinidad society these patterns had never previously been recognized and defined creatively outside of the calypso tents. By transforming popular local biases into literary stereotypes, the barrack-yard writers were able to recreate a recognizable social milieu, which, if anything, enhanced the credibility of the handful of characters in a particular story who were given a fuller treatment, and portrayed as being capable of emotions of love, hate, trust, and guilt that the reader could recognize and identify with.[26] In this way the barrack-yard genre was able to translate the social realism of the European tradition and the comic satire of the calypso tradition into a new, intermediary form around which an indigenous literary tradition could be built. When one bears in mind the significance of this achievement for the novelists who emerged from the *Beacon* group and the Trinidad writers who followed them in later years, the unique place of the early barrack-yard stories in the history of West Indian literature can be fully appreciated.

NOTES

1. Alfred H. Mendes, "A Commentary," *Trinidad*, 1, 2 (Easter, 1930), 65.

2. Ibid., 67.

3. Ibid., 66-67.

4. *The Beacon*, 1, 10 (Jan.-Feb., 1932), 1.

5. Albert Gomes, *"The Beacon,"* Kraus *Bibliographical Bulletin*, 21 (August, 1977), 159.

6. See Alfred Mendes, "Talking about the Thirties," interviewed by Clifford Sealy, *Voices*, 1, 5 (December, 1965), 5.

7. *Trinidad*, 1, 1 (Christmas, 1929), 53.

8. Ibid., 54.

9. *The Beacon*, 1, 12 (April, 1932), 27.

10. *The Beacon*, 1, 4 (July, 1931), 9.

11. R. A. C. de Boissière, "The Old Year Passes," in *From Trinidad: A Selection from the Fiction and Verse of the Island of Trinidad, British West Indies*, ed. Albert Gomes (Trinidad: Frasers Pinterie, 1937), pp. 23-24.

12. Alfred H. Mendes, "Afternoon in Trinidad," ed. John Lehmann, *New Writing*, 2 (Autumn, 1936), p. 100.

13. Ibid., 106.

14. *Trinidad*, 1, 1 (Christmas, 1929), 31.

15. Ibid.

16. *The Beacon*, 1, 12 (April, 1932), 7.

17. Ibid., 8.

18. *Trinidad*, 1, 1 (Christmas, 1929), 15-16.

19. Ibid., 16-17.

20. Ibid., 25.

21. *The Beacon*, 2, 10 (April, 1933), 13.

22. Kathleen Archibald, "Clipped Wings," in *From Trinidad*, ed. Gomes, p. 54.

23. Ibid., pp. 46-47.

24. Ibid., p. 51.

25. Ibid., p. 53.

26. Indeed, the protagonist in Mendes's "Sweetman" was so close to the bone that the author was sued by a man named Seppy for defamation of character in what was probably the first case of literary libel in the history of Trinidad.

CHAPTER 4

ALFRED H. MENDES: THE SYMPATHETIC OBSERVER

Alfred H. Mendes (b. 1897) was the most prolific and creative writer in the *Beacon* group. During the 1920s and 1930s he published about fifty short stories in a variety of local and foreign magazines, two novels, and a number of poems and essays. He started by writing poetry, but soon "discovered that this was not [his] dish of tea" and destroyed most copies of a privately published poetry collection, *Wages of Sin* (1925).[1] His first novel, *Pitch Lake* (1934), was completed before he left Trinidad for the United States in 1933, and it appeared with a preface by Aldous Huxley. Mendes began working on *Black Fauns* (1935) soon after his arrival in New York and recalls that he "did the job in six months."[2] This was his last major work to reach the reading public, although before returning to Trinidad in 1940 he wrote seven more novels.

The son of a well-to-do Trinidad merchant of Portuguese descent, Mendes was sent to school in England from the age of eight and received his secondary education at Hitchin Grammar School. When World War I broke out, he joined the First Rifle Brigade and was posted to Flanders and France. Mendes was appalled by the sordidness of the struggle. In a short impressionistic piece entitled "Over the Top," he recalls the horror and desolation of one battle in the Ypres Salient, using images of violation which he shares with the British poets of the Great War:

Sky pregnant with pain: earth too in pain, vomiting all her entrails, rocking in pain, shells pounding her brown-bleeding bosom, putrid nauseous stench rising from her open wounds, wounds huge as houses, ragged-edged, a thousand wounds in which live men accoutred for war: smoking rifles: red-hot pistols: blood-red bayonets: wounds oozing puss, nauseous putrid stench, rising, soaking, air soaked with nauseous putrid stench, saturated, and "it's half past seven," the captain says, eyes blinking over a watch.[3]

Waiting for the expected German counterattack, the writer begins to question his involvement in the war and his reasons for wanting to kill the enemy soldiers:

And the Boshe: where are they? Where are our enemies? But are they our enemies? I was at school with a Hamburg fellow and I loved him very much. His name was Uhlandt. Is he my enemy? But when we parted—a little over two years ago— we shook hands and clapped each other on the back and swore to see each other again. "Come to Hamburg," he said, waving his hand from the railway carriage, "and I will give you a good time."[4]

In spite of his reservations, Mendes seems to have done his fair share of defending British imperialism against German imperialism. In 1917 he was awarded the military medal for bravery in battle in the Ypres Salient. The citation records that "he set a fine example of devotion to duty and every soldierly quality."[5]

While the holocaust of World War I shattered the faith of Mendes and a whole generation of Western intellectuals in the ideals of Western democracy, the 1917 October Revolution in Russia provided them with a new framework within which to interpret modern society. The Russian Revolution brought an end to the war on the Eastern front, and ushered in a new social and economic order. Looking back on this phase of his intellectual development, Mendes comments:

Today, after this long distance from the Russian Revolution, no member of the two generations that followed it can have the faintest idea of how moved, how uplifted and how hopeful those of us were who could sense its implications and its inherent possibilities. World War I with its ghastly disillusionment and its Death, its broken promises and its cynicism had left us eager to clutch at any straw of hope in a drowning sea.[6]

Mendes returned to Trinidad in 1920 fired with socialist ideals. From his new perspective he saw Trinidad as another casualty of British imperialism, and the local middle class, of which he was part, as subservient imitators of the metropolitan bourgeoisie. He was not a political revolutionary, so his attack was directed mainly at the cultural values of the colonial middle class: He challenged the authority of orthodox religion, and attacked conservative attitudes about art and literature. In a commentary published in *Trinidad*, he maintained:

The *Zeitgeist* is one of revolt against established customs and organic loyalties. Since the War, this revolt has been directed not so much against the Puritanism of the 16th century as against a degenerate form of it popularly known as Victorianism.[7]

Mendes's attack on his class was part of a worldwide reassessment of cultural values in the interwar years. Whereas in Europe and North America the intelligentsia turned to the culture of Africa, and "primitivism" in art, music and literature became the order of the day, in Trinidad Mendes turned to the culture of the masses. In the short story he found the form and in social realism the narrative technique to assault the traditional values of colonial society. In this connection his barrack-yard stories are among the best-known examples of his work. Their seminal importance has been noted in this study and elsewhere; however, any appraisal of his writing is incomplete without reference to the other subjects and settings which Mendes covers in his work. He himself insists that his characters are "taken from all walks of Trinidad life."[8] A fair proportion of the sixteen short stories[9] he published in *Trinidad* and *The Beacon* have middle-class settings: Two of these, "Boodhoo" and "Faux Pas," are discussed in chapter 3. In "Colour," a short story set in Grenada, Mendes examines the tensions which develop between a white American and her near-white West Indian husband, as well as portraying the claustrophobia of middle-class life in the smaller islands. In other stories he explores themes that would be taken up and developed by later West Indian writers: "Pablo's Fandango" deals with the life of the rural agricultural class, while "News," a humorous story, presents that peculiarly West Indian obsession—an enthusiasm for cricket.

Like many of the writers who followed him in the 1950s, Mendes was especially interested in winning recognition for his work abroad where he felt he could reach a larger and more prestigious audience. At the end of 1929, a story he had coauthored with Algernon Wharton entitled "Lai John" was published in *The London Mercury*.[10] It reappeared subsequently in E. J. O'Brien's *Best Short Stories of 1929*. In 1932, *This Quarter*, a Paris-based literary magazine, published Mendes's "Sweetman" alongside stories by writers such as Samuel Beckett and James T. Farrell.[11] Before Mendes left Trinidad in 1933, several of his short stories appeared in *The Manchester Guardian* and *The New English Weekly*, and one story, "Bête Rouge," was published in *The Clarion*.[12] Perhaps the most important encouragement came from Aldous Huxley, who, after reading the first issue of *Trinidad*, wrote a letter to Mendes and James congratulating them on the high standard of the magazine. Of the short fiction Huxley wrote: "I was much interested in the stories, particularly the two long ones, 'Her Chinaman's Way' and 'Triumph.' Both excellent intrinsically, as well as interesting, to one who has never visited the West Indies, as sociological documents."[13] It was Huxley who advised Mendes to send the manuscript of *Pitch Lake*

to the London publishers Duckworth, where it was recommended for publication by Anthony Powell, who was one of their readers at the time.

Confident of his talent as a novelist and short-story writer, Mendes left
for New York so as to be closer to the metropolitan literary scene. There
he made contact with a number of American writers including William
Faulkner, William Saroyan, Thomas Wolfe, Sherwood Anderson and James
T. Farrell. He worked for a time as a reader for Whit Burnett's *Story*
magazine, and in 1938 he was commissioned to write a 150-page brochure
for the New York World's Fair as part of the WPA Federal Writers' Project. His work on the Federal Writers' Project brought him into contact
with a number of black American writers who had participated in the Harlem Renaissance, including Richard Wright, Countee Cullen, Zora Neale
Hurston, Langston Hughes and the Jamaican Claude McKay. Though
Mendes has described his years in New York as "the period of heaviest
creativity," hardly any of the forty-odd new stories he wrote during his stay
were published in American magazines, except one or two that had barrack-yard settings.[14] This was the aspect of his work most often picked for
attention by critics and editors with whom he came into contact. As a result
of being "pigeon-holed" in this way, Mendes began to find it increasingly
difficult to extend his range as a novelist: Between 1920 and 1940 he wrote
nine full-length novels but only two were published. The other seven, he
recalls, were "destroyed by burning, even before I had offered any one of
them to my publishers. That was in New York, in 1940—and now I lament
a rash act performed on the edge of a ghastly experience."[15]

Mendes's own limitations as a writer were probably an equally important
factor in the frustration of his attempts to become a major novelist. Looking
back at this period in his life he has commented:

Time and again I tried to plan a novel on the grand scale, the large canvas—but I
just couldn't do it. I began to realise that my novels were small novels, things made
only to please and entertain—in spite of the critics saying that they were universal
in their implications. . . . I grew more and more discontented with my work.[16]

In retrospect Mendes probably does himself less than justice, but his comments offer a critical insight into the impasse reached by the early pioneers
of fiction, especially of barrack-yard literature. The sympathetic recording
of life in the barrack-yard tended to become a dead-end, however important it had been as a beginning. "The grand scale, the large canvas" which
Mendes talks about did not necessarily imply turning away from the lives
of the lower classes as a literary source, but it did mean that the tendency
to view the barrack-yard in exotic isolation had to be transcended. The
limited narrative strategy of realistically recording the day-to-day life of the
yard had to be replaced by a fuller treatment of society as a whole and a

greater awareness of the symbolic possibilities of the yard. C. L. R. James in *Minty Alley* takes one step in this direction by examining the interaction of the barrack-yarders with one representative member of the outside world. Ralph de Boissière goes further and achieves the larger canvas in *Crown Jewel* by committing his writing to a radical analysis of the entire society against the background of the changing political consciousness of the barrack-yarders during a crucial period in Trinidad's history.

Black Fauns demonstrates both the strengths and the weaknesses of the first stages of early Trinidad writing. The self-consciousness of the middle-class writer's attempts to make contact with the world of the barrack-yard is brought out in Mendes's account of his personal experience:

What I did in order to get the atmosphere, to get the sort of jargon that they spoke—the vernacular, the idiom—what I did was: I went into the barrack-yard that was then at the bottom of Park Street just before you came into Richmond Street, and I lived in it for about six months. I did not live completely there, but I ingratiated myself. They knew of what I was doing; they knew what I felt about their way of life—that I was sympathetic towards it. So I was *persona* very *grata*. I slept there frequently, and a lot of the incidents that appear in my second published novel, *Black Fauns*, were taken almost directly from my experience with the barrack-yarders. I had of course to give these incidents form and shape. I had to synthesize them into one whole—one novel with a beginning and an end.[17]

From his own description Mendes seems to have taken on the role of an anthropological field-worker or investigative journalist, anxious to produce a sympathetic documentary on his chosen subject without departing too radically from the objective reality. In one sense he acts as an interpreter of the barrack-yard, bringing it to his middle-class or foreign reader in a form that can easily be grasped. However, this approach precludes any examination of the relationship between the researcher and his subject. We have no way of knowing how the yard responded to the presence of the narrator, or of gauging his own reaction to what he saw and heard. The characters are allowed to speak for themselves with carefully neutral explanatory passages inserted by the "editor" to provide the necessary background to the events presented. At times this narrative strategy reduces the novel's social realism to the level of sociological documentary so that its subjects become objects.

The community depicted is a community of women.[18] Most of the women are supported by keepers but, as the narrator explains, "The women . . . saw so little of them that on such occasions there was more often than not just time enough in which to eat, drink, make love and sleep" (p. 17).[19] Apart from Ma Christine's son, Snakey, whose visit from America produces much of the conflict within the yard, there is a conspicuous absence of men. Of the two keepers who do make an appearance, the first is killed off in a car accident in the first few chapters of the novel while the second, Mannie, is arrested shortly afterwards for smuggling opium. Mannie, better known as Lord Invincible, is a calypsonian. The narrator seems to have introduced him to inform the reader of the two aspects of Trinidad folk culture, Carnival and the calypso:

For Mannie, the end of one Carnival meant the beginning of preparations for the next; and whenever anything of topical interest occurred, like an important fire, an inter-colonial cricket tournament, or a political scandal such as happened once when the East Indian legislative member for Caroni was slapped resoundingly in the face by the white member for Port-of-Spain in the Legislative Council Chamber itself— at such times the Lord Invincible could always be found in the throes of creative labour. (p. 83)

The narrator could have added that the drama of life in the barrack-yards also provided Mannie with material for his calypsos. Mendes seems to be acknowledging a literary debt to the calypsonian when he comments, "His verses might not have been models of form and feeling, but the island has yet to give birth to a poet with a finer sense of native atmosphere and indigenous wit than the Lord Invincible, Attila the Hun, the Duke of Normandie, Lion and that lot" (pp. 83–84).

The two other males who enter the barrack-yard occasionally are intruders. One is a policeman, who attempts to settle squabbles between the women and whose interference is invariably resented. The other, Mr. de Pompignon (called "Mr. Pompom" by the women), is the rent collector and tries unsuccessfully to win the favors of Martha, one of the yard's younger tenants. This is the closest we come to seeing how the women interact with outsiders who have more power or privileges than they do. It is clear that they resent any intrusions into their world and are constantly on their guard against any attempts by outsiders to undermine their community. Significantly, the group's solidarity is ultimately undermined by another outsider, Snakey. Though Snakey does not arrive until halfway through the novel, the letter which initially announces his visit is referred to constantly and becomes an ominous refrain which links various segments of the plot and anticipates later developments.

Black Fauns has a loose, episodic form, rather like a series of linked short stories, which allows the author to develop each of his female characters in turn. Ma Christine, Snakey's mother, is portrayed as the matriarch of the yard. She is held in respect by the younger women, who often approach her for help and advice. Like other *confidante* figures in barrack-yard stories, she is versed in the art of obeah which she uses on occasions to help the other women find new keepers or to counter a spell of bad luck. Paradoxically, she is also associated with an element of middle-class respectability as, unlike most of her neighbors, she has seen better days as the wife of a primary school teacher. "Them days, young girls did look for husbands, not for keepers. Them days, young girls did live in the fear of the Lord. Now, they walkin' hand in hand with the devil just like as if he is their best friend," she tells Miriam and Ethelrida reproachfully (p. 25). The author makes no overt connection, but there is clearly an intended irony in the fact that her son Snakey, who has had the benefit of a comparatively "respectable" upbringing and the chance to improve himself by travelling, comes back to keep one of the yard's inhabitants and be kept by another.

Miriam and Ethelrida are both relatively young women, and seem to disagree with each other on every conceivable issue. The author uses their conflicts to present two contrasting perspectives on life which he encountered in the barrack-yard. One bone of contention between them is the status and contribution of black people within Trinidad society and elsewhere. Miriam, the only member of the yard who can read and write, is full of praise for white people. For example, when Snakey tells them about the technological wonders of New York City, she finds support for her conviction that "white people more smart than nigger people" (p. 241). Ethelrida is not impressed by Snakey's descriptions of what she considers a "crazy country run by crazy white people living in crazy city." She warns him: "If you leave your own land . . . to come back wit' de news dat white people more smart than nigger people, it was more better you was never born!" (p. 241). For her part she prefers "to go to Africa and see [her] own people living like God make them to live" (p. 242). In associating a pro-white position with Miriam, the educated aspirant to middle-class status, the author is able to attack the racial and social prejudices of the colonial middle class. The proletarian Ethelrida is used to voice in the ordinary language of the yard Mendes's own contempt for the middle class.

Miriam and Ethelrida express conflicting opinions on obeah, sex, marriage, the Catholic Church and politics. However, their debates are moderated by Ma Christine and never lead to physical violence. Their views on the political situation in Trinidad give Mendes another opportunity to present the arguments on either side of a controversy in which he also held strong views. Ethelrida sees the reformist measures of Captain Cipriani as a farce and argues for the need for black politicians to fight on behalf of Trinidad's working class. Miriam as usual disagrees, and puts forward a popular argument:

Look the Red House, where the Governor does sit with his council. It have nigger there; yes; but who does stand up for our rights? You call Capting Cupriani a black man when all the time he white like water? The negro in the Council 'fraid their own shadow, my child! An' why? I ain't have to ask you that!" (pp. 13–14).

The division and disunity within the black community in the late 1920s is well captured in this exchange. Miriam's loyalty to and appreciation of Cipriani on the one hand is contrasted with the awakening of more militant sentiments of class solidarity and racial pride in Ethelrida. Both acknowledge the absence of an effective black leadership in the Legislative Council. Mendes only touches briefly on this issue in *Black Fauns*, but in the figure of Ethelrida one can detect the formation of a character similar to Ralph de Boissière's Cassie, the militant working-class leader in *Crown Jewel*.

None of these altercations leads to actual violence, but Ethelrida does come to blows with Mamitz, a mulatto woman, whom the forthright Ethelrida dislikes because she gives herself airs and seems to do no work. It is Mamitz who entices Snakey away from Martha, a quiet and withdrawn girl whose violent attacks on other members of the yard sorority provide some of the most sensational moments in the novel. The author uses Martha's introversion and ultimate breakdown to highlight the pressures on privacy which the yard environment makes inevitable. He also seems to suggest that the communal nature of life within the yard with its forced sharing of joy and sorrow provides a therapeutic outlet for its inhabitants' frustrations, which they reject at their own peril. Martha from the outset never makes use of this outlet, and is presented as distinct from her quarrelsome and convivial neighbors. This does not stop the other members of the yard community from offering her their support. Like most of them she augments her income as a washerwoman by "friending" with men who keep her for as long as their affections last. When at the beginning of the novel she loses her keeper, Ma Christine offers to help her by using obeah. Martha's quest for a new keeper, a familiar motif in the barrack-yard story, is more than a search for material support. She has had an unhappy childhood and a traumatic introduction to sex at the age of fourteen, which have left her emotionally insecure. Drifting from one relationship to another, she seems to be hoping for emotional as well as material support, an ideal which is ridiculed by the other women in the yard, who have long since come to terms with the transient nature of male-female relationships within the cramped and poverty-stricken confines of the barrack-yard, and see the economic and emotional security of marriage as a luxury only the rich can afford to indulge. Estelle ridicules Martha's notions of love:

Love? Love me foot! You give them love an' they give you kicks in return. I prefer to give them somet'ing else and get money in return. It got more sense that way. Love ain't make for us so. I never love a man yet—an' the day that happen to me I going to t'row meself straight in de sea! (p. 217)

Mamitz adopts an even more cynical attitude:

I don't know the difference between that somet'ing else you talk about and love. . . . For me, they's de same t'ing. I willing to love any man who willing to pay me for it. (p. 217)

It is against these two women and their values that Martha comes into passionate conflict. Estelle exploits Martha's need for love by developing a lesbian relationship with her and forcing her to steal from the other inhabitants of the yard. This plunges the yard into a crisis of suspicion and intrigue, which threatens to destroy its communal spirit. Martha only ceases to put her emotional dependence on Estelle before her loyalty to the yard when she realizes how little Estelle cares for her own child or for anyone else. She reacts by violently attacking Estelle.

The history of the money which Martha steals for Estelle is one of the main threads tying together the various interrelated plots of the novel. The uses to which it is put in the yard give an indication of the moral standing of each of the people who possess it. Their standards bear little relationship to the generally accepted moral criteria outside of the barrack-yard. It is first stolen from a Chinese shopkeeper by Mannie, shortly before his arrest for opium trafficking. After Mannie's arrest it is smuggled out of prison by Ethelrida, who uses part of it for the benefit of the whole yard community as she pays off the debts of all the tenants who are in arrears with their rent. Even when the rest of the money is stolen by Martha for Estelle, it continues to be of benefit to the yard as Estelle uses part of it to buy food and drinks for everyone at the celebration of her baby's christening. The picture changes when Martha steals the remaining money back from Estelle in order to lavish it on Snakey, to whom she has now transferred her affections in the hope that she can win his devotion. Snakey gives the money to Mamitz, with whom he is also having an affair. It is the discovery of this betrayal which provokes Martha's fatal attack on Mamitz. Everybody agrees that the only real owner of the money is the Chinaman, and because of this they consider that the subsequent movements of the money can hardly be considered "stealing." Mendes uses the resulting confusion and intrigue as an ironic comment on the irrelevance of capitalist notions of property and security within the financially unstable world of the yard.

Though *Black Fauns* constantly asserts the values of the barrack-yard against the double standards of middle-class life, the novel ends on a note of tragedy and disunity. Snakey leaves, having through his selfishness driven Martha to murder Mamitz; Ethelrida and Estelle are involved in another fight over the stolen money and both of them are arrested. All semblance of joy or defiance of life's problems seems to disappear. As one observer from a neighboring yard comments:

Eh-eh . . . it looks like as if God vext with this yard in truth. Miss Et'elrida in jail, Miss Estelle in jail, nobody know what going to happen to poor Mart'a; Mannie in jail, Seppy dead, Snakey gone, Miss Mamitz in the hospital lying down like as if she dead, with her face all cut up and her bosom all cut up and a stab in her back—eh-eh, it is a good t'ing me an' Lestang ain' living here! (p. 326)

Black Fauns was written in the early thirties, before the consolidation of militant working-class organizations in Trinidad and before the social upheavals of 1937 had challenged colonial rule. It is not a political novel but it does register the growing frustration and dissatisfaction of the lower classes with their lot. On the surface the violence that breaks out in the barrackyard and consumes its inhabitants at the end of the novel is a result of personal jealousies and rivalries. Frantz Fanon in his observations on inner-directed violence in colonial societies has suggested that such violence is the result of the inability of deprived colonial peoples to recognize the source of the political and economic power which relegates them to poverty and political impotence. Only an understanding of the system could divert this self-destructive violence into a unified attack on imperialism. Mendes, like other writers in the *Beacon* group, seems to have sensed the potential of the masses, but he could hardly have foreseen the dramatic turn of events which would transform this potential into action. He concentrates instead on defining and analyzing the positive aspects of barrack-yard life beneath the surface violence and personal tragedy. For large sections of the novel he portrays the women of the yard as a closely knit community. Their physical proximity provides the yard's inhabitants with a sense of identity and shared experience. They participate in each other's triumphs and problems, and when necessary individuals can fall back on the group for advice and material assistance. Ethical mores associated with property rights and sexual purity are subordinated to the more important struggle to satisfy the basic needs for food, clothes, and financial security. Tragedy only enters the yard when its inhabitants break their own code of moral values and betray each other's trust. Within the limitations of their economic conditions the women still manage to find the means to celebrate occasions of special significance to the community such as the christening of children or the welcoming of guests. Mendes emphasizes these positive aspects of barrack-yard life and in so doing makes an implicit criticism of the hypocrisy and selfish individualism that he considered characteristic of the middle class.

Mendes and the rest of the *Beacon* group were impressed by the cultural resilience they discovered within the lower class, and saw in this a way of challenging the imitative cultural forms of their own class. In their work they tried to use this indigenous source as the basis for a new nationalist literature. They also hoped that by writing about the barrack-yard with sympathetic insight they would be able to involve members of their own class imaginatively in the problems and potential of the masses. However, the new colonial bourgeoisie was especially reluctant to be reminded of its origins as the descendants of slaves, indentured laborers, and the illicit offspring of unions between master and servant. *Pitch Lake*, Mendes's first novel, focuses on this desire within the Trinidad middle class to obliterate its past. It satirizes the Portuguese middle class in particular, and demonstrates the way in which misguided social aspirations contributed to the development of racist attitudes among Portuguese creoles towards other ethnic groups in Trinidad. Whereas in *Black Fauns* Mendes attempts to convey a sense of community by focussing on a group of characters, in *Pitch Lake* he explores the alienation and isolation which he sensed within his own class, and for this purpose he concentrates on a single protagonist. In *Black Fauns* each of the women in the yard is allowed to speak for herself and there are few overt authorial intrusions. In *Pitch Lake*, though there is no first-person narrator, events are perceived through the consciousness of the central character and, apart from him, very few individuals are fully developed.

Joe da Costa, the central character in the novel, is a first-generation Portuguese creole whose father runs a ramshackle rumshop in San Fernando. When his family decide to emigrate to New York, Joe (who is twenty-two) decides to stay behind and try to join the white-collar circles of the Portuguese elite in Port of Spain. He knows that he can only be accepted there if he cuts all ties with the lower-class people among whom he has lived and worked as his father's assistant. He therefore ends his protracted relationship with a colored girl named Maria, who lives with her mother in a San Fernando barrack-yard, and moves in with his brother Henry in Port of Spain. Henry has married into a Portuguese family of good social standing. He and his wife Myra introduce Joe at the exclusive Portuguese social club and help to arrange a match between him and a wealthy young Portuguese creole, Cora. Joe eventually finds a job in a respectable city firm but is haunted by figures from his past. These include his shabby father who passes through Port of Spain en route to New York, his old girlfriend, Maria, who turns up with her mother and publicly demands money from him, and an old crony from his San Fernando days, who keeps on trying to draw him into what Joe now considers "low" company. Just as he seems to have rid himself of all these embarrassments and looks set to marry Cora, his brother's Indian maid Stella, with whom he has been having a clandestine affair, becomes pregnant. Fearing a scandal which might ruin his social position, Joe murders Stella.

The plot of *Pitch Lake* resembles that of many naturalistic novels written at the end of the nineteenth century. The philosophy behind such works was that an individual's fortunes were predetermined by biological, environmental or cosmic forces, or some combination of these. In the naturalistic novel which portrays the hero's life as determined by his environment, the character is first shown in the milieu which conditions him. He is then allowed to make an apparently successful escape from this environment, but is finally reclaimed by it and destroyed. Mendes has agreed that the plot of his novel was influenced by Theodore Dreiser's *An American Tragedy* (1925), in which the hero is defeated by a similar series of environmental factors.[20]

Although he plans to murder his pregnant girlfriend and is charged with the crime, Dreiser's protagonist does not actually kill her because she accidentally falls overboard during an excursion in a row boat. Dreiser clearly attempts to extenuate his protagonist by introducing a defense lawyer who argues the protagonist's innocence in court by drawing reference to the way that the demands of American society have conspired to place him in an impossible situation. By contrast, Mendes makes no attempt to dismiss Joe's responsibility for the crime he commits. The book ends with a brutal and deliberate murder, and there is no trial scene or counsel for the defense to elicit sympathy for Joe.

In *Pitch Lake*, Mendes step by step explodes the myth that racial prejudice in a society such as Trinidad is inevitable. Joe's prejudice is shown to stem from his warped social values and aspirations. By following these perversions to their logical conclusion in the mind of a weak and selfish individual, Mendes demonstrates the ultimate self-destructiveness of such attitudes for the society that espouses them. From the start it is clear that Joe has only contempt for those around him, and he never acknowledges that the people he despises are the source of his family's livelihood and therefore worthy of some consideration. "It hurt him to think that he had wasted so many years of his life in selling rum and cigarettes to common niggers and coolies who were not fit even to tie his shoe-laces" (p. 14).[21] He seems to be convinced that because he comes from European stock, society automatically owes him respect and a comfortable life, and he has only contempt for other Portuguese who have not yet made it into high society:

That was why he said to himself that the Portuguese, of all the white communities in the island, were the most despised: they made themselves too cheap by running the shops of the island and coming into contact with the common coloured people. (pp. 14–15)

In a sense Joe's weakness when it comes to associating with members of the lower class is the one redeeming feature which wins him some sympathy with the reader. Joe is drawn to Maria and Stella for the simple reason that he is a young man and they are both attractive women. Moreover, because of his background they are both people he can communicate with easily, unlike the sophisticated women he encounters at the Portuguese Club. Joe himself never seems to understand that such attraction of common spirits is natural and need not be debased or exploitative. Instead of seeing the alienation of the other Portuguese creoles from colored people and even their own poorer relatives as an aberration, he feels threatened and ashamed of his inability to act in a similar manner. The narrator captures the curious perversion this leads to in his attitude to his first girlfriend, Maria:

A little before closing-time [Maria] entered the shop and stood in a corner waiting. She was a brown-skinned girl with a full squat figure and a pretty face. She looked at Joseph slyly. There was an unmistakable touch of the Chinese in her eyes. Her black sleek hair fell down her back in a long plait. Joseph looked at her and took his eyes away at once. A sudden shame came over him and showed itself on his face for a moment, but immediately afterwards he controlled himself and then felt exasperated. (pp. 15–16)

The contradiction between Maria's obviously attractive appearance and Joe's shame at having to acknowledge that he finds her attractive, even when there are no critical middle-class Portuguese creoles looking over his shoulder to observe their relationship, is one indication of how completely Joe has internalized the values of the class to which he aspires, even before he attempts to enter its ranks. His racist feelings about Maria surface when Miss Martha demands that he marry her daughter and he blurts out: "You've got a blasted cheek asking me to marry your daughter. What do you take me for? Go and ask one of those little coloured boy friends of hers to marry her, not a white man. To hell with you" (p. 45).

His changed circumstances and the greater strength of his attraction to Stella in Port of Spain make it even more difficult for him to rationalize this second relationship. At the beginning he sees himself as Stella's protector, a fantasy that is reinforced when he discovers that she is an orphan and unlikely to produce a fierce mother like Maria's to terrorize him. With admirable insight he observes that "every circumstance was against this child . . . and let her but find herself without a job for any length of time and only the trade of the night-streets would be left open to her" (p. 85). It is difficult to follow the train of thought that leads him to decide that the best way to keep her off the streets is to make her his mistress. For one moment his finer feelings lead him to an even more fertile flight of fancy:

If only he could fly away with her to where there were no human beings at all, to a small deserted island, where there would be no one to point a finger at him for taking to himself one not of his own colour. (p. 94)

It never seems to occur to him that the only person who showed disgust at his earlier liaison with a colored woman in San Fernando was himself. As soon as Joe becomes sexually involved with Stella his racial prejudices begin to reassert themselves. He is terrified at the thought of his family and friends discovering their relationship and swears Stella to secrecy. Even so he still persists in pretending to himself that the motives for his involvement with Stella are not selfish and exploitative. He argues mentally that "his affection for Stella was of an entirely different *kind* from what his affection had been for Maria" (p. 225), but at the same time acknowledges that "sooner or later he would have to break with her" (p. 224).

Joe's disgust with his associations with colored lower-class women is matched by his discomfiture in the presence of women whom he considers his equals but who it is clear he fears may be his superiors socially. His pangs of shame at the sight of Maria are second only to his pangs of inferiority when he is first introduced to Cora, and he finds himself wishing for less demanding companionship:

> He was on tenterhooks of shyness trying his best to appear at home in Cora's presence. This was what he had been looking forward to all these months. This was the sort of girl Philip was accustomed to associate with; the sort of girl he had been trying to meet, and now, try as he might, he could not bring himself to be easy with her. How simple speaking to Stella was! How difficult and trying speaking to Cora! (p. 108)

In spite of her authoritarian tendencies, Cora is one of the few characters in the novel with whose attitudes the author seems to identify on occasion. Mendes gives her the benefit of a British education like his own, which exposes her to more liberal postwar attitudes toward class and the status of women than were current at the time in Trinidad. Back in Trinidad she is considered the *enfant terrible* of the Portuguese middle class but is tolerated by all because she is pretty, well-travelled and wealthy. Her favorite statement is "I don't care a damn about society," and she enjoys ridiculing the pomposity and narrow-mindedness of the Portuguese elite circle. She is convinced, for example, that social status is not important to her in her choice of a husband:

> I tell you I don't care about all this social fuss. People here amuse me with it. They all try to appear more important than each other: strutting like turkeys; and nobody is better than anybody else. If I like a fellow I'm quite willing to show him that I like him; and if I like him well enough I'm quite willing to become his wife in spite of his social inferiority or otherwise. (p. 161)

Cora has real musical talent and is dismayed by the absence of any cultural interests within the middle class. On several occasions she comments on the oppressed conditions of women, especially middle-class Trinidadian women, and the claustrophobia of colonial life. However, her stance smacks of the liberal aristocrat, and her criticism of Trinidad life rarely extends beyond issues of immediate concern to her own class. She clearly takes certain social divisions for granted, and though she has some fine sentiments about the lower classes they remain fine sentiments only.

Cora is perhaps one of the most sensitive and positively portrayed characters in the novel. Her limitations hint at the pessimism with which Mendes viewed the possibilty of even the best individuals in his class making a constructive contribution to social reform in Trinidad society. In a sense, Mendes seems to have shared some of his character's limitations at the time when this book was written, as the lower-class women in *Pitch Lake* are in the main presented as objects of pity. *Pitch Lake* preceded most of Mendes's barrack-yard stories, and there is a striking contrast between Joe's two comparatively passive mistresses and the female barrack-yarders of the later works. Only Miss Martha with her bold demands and contempt for Joe has anything like the resilience and pragmatism of the women in *Black Fauns*. It is Miss Martha who stands up for her daughter's rights and refuses to be cowed by considerations of class or race. As she tells Joe in their last encounter:

Not ten like you go put me out of dis yard, you stinking Po'teegee. Not ten like you! I come fo' me rights an' I ain' leavin' till you gie me satisfaction. You hear? I ain' leavin' till you gie me satisfaction! No white man go come an' take dis gerl like a dog take a bitch, you hear? You low dong Po'teegee, you hear? (p. 215)

It is also Miss Martha who expresses what the lower class as a whole was to realize during the latter part of the 1930s—that only a show of force would frighten the elite into action. As she explains: "Me rights, that's wha' I wants, an' how I go get dem if I ain' make a row fo' dem?" (pp. 216–217).

For the most part, however, the attack on the Portuguese middle class is made through the narrative voice. Side by side with his exploration of the growing inability of the protagonist to deal with reality, Mendes gives us glimpses of various aspects of middle-class life. Myra, Joe's sister-in-law, has no qualms about the decision of the Portuguese Club to refuse membership to first-generation Madeiran immigrants who lack the refinement and genteel professions of the Portuguese creoles. Even Joe squirms uncomfortably on his father's behalf when she declares that members of her group "shouldn't be associating themselves with the shopkeeping class" (p. 60). Philip, one of Joe's well-to-do cousins on his mother's side, is less concerned with the unnaturalness of excluding members of his family from the club than with the practical problems of making a club with such a limited membership viable:

At present, I believe there's only a membership of round about a hundred and fifty . . . under the existing rules you can only be a member if you are of Portuguese descent. The Portuguese community here from which we can draw members is small. I don't agree, though, that non-Portuguese should be allowed membership. All sorts of complications will have to be faced then. The colour question, you know. (p. 130)

Mendes portrays the Portuguese middle class as a group that would rather die from social suffocation and isolation than risk social contamination from their poorer relatives or other racial groups. Just as Joe's personal insecurity stems from a desire to be acceptable within this group, the group's insecurity stems from the desire of its members to rival or be accepted by the British colonial ruling class, who occupy the pinnacle of the local social hierarchy.

Apart from their self-destructive social isolation and their pernicious racial prejudice, Mendes also accuses the Portuguese community of greed and materialism. As with their other social deformities, the signs of greed in the novel become increasingly sophisticated the further up the social scale they occur. The author uses Joe at times to comment on this materialism though he is not immune to its influence. In old da Costa this materialism takes the form of miserliness. Mendes does not romanticize the old man by giving him the status of a pioneer. Just in case the reader is tempted to see the old rumshop keeper purely as a victim, Mendes reminds us of his function in the chain of exploitation that perpetuates the *status quo*:

Porters and cartermen and stevedores . . . could not live without their rum. They might be ill and exhausted by a fever: they would recover without medicine; but the day's work of packing flour, pushing hand-carts or unloading a ship's cargo had its only compensation in drinking rum until they were drunk. This again held no significance for old Antonio. The more drunk his customers were, the bigger were his sales. (p. 27)

Although old da Costa can bear his family's contempt and rejection with admirable stoicism, he flares up the moment Joe so much as spills a drop of gin:

"You getting crazhy, Joseph"—old da Costa accented the last syllable of the name— "why fo you t'row 'way de gin? You non know I pay for it, it cos' me money, an' you t'row it 'way like dat? You getting crazhy; after all dezhe yearzh I work fo' de money, now fo' you to t'row it 'way?"

"It's always money, money, money," Joseph said, not looking at old da Costa; "just as though money is everything and there is nothing else in this world but money." (p. 22)

Perhaps the most eloquent illustration of the refined acquisitiveness within the Portuguese middle class is Mendes's picture of Joe's brother Henry, who in his attempts to fit in his wife's social circles has lost all other signs of animation:

He sat there staring at Joe with one expression on his face, as though his face were a mask, and hm-ing and yes-ing and no-ing in a dull flat voice that made Joe suspect at times that his mind was far away from what was being said. "Can this be my brother?" Joe thought. "There is nothing in common between us," he said to himself. (pp. 58–59)

The only time that Henry comes to life is when he is left on his own to gloat over his expensive stamp collection.

Joe sees no resemblance between himself and his brother, but the narrator makes it fairly obvious that if he marries Cora and satisfies his lust for wealth and social prestige Joe will probably end up becoming a vegetable like Henry, incapable of any emotions except greed and fear of social ostracism. The world of the Portuguese middle class is depicted as a sterile, materialistic trap which can only offer Joe a choice of ways to die. Though Joe chooses the most brutal and final way of destroying himself, the author seems to suggest that there could be no optimistic end to the novel even if Joe had rejected the glitter of the Portuguese elite. Neither the unambitious Antonio da Costa nor the enlightened Cora achieve anything more through their way of life than Joe, Myra, or Henry. The only other alternative, meaningful involvement with the rest of the society, is never fully explored, though by implication we are always aware that this option is being rejected by the major characters. The patterns of social interaction in Trinidad in the late 1920s must have seemed fixed and practically unassailable except through the intellectual eccentricities practised by groups such as the *Beacon* fraternity. It is perhaps futile to speculate about what effect the events of the late 1930s would have had on Mendes's assessment of the society had he been there to witness and participate in them. Perhaps such an involvement might have helped him to overcome the creative impasse implicit in the negative endings of both of his novels and explicit in his inability to extend his range as a novelist after 1940.

Mendes's socialist leanings helped him to appreciate and sympathize with the lot of the lower classes, but there is no evidence in his work that he ever made the crucial step of fully identifying with their aspirations. His American writing is in tune with his earlier work but, significantly, it does not reflect any major influence from his exposure to radical ideas current among both black and white American creative writers. His relative failure to find outlets for new work in the United States has already been noted. Perhaps it may also have been due to the fact that within the context of the American literary scene, particularly the black American literary scene, his work had become anachronistic. He was still writing stories that fell into the Trinidad equivalent of the Harlem Renaissance genre at a time when most of his American contemporaries had passed this phase and turned to more radical protest writing.

After Mendes returned to Trinidad, he took a general interest in the new cultural and political scene. He reviewed arts exhibitions and wrote a number of important articles on the steel band, calypso, and the recently formed

Beryl McBurnie Little Carib Dance Group. A number of the short stories he had written in America or published previously appeared in West Indian magazines and *The Trinidad Guardian Weekly*.[22] He was involved in the formation of the United Front, a small socialist party which contested the elections of 1946. However, he soon began to devote all his energies to his new and demanding job in the Civil Service and was eventually appointed General Manager of the Port Services Department. Having abandoned all hopes of becoming a major creative writer, Mendes seems to have flung everything into his respectable civil service career. It is one of the ironies of fate that one of his early office mates was Edgar Mittelholzer who, while Mendes grappled with the intricate business of Port administration, spent his time at his desk writing *A Morning at the Office* (1950). Mittelholzer was soon to repeat Mendes's journey into exile and establish himself as a major West Indian novelist.

There can be no doubt that Mendes (with C. L. R James) was the first to write about the Trinidad barrack-yard, and his achievement in this respect has begun to gain recognition: The University of the West Indies awarded him the honorary degree of Doctor of Letters in 1972, for his pioneering contribution to West Indian literature. However, his work has only just begun to receive the critical attention it deserves.

NOTES

1. Alfred H. Mendes, personal communication, January 7, 1979.
2. Ibid.
3. *The Beacon*, 1, 2 (May, 1931), 26.
4. Ibid.
5. Mendes, personal communication, January 7, 1979.
6. Mendes, personal communication to Ramchand, September 10, 1964. Quoted in Kenneth Ramchand, "The Alfred Mendes Story," *Tapia*, 7, 22 (Sunday, May 29, 1977), 6.
7. Alfred Mendes, "A Commentary," *Trinidad*, 1, 2 (Easter, 1930), 64.
8. Mendes, personal communication, January 22, 1979.
9. These sixteen short stories are: "Her Chinaman's Way," *Trinidad*, 1, 1 (Christmas, 1929), 15–25; "Faux Pas," *Trinidad*, 1, 1 (Christmas, 1929), 54; "News," *Trinidad*, 1, 2 (Easter, 1930), 119–126; "Pablo's Fandango," *The Beacon*, 1, 1 (March, 1931), 29–32; "Over the Top," *The Beacon*, 1, 2 (May, 1931), 24–27; "Two Candles," *The Beacon*, 1, 4 (July, 1931), 21–23; "Five Dollars' Worth of Flesh," *The Beacon*, 1, 6 (September, 1931), 13–15; "Sweetman," *The Beacon*, 1, 7 (October, 1931), 1–6; "Water Piece," *The Beacon*, 1, 8 (November, 1931), 6–7; "Without Snow," *The Beacon*, 1, 9 (December, 1931), 6–10; "Boodhoo," *The Beacon*, 1, 11 (March 1932), 18–25; 1, 12 (April, 1932), 23–27; and 2, 1 (May, 1932), 9–11; "Damp," *The Beacon*, 2, 4 (August, 1932), 17–20; "Scapular," *The Beacon*, 2, 5 (September, 1932), 8–10; "Snap-shots," *The Beacon*, 2, 7 (December, 1932), 11–17; "Ursula's Morals," *The Beacon*, 2, 8 (February, 1933), 21–23; "Colour," *The Beacon*, 2, 12

(June, 1933), 14–18; 3, 1 (August, 1933), 9–10; 3, 2 (September, 1933), 33–35; 3, 3 (October, 1933), 52–55; and 3, 4 (November, 1933), 76–79.

10. *The London Mercury*, 19, 11 (January, 1929), 256–262.

11. *This Quarter*, 5, 2 (December, 1932), 321–337.

12. *The Manchester Guardian* published: "Hurricane 1," (November 29, 1932); "Profit on Opium" (March, 1932); "Escape," (August 5, 1931); "Juan's Cocoa," (March 6, 1931); and "On the Seventh Day." *The English Weekly* published: "A Life" (April 13, 1933) and "Walkin' on de Waters" (August 31, 1933). "Bête Rouge" appeared in the January 1932 issue of *The Clarion*.

13. This letter from Aldous Huxley, dated September 8, 1931, was published in *The Beacon*, 1, 7 (October, 1931), 24.

14. The following stories were published in America: "In Port of Spain," *The Little Magazine*, Sept.-Oct., 1934; "Lulu Gets Married," *Best Short Stories of 1936*; and "Marie and Rampatia," *The Magazine*. During this period the following stories were published in England: "Afternoon in Trinidad," ed. John Lehmann, *New Writing*, 2 (Autumn, 1936), and "Lulu Gets Married," *New Stories*, Oct.-Nov., 1935.

15. "The Turbulent Thirties in Trinidad: An Interview with Alfred H. Mendes," *World Literature Written in English*, 12, 1 (April, 1973), 79. According to information provided by the author, three of the novels destroyed contained similar material to that of *Black Fauns* and *Pitch Lake*: two were barrack-yard novels (one a sequel to *Black Fauns*) and one a satire on the Portuguese business community.

16. Mendes, personal communication to K. Ramchand, September 10, 1964. Quoted in Kenneth Ramchand, "The Alfred Mendes Story," *Tapia*, 7, 23 (Sunday, June 5, 1977), 6.

17. Mendes interview, *WLWE*, 71.

18. On the predominant role of women in early West Indian fiction, see Rhonda Cobham's "Introduction" to the 1984 republication of *Black Fauns*.

19. In this section of the chapter all page references in parentheses are to Alfred H. Mendes, *Black Fauns* (London: Duckworth, 1935).

20. See Mendes interview, *WLWE*, 74.

21. In this section of the chapter all page references in parentheses are to Alfred H. Mendes, *Pitch Lake* (London: Duckworth, 1934).

22. Among the stories published in *The Trinidad Guardian Weekly* are: "Ranjit Dass" (June 15, 1947); "Village Lothario" (May 18, 1947); "Twelve Cents" (October 9, 1949); "Hurricane 1" (January 11, 1948); and "Hurricane 2" (July 27, 1942). Jean de Boissière's *Callaloo* reprinted "Afternoon in Trinidad," 1, 5 (December, 1940), and "Lulu Gets Married," 2, 2 (October, 1941). Mendes's "Torrid Zone" appeared in *Bim*, 3, 11 (December, 1949), 209–213.

CHAPTER 5

C. L. R. JAMES: THE AMBIVALENT INTELLECTUAL

C. L. R. James was born in 1901 in Tunapuna, Trinidad. At the age of nine, he won an exhibition to Queen's Royal College. After leaving college in 1918, he taught for a time at his old school and at the Government Training College for Teachers. In 1932 he left Trinidad for England where he lived until 1938, working first as a sports correspondent for *The Manchester Guardian* and later as editor of the journal of the International African Service Bureau, the organ of George Padmore's Pan-African movement. Between 1938 and 1952 he lectured widely in the United States. After internment during the McCarthy era and deportation from America, he returned to Trinidad and had a short-lived association with the People's National Movement as editor of the party's official newspaper, *The Nation*. Since then he has continued to write and lecture in Europe, America and the Third World, and has gained an international reputation as an intellectual and man of letters.[1]

James's early background is typical of the new class of educated black West Indians that began to emerge at the turn of the century. As the son of a schoolmaster he belonged to the privileged sector of the local black community. James has described the position occupied by schoolmasters of his father's stature in Trinidad when he was a child:

The schoolmaster was an important person. Next to him were the Anglican parson and the Catholic parson, but the third stage was the teacher. If you wanted to know what was happening in the British Parliament, or . . . about the revolution in Turkey, or if you wanted to know what was happening in Barbados . . . or . . . what books Dickens had written, or who Henry VIII was, or what Magna Carta was—whatever it was, you came to the local teacher to find out. And if he didn't know, he went to the two parsons, and if they didn't know—well, nobody knew. That was the intellectual life of a rather narrow area. But the local teacher recognized his responsibility. . . . [He] taught you everything you needed to know: reading, writing, arithmetic, proper behaviour, good manners, how you were to wear your clothes—everything.[2]

The secondary education available to young West Indians in the early twentieth century was conducted along strictly orthodox lines and laid considerable stress on the classics. Though the educated black community had already produced "black-conscious" spokesmen such as J. J. Thomas, it saw itself as part of the tradition of Western European civilization and turned to Europe for its intellectual inspiration and aesthetic standards. Even after he developed a more radical approach to social reform, James retained his early reliance on Western models, as he has indicated:

I, a man of the Caribbean, have found that it is in the study of Western literature, Western philosophy and Western history that I have found out the things I have found out, even about the underdeveloped countries.[3]

The class position of James's family in the early twentieth century would hardly have provided him with any other tools with which to examine his society. After leaving elementary school, James would have had little direct social contact with lower-class black Trinidadians and would probably have had only a superficial knowledge of their African-derived culture. Few middle-class, black West Indians questioned the cultural bias of their orthodox education. They saw the mass of ignorant, uneducated people around them as deserving of their sympathy and guidance, but they would hardly have considered such people capable of teaching them anything in the way of moral or cultural values. When as a young man and a member of the intellectual group around *Trinidad* and *The Beacon*, James began to look more closely at the lifestyle and values of the lower class, he had to deal with the inherent ambivalence in his attitude. The relationship between the educated black man and the uneducated black masses is a recurring preoccupation in his early writing.

In Trinidad, James wrote several pieces of short fiction[4] and a novel, *Minty Alley*, which was published by Secker & Warburg in England in 1936. Two of the pieces which appeared in *The Beacon* are extended anecdotes. They seem to contain the material for unrealized short stories and provide a possible insight into James's methods of collecting material for his fiction. Both pieces take the form of interviews, and in both it is the narrator's curiosity which draws the full details of the recounted experience from the informant. The first piece, "Revolution," reproduces an encounter with a Venezuelan exile living in Trinidad who had participated in a revolution in his native country. The second piece, entitled "The Star that Would Not Shine," also takes the form of a reproduced conversation. This time a chance meeting with a stranger gives the narrator an opportunity of hearing a rather bizarre little tale about the stranger's son who had passed up a career as a "fat boy" in the movies because he had been asked to play the role of a character called "Fatty Arbuckle," the hated nickname with which he had been taunted by his schoolmates. Neither of these pieces is fully developed, but both give an indication of James's lively curiosity about the people he encountered in his daily life.

Both "Triumph," which is discussed in chapter 3, and "La Divina Pastora" are successful short stories based on encounters of a similar nature. James even uses the same narrative device of the reporter in the opening paragraph of "La Divina Pastora":

Of my own belief in this story I shall say nothing. What I have done is to put it down as far as possible just as it was told me, in my own style, but with no addition to or subtraction from the essential facts.[5]

The plot revolves around an attempt by a cocoa worker called Anita Perez to invoke the aid of the saint La Divina Pastora in bringing her hesitant suitor Sebastian up to scratch. As an act of supplication, Anita goes to the shrine of La Divina Pastora and offers the saint her most treasured possession, a golden chain. On returning home she finds that during her absence Sebastian has missed her, and has suddenly realized how much he has always taken her presence for granted. He asks Anita to go with him to a dance. In her elation, Anita discounts the intervention of the saint: "It was too sudden. As if the saint had had nothing to do with it." Dressing for the dance, she even regrets momentarily that she no longer has her golden chain. As it turns out, the evening is not the success she had hoped it would be. Anita returns home and discovers to her shock that "there, in its old place in the cigarette tin, lay a little chain of gold." The reader is left to speculate as to how this development will ultimately affect the relationship between Anita and Sebastian and as to whether the reappearance of the chain is a psychological illusion or a miracle.

Like "Pablo's Fandango" by Alfred Mendes, James's "La Divina Pastora" is one of the few early Trinidad stories to deal with peasant characters in a rural setting. Both writers made a clear distinction between the settled patterns of a rural existence and the turbulent competitive life of the urban poor. Mamitz's flamboyant independence in "Triumph" is a far cry from Anita's approach to life:

Anita Perez . . . had one earthly aim. She considered it her duty and business to be married as quickly as possible, first because in that retired spot it marked the sweet perfection of a woman's existence, and secondly, because feminine youth and beauty, if they exist, fade early in the hard work on the cocoa plantations. Every morning of the week, Sundays excepted, she banded down her hair, and donned a skirt which reached to her knees, not with any pretensions to fashion, but so that from seven till five she might pick cocoa, or cut cocoa, or dry cocoa, or in some other way assist in the working of Mr. Kayle-Smith's cocoa estate. She did this for thirty cents a day, and did it uncomplainingly, because her mother and father had done it before her, and had thriven on it. On Sundays she dressed herself in one of her few dresses, put on a little gold chain, her only ornament, and went to Mass. She had no thought of woman's rights, nor any Ibsenic theories of morality. All she knew was that it was her duty to get married, when, if she was lucky, this hard life in the cocoa would cease.[6]

Not only does James play up the difference between rural and urban approaches to life, he also places great emphasis on the hardship and deprivation of rural life, features which are usually played down in the barrack-yard stories.

In James's novel *Minty Alley* there is also little reference to the physical hardships experienced by the lower-class tenants of the yard and house at No. 2 Minty Alley. It takes Haynes, the middle-class protagonist, a full year to notice the harsh conditions in which his landlady, Mrs. Rouse, makes a living baking cakes:

One day, nearly a year after he was living in the house, he went into the kitchen for the first time. As soon as he was fairly inside, he felt that he was in the mouth of hell. The big three-decked stove was going, the coal-pots with food, the concrete below so hot that he could feel it through his slippers, and above, the galvanised iron roof, which the tropical sun had been warming up from the outside since morning. He could scarcely breathe and involuntarily recoiled.

She came to the door smiling as usual.

"You find it hot, Mr. Haynes?"

"How can you stand it, Mrs. Rouse?"

"Poor people have no choice Mr. Haynes. It's hard, but it is better in the hot season. When it is raining you have to leave the hot stove to go out into the wet yard and so you catch cold." (p. 187)[7]

This is the only passage in *Minty Alley* in which the narrator describes directly the hardships under which his lower-class characters functioned. Such passages are rare in Trinidad barrack-yard literature, and this distinguishes the work from the later yard novels of Jamaican writers such as Roger Mais which dwell at length on the poverty and suffering of the urban slum-dweller.

Minty Alley shares a number of the characteristics of the barrack-yard stories and Alfred Mendes's *Black Fauns*. Like them it presents the yard as a closely knit community, and hardly goes outside its walls for its subject matter. The yard at *Minty Alley*, however, is not quite the same as the yards depicted in "Triumph" or *Black Fauns*. James, it would seem, was realistic enough not to have his middle-class protagonist move into a real slum, and chooses instead to place him in the type of lodgings which he himself as a young man living away from home might have had to use. James has acknowledged an autobiographical link with his work:

I was about 27 or 28 at the time when I went to live in that household described in the novel . . . the people fascinated me, and I wrote about them from the point of view of an educated youthful member of the black middle class . . . Many of the things that took place in the story actually took place in life.[8]

The front house at No. 2 Minty Alley is a small but respectable-looking dwelling, but the yard behind the house contains a number of outbuildings which the landlady Mrs. Rouse rents out to augment her income. The interaction between the lower-class tenants and the middle-class protagonist is central to the novel's development. From the start the social distance between the two groups is made quite clear even though Haynes is only a struggling clerk in a bookstore and can hardly afford to live elsewhere. Haynes is the son of a school mistress, who until her death had lived in a comfortable though heavily mortgaged house and kept servants. As Ella, Haynes's faithful old retainer, points out, the inhabitants of Minty Alley "are ordinary people, sir. Not your class of people" (p. 21). Haynes's next-door neighbor in Minty Alley is a kept woman, while his landlady is a cake seller who lives with her sweetman. Mrs. Rouse's niece Maisie and the Indian girl Philomen function as servants in the house. The only occupant of the yard with any claim to social pretensions is Nurse Jackson, but as the mother of an illegitimate child and (according to Mrs. Rouse) a former prostitute, her claims to respectability are of the slenderest nature.

The narrator takes great pains to explain Haynes's decision to abandon his middle-class home for the room in Mrs. Rouse's backyard. At the age of twenty his mother dies after a long and expensive illness, and Haynes finds it financially impossible to remain in their home if he is to carry out his mother's dying wish that he pay off the rest of the mortgage on the house. The crisis is not merely a financial one. Haynes as the only child of a widow has "grown up under the shelter of his mother, to whom he was everything and who was everything to him" (p. 22). Mrs. Haynes's death deprives her son of her emotional and psychological support and brings his long adolescence to an abrupt end. Haynes's mother had envisaged his job at the bookstore as a stopgap, while she paid off her mortgage and saved enough money to send him abroad to study to become a doctor. Freed from the pressure of his mother's ambitions, Haynes feels the need to escape, if only temporarily, from the demanding career that has been mapped out for him:

> He wanted a change. . . . It would be better to live cheaply, for a time at least. . . . And at the back of his mind unformulated, but nevertheless a steadily growing influence, was the desire to make a break with all his monotonous past life, school, home and the drowsy bookshop. . . . His life was empty. . . . The sea of life was beating at the walls which enclosed him. Nervously and full of self-distrust, he had been fighting against taking the plunge, but he would have to sometime. (pp. 22–23)

Financial necessity, boredom and the urgent call of manhood all conspire in Haynes to make him abandon "the pleasant furniture, the mahogany sideboard with its spotless china and the silver pieces" for the drab environs of No. 2 Minty Alley.

Although the story is not told by a first-person narrator, the narrative perspective is limited to only those things that Haynes can see or hear, quite unlike the omniscient narrator in the barrack-yard story, "Triumph." Kenneth Ramchand has suggested that through the use of this limited narrative perspective "the characters retain autonomy as familiar but not fully known beings" and "we are made to feel that there are hidden resources even in the hedged-in people of the yard."[9] The physical and psychological limitations of Haynes's perspective are summed up in the passage below. The way in which it is presented offers an ironic commentary on the methods of the middle-class writer who wished to write about the lower classes, and the dilemma in which these methods involved him:

> [Haynes] heard voices in the yard. In the stillness of the early morning, they were very clear. One voice was deep. Benoit's, but talking in a low tone. Through the thin wood of which the house was built sounds from outside came through distinctly. Haynes's eyes, looking idly at his toes, were caught by a wide crack of light between two of the boards. It had been pasted over with paper, but the paper had burst or been punctured long ago. He threw the pillow to the bottom of the bed, put his elbows on it and peeped through.
>
> Benoit stood by the kitchen door and Wilhelmina, the servant girl, stood washing at the sink.
>
> "Come here," said Benoit.
>
> "Wait till I wash my face. This cold morning you so hot!"
>
> "Me. I am always hot," said Benoit.
>
> Wilhelmina wiped her hands on her dress and came up to Benoit.
>
> "Well! What you want?"
>
> "What I want?" He held her and placed her against the kitchen door. Then he leaned himself against her.

"This is what I want," he kissed her savagely. "And this," he kissed her again. "And this, too, and this."

She pulled herself away.

"You are hurting me," she said.

He made to hold her again.

"No," she objected, and shook her head, "you said you was comin' last night and you didn't come. This is the second time."

They went into the kitchen.

Haynes fell back on his bed, his eyes hurting him from the strain. He was suddenly no longer sleepy. Instead, he was very much alive. In fact, he behaved quite idiotically. He balanced himself on the small of his back and kicked his feet up in the air. (pp. 36–37)

Haynes's role as eavesdropper—or, as Merle Hodge has put it, "peeping Tom in the nigger yard"[10]—is an exact parallel of the position of the middle-class writer of barrack-yard stories. The lives of the barrack yarders provide him with excitement and sexual titillation of a kind unknown in his usual environment. In responding to the spectacle Haynes at times loses sight of the deeper human conflicts he witnesses. However, as time passes, he begins to see his neighbors as real people rather than characters out of some exotic, X-rated film, and in spite of his inhibitions he emerges from behind his peephole and becomes personally involved in the "terrific human drama" which he sees unfolding around him (p. 38).

During Haynes's stay at No. 2 Minty Alley a number of conflicts develop and come to a head. The central conflict involves Mrs. Rouse, Mr. Benoit and the light-skinned mulatto lodger, Nurse Jackson. Mr. Benoit, whose aggressive sexual exploits have already been noted, is Mrs. Rouse's sweet-man, but in spite of his womanizing tendencies, his relationship with Mrs. Rouse has lasted for eighteen years and at the outset of the novel seems to have been mutually beneficial to them both, as he assists Mrs. Rouse with the business side of her baking. Nurse Jackson however provides a special attraction for Benoit, as he explains to Haynes:

The white woman is too sweet. She is like jelly. I am not going to give her up. Look! Where she work the other day they send for her, give her a big bottle of lotion, a bottle with a gold stopper and ten dollars as a present. Five was mine. Give her up! No man. This one [Mrs. Rouse] is too stupid. I live with you nearly eighteen years. I not going to leave you. But she ain't going to prevent me going out when I want. (p. 67)

Haynes, who is initially a mere spectator, is drawn willy-nilly into these conflicts, and *Minty Alley* records his growing involvement in the yard and changing attitudes towards lower-class life. At the start of the novel especially, he repeatedly regrets his decision to move from his middle-class environment. At one point he becomes disgusted with "this blasted place with its eternal smell of cake" (p. 36). When, at the height of the affair between the nurse and Benoit, Mrs. Rouse attempts to kill Benoit, his moral sensibilities are offended: "He would be sorry to go, but when it came to knives and stabbing, however much his leaving would hurt Mrs. Rouse, he would have to go elsewhere" (p. 89). However, on neither occasion do his words result in action. Throughout the novel he retains a degree of ambivalence about his situation, but the more he gets to know about his neighbors, the more he feels obliged to stay.

Haynes's actual involvement in the affairs of the yard begins with a small incident which forces him to take sides. When Nurse Jackson, whose uncontrollable temper is well known in the yard, threatens to beat her son in a fit of rage, the boy runs into Haynes's room for refuge. Everybody expects Haynes to protect the child, but he can only plead weakly, "Spare him, Nurse" (p. 45). When the nurse disregards his plea he feels helpless:

Haynes locked his door, and overwhelmed with shame tried in vain to shut out the thud of the cane on the little body, the yells and screams and the "Hush, I tell you, hush" of his mother. He felt that he should have done something, that he should do something. At each blow he winced as if it had fallen on his own flesh. (p. 46)

After this incident, however, he can no longer remain a mere observer, as the members of the yard take the child's lead and confront him directly with their problems. Whether he wants to or not, he feels bound to act when Mrs. Rouse approaches him to have a word with Benoit about his affair with Nurse Jackson. The situation is one for which Haynes's sheltered upbringing has hardly prepared him; as he realizes, "It would be the first time in his life that he had ever voluntarily interfered in anybody's private affairs" (p. 70). To complicate matters still further, Benoit also confides in him, and he is divided between loyalty to Mrs. Rouse and sympathy with Benoit's position. After Benoit leaves, Haynes acts as Mrs. Rouse's man of business; as Benoit observes during a chance encounter on the streets, "I hear you writing letters, making receipts, giving advice and so on. In fact you take my place" (p. 139). Subsequently, when Haynes loans some money to Mrs. Rouse to tide her over a particularly difficult period, the narrator comments:

After that he was the master of the house. Nothing was ever done without consulting him. He made up Mrs. Rouse's accounts, told her what to pay, and wrote letters to the more difficult creditors, endorsed a note for her (the business simply would not go well), and as Mrs. Rouse told him one day was of far more help to her than Benoit had ever been in his life. (p. 173)

While Haynes continually has to make a conscious effort to suppress his middle-class reservations about his new environment and the people who inhabit it, the yard-dwellers seem to exhibit no reservations whatever in welcoming him into their community. There is apparently no envy of his comparative wealth or mistrust of his social position. Indeed, most of the women seem to hold him in awe. Benoit's attitude to Haynes imposes the least strains on our credibility. He treats Haynes as a masculine equal to whom he can recount his sexual exploits. Although most of the other inhabitants of the yard chat freely with Haynes and share their confidences with him, they seem to accord him a special status because of his superior education, as if they share his mother's ambitions for him. Merle Hodge has taken issue with James's portrayal of the yarders' attitude to Haynes, who, after all, is a mere twenty years old. In her article on the novel she maintains:

The extreme awe in which he is held by the entire yard is quite unlikely. Surely the ordinary worker is more self-possessed than this, even before the "middle class," and especially when the middle class encounters him on his own ground. James lets the whole yard fall at the feet of this young and obviously inexperienced man, makes them accept him as a confidant, arbitrator, guide and mentor, all on account of his perfect English, it would seem, for this is about all there is in the situation to distinguish him from his co-tenants in these shabby lodgings. It is like old European mythology—the Princess and the pea, royalty asserting itself under all circumstances, patronizing, commanding respect.[11]

Though Mrs. Rouse's total confidence in Haynes seems difficult to swallow, Merle Hodge's criticism introduces a postcolonial bias into the situation depicted in *Minty Alley* which is hardly warranted. Today, when secondary education in the West Indies is available to a relatively large section of the population, the educated black West Indian is not the rarity that he indeed must have been in the 1920s. At twenty, Haynes must have embodied the most cherished dreams of personal fulfillment for the other black members of the yard, and in the man-starved world of the barrack-yard he comes to act as surrogate husband, father and son to the women and children who live there. It is this identification with his aspirations rather than a sense of personal awe which makes Haynes the darling of the yard. As Miss Atwell, the kept woman in the room next door, points out: "Education. That's what it is. Education. If I had a child I would sacrifice anything to give him education" (p. 152).

The only relationship that Haynes develops in the yard in which he is portrayed as being on the receiving end throughout is his relationship with Maisie. From the start Maisie accepts that she can expect no permanent gains from an affair with Haynes, as marriage between people from their respective classes could hardly be contemplated. James presents this limitation on their relationship with very little comment and, like the casual way in which Haynes is allowed to drift out of his involvement with the yard at the end of the novel, this seems to indicate the extent and nature of the interaction betwen the classes which he perceived as possible—or even desirable—at the time. Maisie's pragmatic approach to life in general, and her relationship with Haynes in particular, are reminiscent of the hard-nosed approach to marriage and money displayed by Mendes's barrack-yard women in *Black Fauns*. It protects her from being exploited by men like Haynes, while allowing her to give him a much-needed initiation into sexual and worldly matters.

James's portrayal of the development of the sexual relationship between Haynes and Maisie provides the novel with some of its best comic scenes. At the same time, James treats Haynes's naivety with a sympathetic insight which precludes caricature. Haynes's sexual inexperience is implied early in the novel in the false bravado with which he sizes up Maisie as "a damned, pretty girl . . . who would be very nice to sleep with" (p. 78). It soon becomes clear that in spite of graphic instructions from Benoit and Maisie's obvious encouragement, Haynes has no idea how to go about initiating a sexual affair. He blames his inhibitions on a reluctance to frighten Maisie, but it is quite clear that Maisie does not scare easily. It is she who maneu-vers Haynes into situations of intimacy and even manages to spur him into action by telling him that she has slept with one of his friends. In this comic reversal of the male-female roles in courtship, James successfully captures the self-consciousness of Haynes's first advances:

"Have a cigarette, Mr. Haynes," said Maisie. "Let me light it for you." And she brought it for him and sat down on the bed beside him.

She lit the cigarette, but did not move. Haynes puffed twice and then put it on the table. Now he was in the very lists of love. Maisie lifted the cigarette from the table and put it in the ashtray. When she brought her hand back she put it on the bed. Haynes could feel it resting against his leg. She left it there. Now certainly was the time. Better hold her hand first so as not to startle her. If he acted too suddenly she might scream or utter a cry and those next door might hear. Yes, he had to guard against that. There was a lot of talking and laughing next door, but if he startled Maisie in any way and she shrieked they would certainly ask what was that. His hand moved furtively towards hers. (pp. 132–133)

On this occasion Haynes is rescued from the brink of decision by a call on him to act the role of patron to Mrs. Rouse. It is only after a number of similar episodes that Haynes, acting on Benoit's advice, "held her and kissed her, and then to his astonishment did what he liked with her" (p. 168). Perhaps the most remarkable feature of this sexual initiation is the tact Maisie shows in allowing Haynes to make the first move so that he comes out of the experience feeling that he has proved himself a man. But Maisie does more for Haynes than introduce him to sex. A friendship develops between them which, in spite of the limitations of their sexual relationship, is the first genuine friendship with a woman of his own age that Haynes has experienced. In spite of his middle-class prejudices he finds himself wondering, "if the girl of his dreams, the divine, the inexpressible she whom he was going to marry one day . . . if in some things she would be to him what Maisie was in all" (p. 212).

Maisie is not only Haynes's lover and friend, she also becomes his teacher in the art of coping with life. When for example Haynes hesitates to ask his employer for a raise in his salary, it is Maisie who insists that he should demand it as his due. Under Maisie's influence Haynes becomes more and more self-confident in his dealings with people in general—including Maisie herself. When he lectures her at one stage for being rude to Mrs. Rouse she remarks: "Ha. . . . You are getting on, Mr. Haynes. When you first came here you couldn't say boo to a goose" (p. 205). As the narrator puts it, "Little by little she was making a human creature out of him" (p. 202). When Maisie leaves for America, Haynes's period of initiation comes to an end and he leaves the yard.

It has been suggested that "the intended thesis of the novel is that the meeting between middle class and lower class is mutually beneficial."[12] The discussion so far has in a sense illustrated that this might very well have been C. L. R. James's intention when he wrote *Minty Alley*. The impact of the novel as a whole, however, does not seem to fully bear out this interpretation. Haynes may have gained a great deal of experience in the yard, which he is able to take with him when he leaves, but there is nothing to suggest that this contact has produced any lasting benefits for the other inhabitants of Minty Alley, or that Haynes's basic attitudes towards the lower classes have been significantly altered. Though at first he makes a point of visiting Mrs. Rouse after he moves, he eventually drifts away until his only contact with the house is incidental: "Whenever Haynes passed there in the tramcar he used to make it a point of duty to look. But of late he forgets more often than not" (pp. 243–244). At the end of the novel Haynes is perhaps a bit more experienced and a lot more self-assured, but he seems as alienated from the majority of his less-privileged countrymen as he was at the beginning of the book. On reading *Minty Alley* after its republication in 1971, C. L. R. James himself seems to have been struck by this feature of the work. "I saw," he says, "embedded in the novel a fundamental antagonism in West Indian society between the educated black and the mass of plebians . . . [yet] when I wrote it down fifty years ago I did not have one iota of feeling that I was posing a social or political situation."[13] Whatever the concessions which time and involvement force him to make in his relations with the rest of the yard, Haynes's distance from the other inhabitants of Minty Alley is maintained throughout. Even Maisie, his most intimate friend, addresses him as "Mr. Haynes," and at times it is clear that Haynes accepts this status in the household as his right. When for instance he is asked to give the toast at their Christmas gathering he accepts, "confident of his intellectual superiority" (p. 150). While the other members of the yard speak in creole, Haynes's language is indistinguishable from the standard English used by the narrator.

Apart from its preoccupation with the meeting of the classes, the pioneering achievement of James's novel lies in its presentation of lower-class life itself. The length of the work gives James the scope to explore some of the less exotic features of barrack-yard life, such as the position of children in the yard and the details of everyday existence, which the short stories often overlook. This makes even the more colorful features of barrack-yard life such as the sexual intrigue and the belief in obeah tangible, familiar, and unobtrusive. Obeah for example is usually referred to as "science"— the less emotive term used for it within the lower class, and a term which highlights its use for practical rather than melodramatic purposes. The narrator refers to the subject in a matter-of-fact way when Benoit's marriage to the nurse seems imminent:

But Mrs. Rouse was not giving him up without effort. Three times a day the scent of incense and asafoedtida burning in her bedroom poisoned the atomosphere. She was using all the science she knew to win back Benoit. But Benoit was a man of science too. (pp. 100–101)

More vivid accounts are given by the barrack-yarders themselves, but here too the accounts are in keeping with what we know of the characters who give them, and serve the purpose of dramatizing the personalities of the tellers rather than calling attention to the outlandishness of their beliefs. Maisie's gift for histrionics is well portrayed in her account of how Benoit and Mrs. Rouse help the nurse to pass her examinations:

Mr. Haynes, you don't know. Benoit say he know science. He tell the nurse what to do to pass. And they write the doctor's name on a piece of paper and they put it in the nurse's boots. So whenever she walk she mash him down. And when he was talking to her, that's when she used to fail, in the talking part, she press hard on him. And they make a little image of the doctor, and all through the day of the exam Mrs. Rouse was bathing it. That was to keep him cool. (p. 94)

Benoit's version of the same incident characteristically stresses the opportunities for sexual excitement which his practice of science provides, and he gives Haynes a spicy account of how he once had to bathe the nurse in special herbs "naked as she born" (p. 63).

In *Minty Alley*, as in "Triumph," James is particularly successful in his portrayal of lower-class women. Here too he emphasizes their humanity rather than their colorful or exotic features. Unlike the Amazonian racial hybrids of the barrack-yard stories, Miss Atwell, the kept woman who lives next door to Haynes, is a nosy little woman, scraping together a livelihood when her luck is down and trying hard to impress Haynes with her respectability. Mrs. Rouse and Maisie are perhaps the best-realized characters in the book, and all three women show the same strength and courage in the face of adversity which the middle-class writers in the *Beacon* group so often emphasize in their barrack-yard stories. Mrs. Rouse's devotion to Benoit is presented with compassion and understanding, but when he leaves she battles on with the business of making a living with all her old tenacity. Maisie, in spite of her vitality and wit, is by no means idealized. She is presented as equally susceptible to the racial prejudices of the rest of the society—she hates the Indian maid Philomen—and her rudeness and sarcasm to her aunt and Miss Atwell are at times inexcusable. At the same time she is the most ambitious member of the household, and James makes her a symbol of all that he considered progressive in the lower classes. She is too spirited to accept the poor working conditions and wages which have broken other women around her and is not afraid to abandon the relative security of life with her aunt in order to better her standard of living:

For staying at home she had no plans. But she wanted to go to America to work for good money. In America you worked hard but you got good food and pay and had a fine time. Why the hell should she starve and slave to get a few shillings a week from some employer in the town? (p. 206)

Maisie's rebelliousness and self-imposed exile seem to indicate the limits of James's evaluation and understanding of the mood of the Trinidad working class in the late 1920s. Like Mendes at the time he was preoccupied with cultural matters and saw the lower class as a fitting subject around which to build an indigenous literature. James recalls that he and Mendes "didn't interfere with politics,"[14] and so he makes no attempt to exploit the potential of Maisie's rebelliousness as a symbol of political protest. Like Maisie, James's response at the time to the limitations of his society was a personal rather than a political one—an escape rather than an attempt to fight the system. His political awakening was a result of his exposure to radical new ideas in England, and though he turned his pen to the attack of the old order he did so as a historian and polemicist rather than as a creative writer. As he explains in *Beyond a Boundary*:

Fiction-writing drained out of me and was replaced by politics. I became a Marxist, a Trotskyist. I published large books and small articles on these and kindred subjects. I wrote and spoke. Like many others, I expected war, and during or after the war social revolution.[15]

In England James wrote one further literary work, a play entitled *Toussaint L'Ouverture*. It was written in 1936 and presented in the same year by the London Stage Society in a special performance with Paul Robeson in the lead role. It preceded the publication of James's major historical study, *The Black Jacobins: Toussaint L'Ouverture and the San Domingo Revolution*, by two years. While still in Trinidad, James had become interested in Toussaint L'Ouverture and his role in the first successful slave uprising in the Caribbean. His earliest comments on the Haitian leader appeared in an article in *The Beacon* entitled "The Intelligence of the Negro: A Few Words with Dr. Harland," in which he attacked Dr. Harland's article on the intellectual inferiority of the negro race. In 1931 James mentioned that instead of arguing with people like Dr. Harland he "would have far preferred to write on Toussaint L'Ouverture."[16] The play of 1936 was his first attempt to present Toussaint's rise and decline, and was probably a by-product of his research on the Haitian revolution for his book *The Black Jacobins*. The original version of the play was never published and no copies of it were available for the present study. The following analysis is based on the revised version of the play which was published as *The Black Jacobins* in Errol Hill's collection *A Time . . . and a Season: 8 Caribbean Plays* (1976). The new version was first produced by Dexter Lyndersay at Nigeria's University of Ibadan during the Nigerian Civil War. It has not been possible to assess the differences between the original and the revised versions of the play. James has merely stated: "After 25 years the colonial revolution had made great strides so about that time I began to rewrite it in view of the new historical happenings."[17]

James's comment highlights one of his underlying motives in producing the drama. It was written at a time when the African nationalist movement, which coalesced around Padmore's International African Service Bureau in London,[18] had just begun to attract attention. James probably saw his play as a contribution to the ongoing debate as to what constituted the best intellectual framework within which the struggle against colonialism could be initiated and carried through. He seems to have felt that the example of Haiti could serve as the basis for an analysis of the ideology behind colonialism, and could provide examples of the problems of leadership which the new nationalist movement would have to resolve.

James's play does not put forward any "Négritude" sentiments, nor does it concentrate on celebrating the military feats of the slaves who took part in the Haitian revolution. Instead the playwright's concern is to reveal and examine the strengths and the weaknesses of the revolution's black leadership. In his play James seems to be advancing the view that Haiti's independence, although in itself a significant achievement, did not result in freedom for the Haitian people, but ushered in a despotic regime that was in many ways as vicious as the earlier French colonial system: White masters were exchanged for black ones; slavery, though abolished in name, persisted; and the dream of liberty, equality and fraternity was dissipated.

The play is the work of a theoretician and historian who utilizes the medium of drama to analyze the protagonists involved in the twelve-year struggle in Haiti. Most of the major male characters are based on actual historical personalities, and their speeches are often taken word for word from their personal letters and other historical records. Apart from Toussaint, Dessalines and Bonaparte, they include two more Haitian leaders, Christophe and Moïse; two French military figures, General Hédouville and Colonel Vincent; two Englishmen, General Maitland and Cathcart; the Spanish General Marquis d'Hermona; and the American Consul in French San Domingo. In presenting these characters, little effort is made at individual characterization. Each becomes a mouthpiece for a particular ideological position and, with a few exceptions, their positions are portrayed through speeches rather than action. Most of their conversations are restricted to the other major characters and we rarely see the leaders interacting with their followers directly. Occasionally we hear them confiding in the two major female characters, Madame Bullet and Marie-Jeanne, who are also partly modelled on actual characters.

James divides his play into three acts. The dramatic division reflects three recognizable stages in the historical development of Haiti from colonial status to independence in 1803. The first act covers the period 1791 to 1798 and focusses on three major events: Toussaint L'Ouverture's decision to join the 1791 slave uprising; the sudden end of his alliance with the Spanish when France abolishes slavery in 1794; and his victory over the British and mulatto forces in 1798, which establishes his position as governor of French San Domingo. The second act highlights the growing conflict between Toussaint and Bonaparte in the closing years of the eighteenth century. Enraged by the ex-slave's audacity in publishing a new Haitian constitution guaranteeing the island self-governing dominion status, Bonaparte decides to send a punitive expedition out against Toussaint under the command of Leclerc, his brother-in-law. The final act depicts Dessalines's rise to power after Toussaint's surrender to the French forces. Dessalines secretly encourages Leclerc in his ruse to remove Toussaint, but once his leader has been removed he enters an alliance with the mulattos and resumes the struggle against France. The play ends with Dessalines's victory over the French, his assumption of the title of Emperor and the beginning of his policy of eliminating all the whites in Haiti.

James blames the disastrous outcome of the revolution on the decline of Toussaint's power as a leader, which creates weaknesses in the Haitian line of command that are easily exploited by Dessalines. From the start of the play these two leaders are contrasted. We first encounter them in the prologue when news reaches San Domingo of the slave uprisings in Martinique and Guadeloupe. Dessalines, watching the street crier who carries the news, *"looks up with determination and hate on his face. He raises a fist to the sky and shouts, 'We will kill them all. Every one'"* (p. 361).[19] Toussaint on the other hand is engrossed in the reading of Abbé Raynal's *Philosophical and Political History of the Establishments and Commerce of the Europeans in the Two Indies*, which was published in 1780 and contained passages severely critical of European colonialism and the practice of slavery. In his historical documentary *The Black Jacobins* James quotes the passage from the book which attracts Toussaint's attention in the play:

If self-interest alone prevails with nations and their masters, there is another power. Nature speaks in louder tones than philosophy or self-interest. Already are there established two colonies of fugitive negroes, whom treaties and power protect from assault. Those lightnings announce the thunder. A courageous chief only is wanted. Where is he, that great man whom Nature owes to her vexed, oppressed and tormented children? Where is he? He will appear, doubt it not; he will come forth and raise the sacred standard of liberty. This venerable signal will gather around him the companions of his misfortune. More impetuous than the torrents, they will everywhere leave the indelible traces of their just resentment. Everywhere people will bless the name of the hero who shall have re-established the rights of the human race; everywhere will they raise trophies in his honour.[20]

In the prologue Toussaint is heard repeating the words "a courageous chief only is wanted" (p. 361). However, unlike Dessalines, he wavers for months before finally deciding to join the slave uprising in 1791. Dessalines's reaction is spontaneous and motivated by hatred of the French and a desire for revenge. Toussaint, on the other hand, remains detached and, significantly, his decision to join the uprising is influenced by French revolutionary literature.

The first scene of Act I elaborates this contrast between Toussaint and Dessalines. To the uneducated, "half-naked" Dessalines, obtaining freedom for the slaves is a simple issue. With some of his followers he storms the house of his French master with a drawn sword and shouts: "Revolution in France. Revolution in San Domingo. Freedom for slaves. Kill Master. Burn down plantation" (p. 363). When Toussaint is sent for to intervene there is a significant reversal of roles:

(Dessalines is taken aback. The slaves pause and grow silent. Madame Bullet returns with Toussaint behind her. Toussaint's dress is commonplace, but tidy and neat. He steps forward, all eyes centred on him. He looks around and then speaks.) TOUSSAINT: Dessalines, put that sword away. *(For a moment Dessalines, rebellious, does not know what to do with the sword.)* Give it to Moïse. *(Dessalines meekly hands over the sword to Moïse.)* M. Bullet, you know that the slave revolution broke out in San Domingo over a month ago. All over the North slaves have

set fire to the plantations and killed their masters. Now they are free. M. Bullet, you must leave here at once and never return. Otherwise I cannot guarantee your safety. (*Bullet looks at his wife.*) Madame Bullet I shall send by a special guard, with Moïse here and my brother Paul. They will take her to her friends in Le Cap. (*To Madame Bullet.*) You will be quite safe with them. You will take certain household effects with you. In two carriages. More than that I cannot do. (pp. 363–364)

Toussaint's forceful personality and air of authority place him in absolute control of the situation. He is able to protect his master from Dessalines's vindictiveness but immediately aligns himself with the rest of the slaves by announcing, "I am going where I belong: to join the revolution" (p. 364).

In Act I, scene ii, when news arrives that the French convention has abolished slavery, Toussaint hardly stops to assess whether this announcement has been made in good faith. Strong in his belief in the ideals of the French Revolution, he astonishes the Spanish general by immediately cancelling his alliance with the King of Spain. In the presence of several Haitian leaders and soldiers he explains his change of positions to the Spanish general:

Look at these people, General. Some of them understand only one French word— *Liberté*. (*Moïse is now gesturing to the crowd of men, who are eagerly listening.*) They will join anything, or leave anything, for *Liberté*. That is why I can lead them. But the day that they feel I am not for Liberty, the day they feel I am not telling them everything, I am finished. They are all listening to us now. As soon as you and I have finished speaking, they will know what we have said because Moïse, my nephew, is translating what we say into Creole. Many discussions have taken place in front of these men while Moïse translated. They know that the Spanish San Domingo Government declared slavery abolished here, that they repeatedly sent to us asking us to join the Republic. But they also understand, Marquis, that when the Government in France abolished slavery, I would be joining them; not before. Now that slavery has been abolished, we go at once. Our soldiers are strategically placed in relation to yours; they have always been. (p. 371)

Toussaint's speech illustrates a number of features of his leadership. It establishes the close rapport which exists between the leader and his troops; it also demonstrates his tactical ability when it comes to military maneuvers and his clear-sightedness and decisiveness in all matters which involve his loyalty to France. He shows the same shrewd judgement later in the play when he sees through the British offer to guarantee Haiti's independence and to support him as King of Haiti as a mere ruse to cut Haiti off from the protection of France. As he informs the English emissary, General Maitland: "my position today is what it always has been. It is the French government, the French revolutionary government, which has freed the slaves of San Domingo. No other country in the world has done that or promises to do that. A French colony we are and a French Colony we will remain, unless France attempts to restore slavery. That is the faith by which I live and under that banner I hope to die" (p. 381).

In his speech Toussaint concedes the theoretical possibility that France could go back on her word and restore slavery, but his loyalty to France, a revolutionary France which only exists in the books that he reads, blinds him to the implications of Napoleon's rise to personal power, which threatens the ideals of the Republic at home and overseas. He is politician enough to foresee the necessity of providing his country with a constitution which would guarantee the freedom of the people of San Domingo for all times, but he naively sends the constitution to France for the First Consul's approval. The constitution embodies Toussaint's dream of a free San Domingo still owing allegiance to France. In modern terms, what Toussaint's constitution aims at is dominion status within a larger French Empire. Scenes iii and iv of Act II depict the predictable outcome of Toussaint's naive idealism. Bonaparte reacts by immediately preparing an expeditionary force to "put these impertinent blacks in their place" (p. 392). Simultaneously Toussaint begins to realize that his Francophile tendencies have begun to alienate him from large sections of the Haitian population. Even while he awaits Bonaparte's decision he confides in Madame Bullet his fears and uncertainties as to what action he should take if Bonaparte decides to invade the island. In so doing he leaves his fellow-leaders and his followers completely out of the decision-making process, and falls short of the standard which he had earlier set for himself in explaining his policies to the Spanish general. He knows the ex-slaves do not understand his reasons for inducing the French planters to remain in Haiti, but he no longer attempts to explain these to them. When General Moïse dares to question the wisdom of his policy of maintaining the large sugar estates, Toussaint turns against his trusted nephew and orders his execution.

James presents Moïse as the only Haitian leader with an intellectual capacity equal to that of Toussaint. Dessalines, though he is not afraid to disagree with Toussaint, sees no further than a desire for revenge and personal power. Christophe, the other educated leader, adopts a policy of opportunism, collaborating with whoever happens to hold the balance of power. Moïse, like Toussaint, is a committed Republican and an admirer of French revolutionary thought, but this does not cloud his judgement when it comes to choosing the policies which he considers best suited to Haiti's interests. Early in the play he tells Toussaint, "We want to be free and equal; make San Domingo independent, the people will come with us" (p. 380). Shortly before his execution he urges Toussaint again to abandon his half-measures and he voices the most convincing arguments against Toussaint's policies:

The country does not know where it stands. Is slavery abolished forever? Or is a French expedition coming to restore slavery? The ex-slaves don't know, the ex-slave owners don't know. I have told you to declare the island independent. Expel all those who do not want to accept it. Assure the ex-slaves that slavery is gone forever. That is what they want to know. Break up those accursed big plantations. As long as they remain, freedom is a mockery. Distribute the lands carefully among the best cultivators in the country. Let everybody see that there is a new regime. (p. 399)

Toussaint never transcends his limited vision of a San Domingo protected and aided by France. Rather than sacrifice his dream, he surrenders to Bonaparte's expeditionary force and retires from his position as Commander in Chief. He explains to Christophe and Dessalines that he hopes by this proof of his sincere allegiance to France "to prevent the complete destruction of what we have fought so hard to build up" (p. 406). Dessalines, who has never shared Toussaint's trust in the French, interprets Toussaint's action initially as a temporary truce meant as a ploy to gain time for the Haitian army to reorganize. His final disillusionment with Toussaint's leadership comes when he finds himself fighting on the French side to put down the remaining pockets of guerrilla resistance to the truce. It is at this point that Dessalines decides that Toussaint stands in the way of the success of the revolution and he conspires with Christophe to have him removed to France. With Toussaint away from the scene, the leadership falls into the hands of Dessalines, who without the education of Toussaint or the understanding of Moïse can give free rein to his lust for revenge and personal power; as he points out to Marie-Jeanne, "All I have learnt from the French is that without arms in my hand there is no freedom" (pp. 410–411). He falls immediately into the trap set by the British, declares himself Emperor, and orders the extermination of all Frenchmen living in the island. In his historical documentary, *The Black Jacobins*, James analyzes the relative strengths and weaknesses of the first two leaders of San Domingo after the revolution:

If Dessalines could see so clearly and simply, it was because the ties that bound this uneducated soldier to French civilisation were of the slenderest. He saw what was under his nose so well because he saw no further. Toussaint's failure was the failure of enlightenment, not of darkness.[21]

Toussaint is presented in the play as an intellectual concerned with the ultimate future of his country. However, his awareness of the limitations of his society blind him to its potential self-sufficiency and make it impossible for him to conceive of severing ties with France. His idealism leads him to attempt the impossible, and that, as James points out in his documentary, gives his career a tragic dimension.[22]

James's play presents no easy answers. It leaves it to the audience to assess the relative virtues of the conflicting attitudes to nationalism epitomized in the positions held by Toussaint, Moïse and Dessalines, and in the context of the 1930s nationalist debate this must have stimulated a great deal of discussion. What James leaves us in no doubt about, however, is his opinion on the nature of imperialism, especially British imperialism. Act I, scene iii, is devoted to the presentation of the various imperial reactions to the prospect of an autonomous Haitian state. Though France and Britain are at war, the French and British military representatives are united in their opinion of Toussaint's leadership and the threat it poses to colonialism in the Caribbean region as a whole. In order to curb Toussaint's power, General Hédouville and General Maitland enter into conspiracy with the American consul to create friction between the black and mulatto elements within San Domingo. When Toussaint defeats the mulatto general Pétion and there can no longer be any doubt about his supreme command, General Maitland abandons this policy, and in another demonstration of the hypocrisy and ruthlessness of British imperialism, he promises Toussaint British support if he severs his links with France. Having done so, he dictates an explanatory letter to London:

The British offer is designed to create a split between French San Domingo and the French Government. . . . However, it must be noted that this does not mean any support from the British for a free San Domingo. . . . That would ruin the whole British Colonial system in the Caribbean. . . . A San Domingo at war with France they will support only until the peace. . . . Whereupon the British will either blockade the island and ourselves take it over . . . or they will collaborate with the French towards restoring the old colonial condition . . . mulatto discrimination . . . and negro slavery. (pp. 381–382)

The staging of the scene in which this letter is dictated is one of the most effective moments in the play, as it is played simultaneously with a similar scene in which Toussaint, having seen through the English ploy, dictates the identical text to Paris.

The strongest indictment of British imperialism occurs at the very end of the play when an agent of the British Government is sent to present a similar plan to Dessalines. To ensure that the split between France and Haiti will be final, the English agent Cathcart makes the killing of all Frenchmen in the island a precondition to the opening of cordial relations between Britain and the Haitian state. Even Dessalines, who in his thirst for revenge has already ordered the massacre of the French population, is taken aback by the English request. As he explains:

I know why I am going to kill them. We suffered from them. They made us slaves because they said we were not men. When we behaved like men and fought for our freedom, they called us monsters. Now we behave like they do. But you have

not suffered from them. They are white people just like you. I don't understand.
(p. 418)

James must have taken a grim satisfaction in being able to claim a historical
precedent for this scene. In a carefully footnoted passage in his historical
documentary he draws attention to this act of "calculated savagery of Imperialism." In the historical version, three Englishmen, among them Cathcart, "swore that the English would trade with San Domingo and accord
their protection for its independence only when the last of the whites had
fallen under the axe."[23]

James's play makes interesting reading because of its pervasive concern
with issues of ideology and leadership, but as a play meant for performance
it suffers throughout from the lack of dramatic action. Because it is a drama
it has to sacrifice too much of its historical accuracy to be an alternative
historical account to the later documentary, but it fails to compensate for
this limitation by making full use of the resources of its genre in other
directions. For example, no attempt is made to exploit the opportunity for
spectacle offered by the many military confrontations which were part of
the twelve years of Haitian history covered. There are, however, a number
of elements in the play that do provide a theater audience with some relief
from the overdose of political speech making. The most interesting of these
are the songs and the nonverbal features such as mime, dance, and music.
Mime is used, for example, in the prologue when James attempts to evoke
the atmosphere of slavery on the eve of the 1791 uprising. There are six
short mimes, each depicting different aspects of the hardship of the slaves,
and the way that their resentment develops, as well as the cruelty of the
slave masters. In the third mime sequence, entitled "The Slaves," a song
of defiance is introduced:

> *The five silhouetted slaves mime digging with pickaxes.*
> *They sing:*
>   Eh! Eh! Bomba! Heu! Heu!
>   White man—vow to destroy
>   Take his riches away
>   Kill them
>   Every one
>   Canga Li.
> *The overseer cracks his whip. They stop singing and freeze.*
> *Blackout. Drums continue for two phrases and stop.* (p. 359)

Throughout the play other songs, mostly French revolutionary songs, are
chanted by the soldiers offstage, but there is only one other scene in which
the common people feature as prominently as in the prologue. This occasion is provided by the voodoo ceremony which takes place in the play

following the announcement of the abolition of slavery. The ceremony would certainly provide a gifted director with an opportunity to vary the pace and mood of the play appreciably. James may have been aware of the dramatic limitations of his work when he added the following explanation to his opening stage directions:

In the play it is possible that crowds may assemble at the back and be spoken to from the back of the main central area. Crowds say little but their presence is felt powerfully at all critical moments. This is the key point of the play and comments cannot, must not be written. (p. 358)

James's insistence on practically mute crowds seems to point to an inherent flaw that runs through his play—an inability to see ordinary, uneducated characters as instigating action rather than merely reacting to events. His crowds are allowed to mime, sing or drum—to enliven the play—but they are not allowed to verbalize their approval or disapproval of the actions of their leaders or to interfere in any way with the decision-making process.

James's play demonstrates a significant advance over his novel in his awareness of the political implications of social relationships. Both works are concerned with the state of alienation in which the educated black found himself with respect to the masses in the colonial period. Whether he was largely self-taught, like Toussaint, or whether like Haynes he had received a formal education, the educated colonial was bound to find his relationship to the masses fraught with deep-seated contradictions. Having assimilated the colonizer's worldview, values, morals, customs and speech, it was logical for him to feel separate and distinct from the uneducated masses of the people, and to function at times like a foreigner in their midst. Toussaint lacks the instinctive understanding of the ex-slaves' thirst for revenge, which Dessalines is able to exploit, while Haynes is often out of his depth in the strange world of Minty Alley.

Once in England, James began to appreciate the ways in which education was used as an ideological tool to perpetuate the *status quo* in the mother country itself. Paradoxically, it was one component of this education—the classical component—which provided him with a vantage point from which to assess the dichotomy between the ideals he had been taught to respect and the social divisions which his education helped to maintain:

We among the blacks who received a good education learnt what we knew from the classical writings of Western civilisation. We knew that the principles which were enshrined in those classical works did not apply in the Caribbean. But when we went abroad we found to our astonishment that they did not apply there also. Therefore, in order to live according to the principles which we had imbibed so strongly in our early days at school we turned automatically to revolutionary movements.[24]

James's play *Toussaint L'Ouverture* was written at a time when he was beginning to utilize his understanding of Marxist ideology to examine the problems of alienation and imitation which hampered the development of the colonial intellectual. This new awareness is reflected in his treatment of Toussaint, who for all his heroic stature is implicitly criticized because he consistently underestimates the intelligence of his followers and the strength of their commitment to the ideal of liberty. Moïse by contrast is presented as a colonial intellectual who is able to establish and maintain contact with the lower classes. Unfortunately we are not given an opportunity to see Moïse's ideas in action; he functions only as a foil to Toussaint. James's play is full of undigested theoretical material and this makes it less successful as a work of art than the earlier, more politically naive novel, *Minty Alley*. Perhaps his failure to combine his political insight with his artistic talents in a work of fiction influenced James to abandon creative writing for history and polemic. However, he has transferred much of the wit and flair for anecdote which characterized his early creative work to his consideration of topics as diverse as the social role of cricket in *Beyond the Boundary* (1963), and the politics of the Haitian revolution in *The Black Jacobins* (1938).[25] James continues to write on subjects which reflect his original concern with the role of the intellectual in the transformation of colonial society and he is recognized today as one of the leading theoreticians on social and political issues related to the Caribbean.[26]

NOTES

1. An excellent introduction to C. L. R. James's work is provided in the three-volume collection of selected writings: *The Future in the Present* (1977), *Spheres of Existence* (1980), *At the Rendezvous of Victory* (1984), published by Allison & Busby, London. The third volume contains a comprehensive bibliography of James's work and studies on him.

2. C. L. R. James, "Discovering Literature in Trinidad: The Nineteen-Thirties," *Savacou*, 2 (September, 1970), 56.

3. Ibid., p. 55.

4. Among them are: "Triumph," *Trinidad*, 1, 1 (Christmas, 1929), 31–40; "Turner's Prosperity," *Trinidad*, 1, 1 (Christmas, 1929), 51–53; "Revolution," *The Beacon*, 1, 2 (May, 1931), 14–18; and "The Star that Would Not Shine," *The Beacon*, 1, 3 (June, 1931), 15–17.

5. C. L. R. James, "La Divina Pastora," in *Stories from the Caribbean*, ed. Andrew Salkey (London: Elek Books, 1965), p. 149.

6. Ibid.

7. In this section of the chapter all page references in parentheses are to C. L. R. James, *Minty Alley* (London: New Beacon Books, 1971).

8. "Interview with C. L. R. James," in *Kas-Kas: Interviews with Three Caribbean Writers in Texas*, ed. Ian Munro and Reinhard Sander (Austin: University of Texas, African and Afro-American Research Institute, 1972), p. 33.

9. Kenneth Ramchand, "Introduction" to *Minty Alley*. p. 13.

10. Merle Hodge, "Peeping Tom in the Nigger Yard," *Tapia*, 25 (Sunday, April 2, 1972), 11–12. This article is a review of the 1971 republication of *Minty Alley*.

11. Ibid., p. 11.

12. See ibid.

13. James, personal communication, January 24, 1979.

14. James interview, *Kas-Kas*, p. 33.

15. C. L. R. James, *Beyond a Boundary*, (London: Hutchinson, 1963), p. 149. Among James's studies in Marxist theory and practice are: *World Revolution 1917–1936: The Rise and Fall of the Communist International* (1937), *State Capitalism and World Revolution* (1950), *Modern Politics* (1960), *Marxism and the Intellectuals* (1962), and *Nkrumah and the Ghana Revolution* (1977).

16. *The Beacon*, 1, 5 (August, 1931), 10.

17. James, personal communication, January 5, 1979.

18. See C. L. R. James, *The Black Jacobins: Toussaint L'Ouverture and the San Domingo Revolution* (New York: Vintage Books, 1963), pp. 397–399.

19. In this section of the chapter all page references in parentheses are to C. L. R. James, "The Black Jacobins," in *A Time . . . and a Season: 8 Caribbean Plays*, ed. Errol Hill (Trinidad: University of the West Indies, Extra-Mural Studies, 1976).

20. James, *Black Jacobins*, p. 25.

21. Ibid., p. 288.

22. See ibid., pp. 289–292.

23. Ibid., p. 371.

24. James, personal communication, January 26, 1979.

25. For a discussion of the literary quality of James's nonfictional writing, see F. M. Birbalsingh, "The Literary Achievement of C. L. R. James," *The Journal of Commonwealth Literature*, 19, 1 (1984), 108–121.

26. Several other works by James are important in this respect. They include literary criticism: *Mariners, Renegades and Castaways: The Story of Herman Melville and the World We Live In* (1953), *Wilson Harris: A Philosophical Approach* (1965); and historical works: *A History of Negro Revolt* (1938), *Party Politics in the West Indies* (1962).

CHAPTER 6

RALPH DE BOISSIÈRE: THE COMMITTED PARTICIPANT

Ralph de Boissière was born in Trinidad on October 6, 1907. His father, a solicitor, was a descendant of the unofficial colored line of a well-known French creole family. De Boissière's mother died of yellow fever three weeks after his birth and the author recalls a lonely, unhappy childhood in Trinidad, enlivened by occasional visits to Grenada, where his stepmother's parents lived. In the course of his education, at Tranquillity Boys Intermediate School and Queen's Royal College, de Boissière encountered the typical colonial syllabus:

We learned English history, which seemed to consist mostly of England's military and naval conquests. In geography you had to know what was made in Sheffield and Birmingham. You were required to draw maps of England showing its principal towns and seaports.[1]

Music was de Boissière's first passion, especially the piano, and he dreamt of a career as a performer. When this failed to materialize, he turned to creative writing. To secure a livelihood, however, he underwent training as a typist/bookkeeper and worked in this capacity for various English and American firms until he left the island in 1947.

In the mid-1920s de Boissière was drawn into the literary group around Mendes and James, who encouraged him to write, and his first short stories were published in *Trinidad* and *The Beacon*. At around this time he became an ardent admirer of the work of such nineteenth-century Russian writers as Turgenev and Tolstoy. He felt an immediate affinity with the social situations which they described and came to the conclusion that "life in colonial Trinidad was not at all unlike life in the towns and countryside of tsarist Russia."[2] He was to emulate the Russians' realistic style and social vision in his Caribbean novels, *Crown Jewel* (1952) and *Rum and Coca-Cola* (1956), but it was his first-hand experience of everyday life at all levels in Trinidad society that provided him with his raw material. For several years one of his jobs entailed the delivery of bakers' supplies all over Trinidad: "Every day found me in little shops and hovels and stinking alleys among Chinese, Indians, Blacks, Portuguese and mixtures of all the races."[3] When Trinidad's oilfield workers went on strike in 1937 and the island was engulfed in major social upheavals, de Boissière was not only a keen observer but subsequently became involved in radical trade unionism. He was especially attracted to the Marxist-oriented Negro Welfare Cultural and Social Association, whose leaders included Bertie Percival, Clem Payne, Jim Barrette and Elma François.

De Boissière's political sympathies were anathema to his employers and led to a nine-month period of unemployment for him in 1939. During the commercial boom that followed the establishment of an American military base on the island during World War II he was again able to find a job, but by now it had become evident that a secure existence would not be possible in Trinidad, given the social conditions and his political views. In 1947 he took a six-month course in motor mechanics in Chicago, then migrated to Australia, where his family joined him. His first job was on the assembly line at General Motors in Melbourne, an experience which deepened his understanding of the working-class issues he was exploring in writing *Crown Jewel*, and which provided the subject matter for his third novel, *No Saddles For Kangaroos* (1964). In Australia de Boissière moved more and more to the left. He began to study Marxist literature and literary criticism, became a member of the Realist Writers Group, and finally joined the Communist Party in 1951, remaining a member until 1967. It was a left-wing publishing house, the Australasian Book Society, that published his novels—in fact *Crown Jewel* was its very first title—and both *Crown Jewel* and *Rum and Coca-Cola* appeared in translation in several East-bloc countries.[4] In 1955 he rewrote a section of *Rum and Coca-Cola* as a musical, which he called "Calypso Isle." He himself composed the songs and calypsos and played the part of Charlie the shoemaker in several successful performances of the show at the Melbourne New Theater. In 1957/1958 de Boissière went on a seven-month tour of China, with a brief visit to the Soviet Union. On his return to Australia he remembers feeling that he "had stepped, it seemed, from the future back into the present, which ought to be the past."[5] He nevertheless applied for Australian citizenship some years later and became an Australian citizen in 1969.

De Boissière is the type of writer who continuously rewrites his work: Both the 1981 republication of *Crown Jewel* and the 1984 edition of *Rum and Coca-Cola* differ significantly from the original 1950s editions, which

themselves were developed in a long process of rewriting. In the case of
Crown Jewel this process goes back as far as 1935. De Boissière has ration-
alized the continuous changes with the remark, "My life was my novel,
and the novel my life."[6] He is still working on a novel he began in the
early 1970s entitled *Homeless in Paradise*, which is set in Australia and
Trinidad. To refresh his memory of the Caribbean he visited Trinidad in
1976—assisted by a travel and research grant from the Australian Literature Board—and spent several months there.

In his early short stories, de Boissière followed the trend set by Mendes
and James, and tried to reproduce the customs, speech, and unique cultural features of the lower classes as a means of registering his dissatisfaction with the culture of the middle class, to which he belonged. For example, in "A Trip to Town," a short story which was published in *Trinidad*,
he attempts to recreate the initial response of a youth from South Trinidad
to the glamor of Port of Spain city life and the excitement of Carnival:

An' tailors, now! Boy, de second day—you ain' know somet'ing?—I dress up in
tailor! . . . I put on waistcoat and gloves an' mas', and I take me tape measure an'
meself an' another feller we goin' all about measurin' pipple an' geurls an' enjoyin'
we self. . . . An' all de time de bands and dem passin' and playin' dey music, and
if you see colours! De second day I join a band. I dress up in millionaire, boy, an'
I pick up me little geurl and I dancin' wid she, and de white pipple lookin' on an'
clappin' dey hands.[7]

The country youth thinks at this point that the first nineteen years of his
life have been wasted "digging drains in the cocoa fields, or picking pods
. . . felling trees in the hot sun . . . digging cassava and yam,"[8] until he
is robbed of his money by some strangers in the city and involved in a
fight. Helped by two women, he eventually makes his way to his aunt's
house. After some initial difficulties he manages to find a job and immediately begins "to put by every cent for a six-dollar mask, a costume, and the
joy of being primitive in the streets on the two days of Carnival."[9]

Clifford Sealy in "A Note on Ralph de Boissière," has drawn attention to
two other short stories by de Boissière in the early magazines which touch
on deeper issues involving the lower class that are more fully developed in
his novels.[10] Both "The Woman on the Pavement" and "Miss Winter" ten-
tatively explore the author's own social predicament as a near-white member of the colored middle class. The introspection of the protagonists in
both stories, and their identification of some of the negative attitudes presented in the stories as their own, suggest a sense of self-recognition on
the author's part that is missing in some of the other *Beacon* group short
stories which satirize middle-class attitudes. In "Miss Winter," Alex Bentley's infatuation with the pretty, fair, Gerry Winter comes to an end when
he gets an insight into her attitude toward blacks. During a fishing expe-

dition, one of Alex's friends playfully rocks their boat while they are buying
bait from some black fishermen, causing Gerry to fall overboard in an un-
dignified manner:

> The fishermen's sense of humour, as with most negroes, was strong, and their
> outlook being simple, their expression of it was naturally cruel. They burst into
> laughter that became more loud and vulgar as it was given rein. . . .
>
> Gerry's eyes were flashing, her cheeks were pink. "You niggers; you damned
> stinking niggers! What are you laughing at?" She waved an oar at them. "Alex, row
> home!" she commanded.[11]

Alex does as he is bid, but the narrator comments that he "felt that he had
looked into her soul."

In "The Woman on the Pavement," two incidents are contrasted. The
first involves a middle-class gentleman who is run over by a cyclist and is
immediately given assistance by nearby shop owners and passers-by. In the
second, a black peasant woman goes into a fit on the pavement and everyone looks on passively, including Mr. Edgehill, the gentlemen involved in
the first incident. When finally some lower-class people take charge of the
woman, Mr. Edgehill feels ashamed: "He knew that this was what he should
have done, but what he had been unable to do, because of the people
looking on, people of the middle classes like himself."[12] Clifford Sealy has
pointed to the crisis of conscience and the quest for identity which are the
underlying themes of both stories, and which must both have been especially painful for sensitive members of the colored middle class.[13] Being
neither black nor white, the colored person was alienated from both sections of Trinidad society. Culturally and socially he hankered after European values, only to discover that he was never fully accepted within the
white community. The other alternative of identification with the masses,
however, involved breaking through the suspicions held by the black working class about the sincerity of his intentions. More drastic than this, it
meant risking rejection by the rest of the colored population and abandon-
ing his class.

It is against this background that Ralph de Boissière's encounter with the
Negro Welfare Cultural and Social Association has to be seen. Already disillusioned with the racial and social attitudes of his class, the NWA provided him with an ideological perspective from which he could analyze the
society's ills, and pointed to a solution for his personal crisis. From a mere
observer and recorder of lower-class life, he became a committed participant in the working-class struggle during the post-1935 period. He realized
that in order to portray this class seriously he would have to engage in its
struggle. By the time of the 1937 social upheavals, he was equipped to

interpret these events in what Clifford Sealy has described as Trinidad's "most important political novel . . . the fundamental work of fiction in our society."[14] *Crown Jewel* and its sequel *Rum and Coca-Cola* possess the scope and canvas that Mendes had continually aimed for but could never achieve. They dramatize the ten crucial years in Trinidad's history, 1935–1945, during which the island's working-class movement was formed. In order to achieve a vast social and historical canvas and to suggest the continuous sweep of political events, de Boissière builds up a series of interlocking life histories which develop and reiterate specific motifs that he considers central to his ideological perspective. Thus the patterns of exploitation during the war, for example, are given a personal dimension within the patterns of experiences which the major and minor characters undergo, and each personal choice provides a further permutation of the types of alternatives open to the individual within the society portrayed. Our attention is constantly being shifted from one character to another; from an aspect of the political crisis to a corresponding aspect of an individual's crisis.

De Boissière's semiautobiographical figure André de Coudray is one of the characters who receive the fullest treatment in *Crown Jewel*. We follow his progress from an insecure, guilt-ridden member of the colored middle class to an observer of and finally a participant in the working-class movement. Following an analogous line of development but moving away from committed participation is the character of Joe Elias, while the life of Cassie, the timid barrack-yarder and domestic servant, is documented as she develops into a politically aware and self-assertive member of the working-class movement. The careers of André and Cassie represent the intellectual and political awakening among all sectors of Trinidad society during the late 1930s, while the career of Joe Elias points to the possible ways in which the new awareness could be diverted to opportunistic ends. In *Rum and Coca-Cola* we continue to follow André's and Cassie's development, but two new major characters, Mopsy and Indra Goodman, are introduced. They bear the full brunt of the author's embodiment of the theme of corruption and disintegration which follows the American invasion of Trinidad society.

André's quest for identity is introduced early in *Crown Jewel*:

The de Coudrays belonged to one of those numerous cliques of island "society." André had been unable to find in this set any but people of limited understanding and petty social ambitions. This had obliged him to look among the "lower classes" for men and women who could match his own interest in life and the arts. He had found many such among Joe's friends, who were almost all Negroes. On the one hand, he knew that to mix with black workers meant to suffer economic damnation. On the other hand he knew that to mix only with his set meant that intellectually, spiritually, morally, he would stifle. André had not yet made up his mind which side to take. (p. 3)[15]

On the autobiographical level, André's intellectual involvement with people outside his class is a clear reconstruction of the social interaction within the original *Beacon* group, transposed in time to the years immediately preceding the labor unrest of the late 1930s. The protagonist's ambivalence, his secret fear of getting mixed up with people outside his social and racial group, are clearly expressed. Like Haynes in James's *Minty Alley*, André in spite of his social inhibitions feels the need to break out of the stifling atmosphere of his own class. However, whereas Haynes, after his encounter with the barrack-yarders, returns to his middle-class environment a bit wiser, a bit more liberated from the values of his own class, André's quest is a journey of no return.

For more than half of the novel André remains undecided and plagued by contradictory feelings. He is particularly conscious of his family history and the carefully suppressed knowledge that one of his ancestors was a black slave. He is well aware that, though to the non–West Indian he seems white, to the sharp eye of the shade-conscious Trinidadian the fact that he is colored is easily apparent, and he is merely tolerated in local white society. His association with blacks, by emphasizing this unspoken "disability," could tip the social scales against him and expose him to social ostracism which, as a colonial, he dreads. As the narrator informs us:

Having lived since childhood in an atmosphere of slavish respect for the English, André found it hard to consider himself their equal. Even though in recent years he had been mixing in wider circles and drawing away from the family . . . his attitude to the English had little changed. He felt hatred of them because they looked down on him; but in his secret heart he looked up to them, feared them, and despised himself for it. (p. 133)

The dilemma that André faces in his social and political choices is dramatized in the novel by his attraction to two women who come from different ethnic, cultural and socioeconomic sectors of the community. Gwenneth Osborne is the daughter of an expatriate English judge, and Elena Henriques is the colored daughter of a dressmaker of Venezuelan descent. Both women are part of the network of major and minor characters in the novel whose contrasting developments and interlapping relationships give the novel coherence and structure. André gets to know Elena through her uncle, Popito Luna, who is a clerk at the business-place where André also works. Elena's mother can barely make a living from her work and is constantly harassed by bailiffs and debt-collectors. Though she has managed to preserve herself and her daughter from the worst consequences of poverty, her status is only slightly higher than that of a barrack-yarder. Her only ambition is that her daughter will be able to escape from the poverty and sordidness of their present life and she saves every penny she earns to give her child a secondary education. The attractive, near-white André presents the same temptation to Elena to compromise her standards and ruin her chances of success as the elegant prestigious Gwenneth presents to André to compromise his principles and succumb to his family's slavish admiration of all things English, for although he is strongly attracted to Elena because of her youth, prettiness and intelligence, his deeply engrained prejudices make it impossible for him to see her in a more serious light than Haynes in *Minty Alley* saw Maisie, or Joe da Costa in *Pitch Lake* saw Stella:

As they strolled along the Pitch Walk André passed several people he knew, in motor cars. They looked at the young couple curiously—André de Coudray with a coloured girl. André avoided their eyes and while he hated himself for it, he could not help feeling relieved when at last they reached her home. (pp. 144–145)

After this experience he "understood it was impossible to uproot himself from his class, go into Elena's and make her friends his" (p. 152), but this does not immediately stop him from monopolizing her attentions and engaging her affections.

As with Joe de Costa in *Pitch Lake*, it is André's new attraction to a wealthy and socially acceptable girl that eventually forces him to cut ties with Elena. André's relationship with Gwenneth acts as a catalyst in his personal and political development. At first it alienates him completely from the friends he has made among the lower classes, and he attains the pinnacle of his family's ambitions when it becomes apparent that Gwenneth is in love with him and a marriage seems to be imminent. However, on account of his dubious racial background he is considered *persona non grata* by Gwenneth's parents. Apart from giving in to family pressure, Gwenneth is essentially a flirt who has been attracted to André because of her bohemian and exotic fascination with creole men. André gets his first shock when, like Alex Bentley in the short story "Miss Winter," he discovers the English girl's deep-seated racial prejudices towards black people. When, in recounting to André a story of their former garden boy who she claims had tried to attack her, she refers to the boy as a "nigger," the narrator comments that "the word hit André like a lash" (p. 218). It is his rejection by Gwenneth's English family that gives André the push he needs to overcome his fascination with the English elite. In keeping with his parallel development of personal and political themes, de Boissière makes a direct connection between André's encounter with the Osborne family and his increasingly critical perspective on the colonial establishment:

During Gwenneth's absence André had written for Joe's magazine an article on the City Council. He took up the view that certain Government circles resented the existence of the Council as a vestige of people's self-rule and felt its authority an affront to them; that English residents resented control of their water, sewerage and streets by a black shoemaker, a singer of calypsoes, an Indian of "doubtful reputation" and sundry black members of the Workers' Party; and that this attitude was responsible for the everlasting tirades in the capitalist press against the Council as well as the niggardliness of the Government grant to municipal funds. André had written this article at the time when he saw with what ease important English officials were drawing Gwenneth away from him into their closed and august social circle. (p. 219)

Even after writing this article, André's break with Gwenneth is not complete. He immediately regrets having submitted it but does not have the courage to ask the editor, Joe Elias, to let him have it back. The publication of this article finally ruins his chances with Gwenneth and her family, and prompts a decisive turning point in André's political development. He refuses to become a strikebreaker during a bakers' strike organized by the Workers' Welfare. The change takes even André's boss unaware and again the author links it directly to his personal experiences:

[André's boss] was incapable of understanding André's feelings of humiliation over that visit to the Osbornes. He could not sense André's wounded pride, his desperate need to salvage the integrity he felt he had sullied. It was impossible for him to believe that the barrier built up by birth and breeding between André and the workers had been breached, and that André had "come out of his shell" at last. (pp. 251–252)

De Boissière's insistence on the importance of small, even trivial personal experiences in strengthening the political resolve of his characters underscores his presentation of a progressive, socialist-oriented ideological position as the natural response of a sensitive and thoughtful person to the incidents and experiences which he encounters on a day-to-day basis, rather than a purely cerebral form of assent to an interesting but impractical ideology.

In the same way that André's political involvement comes as the result of personal experiences, his new personal relationships are now influenced by his new political awareness. On business trips to South Trinidad he becomes friendly with the oil-belt labor leader Ben Le Maître. Le Maître is at first puzzled by André's sympathetic political views and becomes suspicious of his motives when he observes that André has struck up a friendship with a young black schoolteacher who "despite the fact that she has received a classical education . . . is with the workers" (p. 340). When Le Maître challenges him one day about his relations with the establishment and the Country Club set back in Port of Spain, André is able to give him a simple and truthful answer:

Look here: that set don't want me. My own coloured set want me only on certain terms. Neither have anything to offer me. And how can one come in contact with the masses without understanding that they have a right to our leisure and luxury, which rests on their backs? (p. 340)

The assurance and conviction with which André is able to satisfy Le Maître's doubts about his interest in the young schoolteacher and the sincerity of his social transformation contrast sharply with his earlier inability to admit even to himself the true nature of his intentions towards Elena and his narrow social aspirations.

Through his friendship with Betsy Solomon, the schoolteacher, André is able to rediscover his relationship with Elena. By opting to marry Elena, André puts everything on the line as far as his family and future are concerned. His father disinherits him and expels him from the family home; Le Maître's predictions about the consequences of aligning himself with the working class begin to come true: "They will hate you for life. They will hound you down. They will try to take your job from you. If you are sincere, you are forever an outcast" (p. 340). For André, however, the act has a positive significance as he realizes: "Only now do I dare to acknowledge their blood is mine. *These* are my people! I want to live, I want to help them fight for the new life they want . . . !" (p. 431). André's marriage underlies the extent to which he has thrown in his lot on the side of the workers rather than the establishment. It contrasts sharply with the attitude of Manny Camacho, one of the young lions of the intellectual circle around Joe Elias's magazine. Manny was a civil servant whose support for the bakers' strike had been dramatic and vociferous within the privacy of the group where he had declared, "Sooner or later we will have to man the barricades! . . . It will come to that. Some of us will die, but we will not run when the police bring their rifles" (p. 202). The political adventurism of this armchair revolutionary is deftly satirized when he is caught up in the confusion of the street battle in San Fernando. Instead of "manning the barricades," he runs for dear life and catches the first train back to Port of Spain.

Joe Elias's development is diametrically opposed to that of André, though at first their actions seem to spring from identical motives and move along similar lines: Like André, Joe feels stifled by his limited social sphere, but he sees alignment with the working class as a chance to achieve fame rather than an opportunity for involvement.

He was the Trinidad-born son of a Syrian merchant, and therefore socially of little account. But he felt that with his intellectual gifts and his personality he should be playing a dominating role in the political life of the island instead of wasting his time in Dollard's lumber yard. (p. 2)

De Boissière prepares the reader from early in the novel for Joe's opportunistic relationship with the Workers' Welfare so as to gain support for his candidacy as a member of the City Council. In his political wranglings with André and the rest of the circle, for instance, we are told that "today he defended the working-class. Tomorrow he scorned the working-class and defended Nietzsche" (p. 6). Joe's obsessive preoccupation with leaving his mark on the world propels him further into his career as an opportunist politician when he inherits the family business after his father's death, and another of Le Maître's insights into human nature is proved correct: As he had once said of Joe, "people like him turn against the workers and support their masters when any real struggles arise" (p. 101). Joe does not succeed in founding his projected Socialist Party, and instead opts for a career in local politics, feeling "courageous in attacking the workers" and asserting "that what was required to pull the island out of the bog of acute depression was not the ascendancy of workers over employers, but reasonable co-operation" (pp. 400–401).

The development of both Joe and André is paralleled, and in a sense overshadowed, by the author's treatment of Cassie, who is Judge Osborne's maid at the beginning of the novel and lives in a barrack-yard next door to the Henriques family. In the course of the novel she develops into one of the most militant members of the Workers' Welfare and finally marries Le Maître. Their marriage is as symbolic as that of André and Elena and emphasizes the degree to which the radical politicization of the working class embraced both its male and female members. As suggested in previous chapters, Cassie is the direct descendant of characters such as Maisie in *Minty Alley* and Ethelrida in *Black Fauns*. Like them she is a product of the world of the barrack-yard. Both her father, an oilfield worker, and her mother have died, and she is struggling to make a livelihood, when she is first introduced:

Cassie had to live, found it impossible to do so on eight dollars a month. Like all young girls she dreamt of love, romance, a measure of security. Along came a policeman who had been a playmate of hers. The importance of a policeman, the uniform, appealed to her. Soon he was keeping her, providing her with furniture on the installment plan. But now he had tired of her. Two weeks ago he had beaten her. (pp. 47–48)

Like her sisters in the short stories, she also has access to a typical *confidante* figure—in this case, the cook at Judge Osborne's house—who advises her to keep her policeman faithful "by putting certain things in his food" (p. 104). However, Cassie belongs to the Shango cult and instead asks the *Orisha*—Shango, Damballa and Ogoun—for help, when the policeman abandons her and all her personal possessions are confiscated by the bailiff because of her arrears on the rent. Soon afterwards Elena's uncle Popito Luna takes an interest in her, and a relationship develops between them that becomes much more serious than the usual kept woman/keeper arrangement. For one thing, Popito, who has become a member of the Workers' Welfare, introduces her to this organization. Although she displays the typical barrack-yard cynicism about any organization which claims to have the welfare of her class at heart, she participates in their activities because they seem to be of importance to Popito. Once involved however, her political awareness develops rapidly and her relationship with Popito becomes that of an equal partner. She even takes him to task for his involvement in opium smuggling, to which he turns after being fired from his job as a clerk because of his militant attitude.

Popi . . . it's not honest labour, man. If it is opium, he not smokin' it himself. It's you helpin' to ruin the lives of Chinee workers. How you could say you fightin' for workers and yet you doin' this thing to them? . . . Get a next job, Popi, Uh beg you! (p. 125)

Popito is also severely admonished by Le Maître and soon abandons his anti–working-class activities, but the police are already on his trail.

Once Cassie has overcome her initial cynicism about the movement, she begins to display an intuitive sense for justice as far as working-class issues are concerned. Her rapid political development is depicted within the context of her personal experiences and as reactions to specific events. Like André, she does not come to her final position merely on account of propaganda that she reads or hears, but because she suffers personal injustices. In keeping with de Boissière's technique of placing his characters in situations typically encountered by members of a certain class, Cassie's hardships are of a much more devastating and violent nature than those André has to face. She is arrested and beaten by a police detective, Duke, in an attempt to make her reveal details of Popito's former opium-smuggling activities, with the result that she loses her unborn child. Later she witnesses the same detective beat Popito to death after they have been together to the *Orisha* to invoke their aid on Popito's behalf. This shatters her belief in the power of the *Orisha* and evokes her own resources and political understanding in the fight against oppression. She becomes one of the most dedicated members of the Workers' Welfare and in particular is able to rally the support of other women for the movement. Her speeches are among the best presented in the novel and are frequently more effective in raising support at public meetings than those of the Welfare's stalwarts, Percy French, Clem Payne and even Le Maître himself. One example of her addresses will have to suffice:

Some of you 'fraid to join the Workers' Welfare, others feel it have no sense in that, you believe Indian and nigger kean't help one another to make life good for all of us. I say, comrades, put that foolish idea out of you' minds. You have children. They will grow up naked, their belly big, their navel swell up. Those who don't go to jail and get the "cat" will have a fight to make eight or nine cents an hour to feed more children to grow up and get the "cat." You never try to work out hummuch servants gettin', but I could tell you. It's three cents an hour. Who that benefitin'? It ain't no benefit to you an' those children. The benefit is for the capitalists. Plenty children, cheap labour! If some dead, what they have to do with that? Plenty more comin' out you' belly. We have to fight for trade unions, fight for higher wages, shorter hours—yes, less work for more money! Make them pay us! You ever see white people children with swell-up belly and big navel, and goin' about naked? No! Our wages payin' to keep them from that. (p. 261)

Cassie's graphic images and grim sarcasm recall the repartee of the barrack-yard characters of the short stories, but instead of using it to score cheap points against a rival in the yard, she puts all the passion and pragmatic wisdom of the yard to the service of the political struggle of her class.

During the deliberations over one of the first strikes in the oilfields, Cassie sides with the most militant members of the movement for immediate action against Le Maître's more cautious approach, and the dramatic tensions between these two strong characters are highlighted. The growth of the relationship between Cassie and Le Maître provides some of the most human, moving passages in *Crown Jewel*. Le Maître, we are told, had been married before, but had lost his wife and children in a typhoid epidemic. Since then he has remained single and unattached because he feels that a married worker "loses all his militancy." As he recalls, "I was married for a short while, and all I could think about was how not to offend the boss, and how many times a night I could have my wife" (p. 78). It is Cassie who breaks down this almost puritanical inflexibility. Initially Le Maître regards Cassie as a fellow worker and comrade, but he begins to appreciate her womanly qualities through a series of shared experiences, especially those which take place during a gruelling hunger march from the southern part of the island to Port of Spain. Their mutual respect for each other turns into a deep feeling of shared emotional need. Perhaps de Boissière's greatest achievement in presenting this relationship is the way in which he avoids using Cassie as the traditional feminine foil to expose Le Maître's human weakness and then undermine his devotion to the cause. The fact that Cassie, in spite of her limited education, is his intellectual equal in matters concerning the struggle of the working class, means that Le Maître can show his Achilles heel without fear of losing the battle. The trust within their relationship is well captured in this exchange:

"Cassie, I wouldn't confess this to anyone but you, but sometimes I wonder if we are benefiting in any way at all from this struggle. When I see how frightened so many of us are, how our spirits are crushed, I wonder what is the good. That is the most terrible thing, that our spirits are crushed!"

"What you sayin', man-hush! Nigger people not so. I never see people wid so much fight as now. It's no time to old talk so. If we don't live to see a change, our children will see it."

"Yours and mine?" he asked softly.

"Eh-eh! I didn't say so, nuh?" She laughed. "Well, I never! . . . Look the moon," she added, breaking off, a note of joy coming into her voice. (p. 354)

Cassie's strength and optimism are shown again at the end of the novel when Le Maître, in hiding from the police after the upheavals in the oil belt, becomes depressed at the prospect of being hunted and trapped and feels like giving up. Cassie merely responds, "You kean't give up! . . . It's to you the workers lookin'. Who else they have to teach them?" (p. 408). By this time she is married to Le Maître, and when he is forced to go underground, she takes over the leadership of the march into the center of San Fernando. Cassie is also involved in the killing of the detective Duke, the symbol of all the oppression and injustice in the island. In the 1981 revised edition of *Crown Jewel*, de Boissière has taken pains to reinforce the symbolism of Duke's death which occurs when he is drenched in kerosene oil and set alight. In the 1952 version of the text, which has been used throughout this discussion, Cassie's involvement in the act is implied. The reader is tempted to see the action as one of personal revenge, however justifiable, for the murder of her former husband and her unborn child. In the new version the initiative is taken out of Cassie's hands and Duke's death becomes a purely symbolic event of poetic justice.

Cassie's development from a kept, barrack-yard woman to a liberated and liberating working-class leader constitutes a major departure in de Boissière's work from the earlier yard literature of such *Beacon* writers as Alfred Mendes and C. L .R. James. This departure is also apparent in de Boissière's treatment of other aspects of lower-class life and customs. In particular, the author of *Crown Jewel* does not share the earlier writers' occasional tendency to romanticize certain aspects of the barrack-yard environment of their uncritical attitude to all folk beliefs. His description of the barrack-yard is closer to that contained in James Cummings's article discussed in chapter 2. Towards the beginning of the novel, Popito goes to visit an acquaintance who lives in a yard "struggling to feed a family of eight on five dollars a week." At this stage Popito has a job as a clerk and as a member of the upper strata of the lower class is unaccustomed to seeing the dire poverty he encounters:

The barrack-yard in which Jacob lived was in Nelson Street. Popito went through a narrow passage between two walls. It was dark and stank of urine. At the end was the yard. Dirty shed-like structures divided into dens bordered three sides of the yard. The doors of the dens were open. Ragged bits of curtain guarded the dark barrenness of each from the gaze of the sun. Two women were washing clothes outside their doorsteps. A third was heating irons on a coal-pot. Each of them was singing a different hymn in a dreary voice as she went about her work. The yard itself was barren as an old hag. Not a blade of grass sprouted. Some boulders, whitened by long use, were heaped about its middle. This was the bleach. On it a tattered pair of khaki pants spread its legs obscenely. Four men were silently playing cards in that part of the yard which the nine o'clock sun was not yet roasting. The stench, the overcrowding, the poverty of the dwellers in the yard oppressed Popito. Involuntarily he looked up at the breadfruit tree near the gamblers. Laden with green leaves and fruit bigger than cannon balls, it towered majestically into the hot sky. It was a symbol of that healthy and normal life that no one in the yard but itself enjoyed. "How the deuce did I get here?" it seemed to Popito to say. But he knew that many a day its fruit had given strength and courage to some empty-bellied worker. (pp. 49–50)

The reader of "Afternoon in Trinidad" or "Triumph" will easily recognize the physical setting of the yard, the arrangement of the rooms and the inevitable bleaching stones. However, these early barrack-yard stories will hardly have provided him with the overwhelming squalor of the total scene, and the lively and exotic kept women who give color to the drab surroundings in the barrack-yard stories are also absent. De Boissière portrays barrack-yard women working and singing in "a dreary voice," and the men "silently" playing cards. The visitor to the yard feels as oppressed by the environment as its inhabitants.

In *Crown Jewel*, the barrack-yarders' communal spirit, solidarity, and cultural resilience are depicted when they are engaged in political action. On such occasions de Boissière, as much as any of the barrack-yard writers, is capable of controlling the nuances of Trinidad lower-class language and of catching the wit and humor it expresses. One of the central political events in the novel before the actual upheavals in the oilfields is the hunger march organized by the Workers' Welfare. The dramatization of this arduous undertaking is effectively carried through, and calls to mind two similar marches in political novels by two African writers: Ousmane Sembène's *God's Bits of Wood* and Ngugi wa Thiong'o's *Petals of Blood*. The repartee of the marchers as they trudge through the gathering darkness gives a good example of de Boissière's success in recapturing the spirit of the occasion.

They left Claxton Bay at eight. Le Maître headed the column. French walked in its rear. On either side staunch comrades hemmed in the womenfolk, and the men who limped morally or physically, and halted the column for the stragglers.

"Hold up, Frederick!"

"Frank, ohi! Hold that, boy."

"What happen, flat tyre?"

"No, we stop for passengers."

"Right-o. All-you in front! Conductor say hold up."

"Well, B'Christ! This is the longest free ride I ever get. Quite from Fyzabad and I ehn't pay a cent."

"Who the hell legs so long in front there?"

Cheerful voices called to one another, halting the column; and then called out still more cheerfully, urging it forward.

"Walk like tourists! Watch the scenery. All-you ever see this part-a you' country yet?"

"In trut', i's no difference. Tourists look at scenery t'rough dark glasses, we look at it t'rough dark night."

"All-you start off bold to walk to town, as if you expect to take a taxi back home," a thin wag of a fellow said. (pp. 301–302)

Elsewhere, de Boissière draws attention to another folk custom, hardly ever mentioned in the barrack-yard stories, which has strong, positive associations. This is the *sou-sou* or communal purse, often utilized as a form of savings in the yard. Each member contributes a certain sum or "hand" every month and all contributors take turns at collecting the whole amount. The system provides evidence of a strong sense of communal responsibility and trust, as well as thrift. In the novel Elena's mother is able to use her "sou-sou hand . . . [to] repair the damages to respectability caused by time or the bailiff, buying clothes . . . or some piece of furniture to replace what had been seized" (p. 18).

De Boissière also deals with aspects of folk belief and superstition, some of which have been mentioned in the discussion of Cassie. However, he approaches these beliefs from a radical political perspective, and hence can avoid being trapped in the peculiar contradiction of other members of the *Beacon* group: on the one hand a rabid antiecclesiastical stance, seen especially in their rejection of popish superstition, and on the other a sympathetic treatment of African-derived religious beliefs. This is not to say that de Boissière does not treat the local beliefs with sympathy and careful attention to accurate detail. His description of the Shango ceremony at which Cassie is ridden by one of the *Orisha* is as powerful as any description of possession in French or English Caribbean literature. However, he implies that when such beliefs are used to compensate for social inequalities, they can be as potentially dangerous an opiate to the masses as the well-organized religions of the capitalist world.

When considering *Crown Jewel* as a dramatization of Trinidad history between 1935 and 1937, it is important to note that de Boissière in a brief "epic" introduction entitled "The Background" places these turbulent years in the context of the preceding four hundred and fifty years of discovery and colonization by the French, Spanish, and English. He highlights the claims of the imported non-European laborers to the land for which they had slaved. De Boissière's introduction takes us up to the year 1935 when "foreign oil companies sprawled all over the south of Trinidad" (p. x). This historical background to the events in the novel prepares the reader for the close correspondence between actual events and the fictional situations depicted. De Boissière has agreed that the novel is "a true social history of the period," but stipulates that it is "not a historical record of events."

The events happened, but not necessarily in just that way or at just that time. Young people, not having lived in that time, will be apt to think of the book as a true historical record of events. Well, it won't do them any harm.[16]

Fiction, as de Boissière implies, has its own methods of structuring, selecting, and rearranging reality: In the absence of written historical accounts of the 1937 upheavals at the time that the novel was written, de Boissière had to rely on what he "saw and felt and was told." It is interesting to note, for example, how de Boissière got the idea of involving Cassie in the burning of Detective Duke. Having much later read Bukka Rennie's account of the event in *The History of the Working-Class in the 20th Century (1919–1956): The Trinidad and Tobago Experience*, he comments:

Rennie says someone dropped a lighted lantern on Charlie King as he lay crippled on the ground. On the other hand a man told me . . . that a woman dashed into the shop (not a house) and demanded kerosene. It doesn't really matter which version is right. The main thing was the hatred of the people for King and what he represented.[17]

De Boissière does not alter the basic event that a police detective was burnt to death during the upheavals, but as a writer of fiction he invests the event with a particular significance within the development of his fictional situation and fictional characters. Except for one named character, Clem Payne, who in real life was not present during the Trinidad disturbances but was indirectly responsible for sparking off similar events in Barbados, de Boissière has changed the names of all recognizable historical characters. Through their descriptions and actions however, at least two major political figures can be identified. One is Captain Cipriani, whose career as a labor leader has been referred to, and on whom de Boissière's fictional labor leader Maurice Boisson is closely modelled. The other is Albert Gomes, whose political beginnings are satirized in the description of the Syrian magazine editor, Joe Elias.

The Workers' Welfare, Le Maître, and Cassie have a much more complicated and interesting relationship to the actual events of the 1930s. The Workers' Welfare is apparently based on the Negro Welfare Association which has been described in the background chapter and which was politically active in the north of Trinidad. However, in the novel the range of the association's activities is extended to include Southern Trinidad as well. This purely fictional decision allows de Boissière to avoid dealing with the historical fact of the existence in the South of Butler's British Empire Workers and Citizens Home Rule Party, which had a wider mass support than the NWA but a relatively limited ideological framework, differences that would only have unnecessarily complicated de Boissière's attempts to suggest the grand sweep of events. However, in responding to questions about these parallels de Boissière does not acknowledge any clear debt to the actual leaders of either of the two historical parties in his creation of Le Maître, in spite of the numerous incidental details of his presentation of the labor leader which seem to tally with the lives of Jim Barrette and Uriah Butler. De Boissière insists that "Le Maître came out of two trade unionists, men who supported socialism, who had no connection with the strike and were never in the South."[18] Cassie, however, is undoubtedly the author's own creation but, paradoxically, the development of her character and political ideas is so convincingly motivated that she gives us a real notion of what the militant working-class women who took part in the 1937 uprising must have been like, and indeed her story calls to mind the documented history of the Trinidad washerwoman and labor leader, Elma François. De Boissière seems not to have known Elma François or to have heard her speak, a circumstance which makes his portrayal of Cassie all the more convincing. Perhaps *Crown Jewel* may well become, as de Boissière has suggested, for "young people, not having lived in that time . . . a true historical record of events"—events which to date have not received adequate historical treatment.

   Crown Jewel does not merely reconstruct Trinidad history during the late 1930s: It interprets this history from a militant, working-class perspective. Ralph de Boissière's involvement with the Negro Welfare Association provided him with the first ideological tools to evaluate the nature of social and economic contradictions in colonial society. However, in the author's note to *Crown Jewel*, de Boissière has pointed out that he only came to appreciate the full significance of the 1937 upheavals after he left Trinidad for Australia; as he recalls:

I worked for a year at the biggest motor manufacturing plant in Melbourne. . . . To remain unaffected by the struggles of the militant Australian workers was impossible. These struggles profoundly affected my outlook, causing me to re-write *Crown Jewel* and make it a better, truer picture of my country and my people.[19]

De Boissière's progression from an ideological supporter of the working-class movement in Trinidad to an actual worker in Australia sharpened his understanding of working-class aspirations and characters. The experience also gave him an insight into the nature of the class struggle in a more advanced capitalist system. In the absence of copies of the earlier versions of de Boissière's *Crown Jewel* manuscript, one has only the author's words to rely on for a description of the way that each of these changes affected his work. However, they suggest a familiar pattern: The very first version, according to de Boissière, was written in Trinidad before the 1937 upheavals and seems to have focussed almost exclusively on André's quest for social and racial identity in purely personal terms. "It included the André-Elena-Gwenneth triangle but in a less developed form. It was not yet linked to the basic social realities that came to light in the second version."[20] The second version, which was completed in 1944, apparently linked André's story with that of Cassie and Le Maître against the background of the sociopolitical developments in Trinidad between 1935 and 1937. The third and fourth revisions to the novel in Australia produced a clearer presentation and development of these two major working-class figures.

In this respect it is important to note that by the third revision (the 1952 edition) de Boissière had begun to employ a technique of writing which the Marxist critic Georg Lukács has called "critical realism." This technique is distinguished from social realism by its commitment to a progressive political perspective, and is distinct from socialist realism because of the author's membership of a class-bound society in the capitalist world, which makes it necessary for him to depict reality in terms of class conflict.[21] De Boissière refers to one aspect of critical realism when he says, "As far as I am concerned, a novel should be not only about what people *are* but what they *can be*."[22] The traditional social realist contents himself with minutely observing and recording characters and events from a seemingly neutral or at most sympathetic perspective: In the context of early Trinidad literature, the short stories and novels of both C. L. R. James and Alfred H. Mendes are examples of this approach. The critical realist, because of his forward-looking and ultimately optimistic perspective, perceives of characters and events as meaningful in terms of underlying movements towards a specific goal. Although his work is as strongly based on objective reality as that of the social realist, the critical realist is frequently able to transcend given aspects of reality by drawing attention to their inherent potentialities. This, for example, would explain why de Boissière did not base his working-class leader Ben Le Maître on either Jim Barrette, the leader of Trinidad's Negro Welfare Association, or Uriah Butler, the leader of the British Empire Workers and Citizens Home Rule Party. Instead he creates a figure that draws on the positive potential of both Butler and Barrette: on Butler's mass leadership and confrontation with the establishment, and Barrette's Marxist ideology and program of workers' education.[23]

In *Rum and Coca-Cola*, Ralph de Boissière was able to sustain the broad spectrum of *Crown Jewel*. As a sequel to the first novel it focusses on the period immediately following the 1937 upheavals and depicts the changes that Trinidad society underwent during the Second World War when the island was overrun with American troops posted to the military bases at Chaguaramas and Waller Field. De Boissière had originally intended to call his novel "The Invaders," but the present title is taken from a calypso by Lord Invader which was made popular in America by the Andrews Sisters in the 1940s:

Rum and Coca Cola
Way down Point Cumana
Both mother and daughter
Working for the Yankee dollar.[24]

The calypso hints at some of the more dubious methods by which Trinidad society earned its American dollars. The building of the American bases required the use of local labor and temporarily eased the unemployment problems of the 1930s, bringing with it a degree of prosperity never witnessed before for the workers, contractors and prostitutes of the island. Like the calypsonian, de Boissière examines the positive and negative effects of this sudden prosperity and the means through which it is achieved, symbolized in the image of the local rum, diluted but made effervescent by the addition of the all-American commercial soft drink, Coca-Cola. Paradoxically de Boissière makes use of a member of the island's old elite class, Henri de Coudray, to voice his criticisms of the effect that the new order had on the lower classes, which extended as far as the calypso tents, formerly one of the most crucial sources of support for the militant working-class struggle in the 1930s. Henri de Coudray, André's father, describes the changes he observes:

Almost every night the new [American] neighbours had some nigger in to make an unseemly racket singing calypsoes. "And what calypsoes!" Mr. de Coudray once remarked. "All slavishly praising the Americans." He was not completely divorced from the people; he understood that calypso, with its power to lampoon personalities, ridicule and criticize the social order, had been a weapon in the workers' resistance to exploitation. He had not approved too much of that sort of thing; but now he approved even less of what was happening: these young calypsonians were singing the praises of the American way of life, wearing garish American "sports" shirts outside their trousers, wearing dark glasses like tourists, smoking cigars they bummed—making themselves regular apes! Put tails on them and they'd swing upside down for the edification of the Americans, no doubt! (p. 97)[25]

Henri de Coudray's criticism of the slavish imitation of American ways among Trinidad's lower classes is an odd mixture of reactionary attitudes to changing fashions, a sense of personal outrage at the impropriety of workers indulging in tourist luxuries, and a perverse sense of cultural betrayal. This last reflects his sense of the impotence of his own class in the face of the American invasion. The French creole elite had not been seriously affected by the workers' uprisings of the late 1930s. As the narrator comments in the last chapter of *Crown Jewel*, "Whatever upheavals may have been caused in various parts of the island, whatever new springs of thought and desire may have arisen among the workers, the tranquil life of St. Clair remained quiescent." André's father Henri de Coudray is faced with demands for higher wages on his estate and "red, frowning, yet calm, he compromised, and the labourers returned to work."[26] Until the advent of the Americans his position and that of the other long-established creole families had remained unchallenged. The decline and death of Henri de Coudray in *Rum and Coca-Cola* epitomizes the way in which the old feudal order, based on landed property and the *droit de seigneur*, is brought to an abrupt end by the advent of more advanced forms of capitalist organization introduced by the Americans.

Henri de Coudray's estate is seized by the Americans since it falls within the area designated for the American naval base; his cook leaves to work for the higher wages offered by his American neighbors and one of his daughters has an affair with an American officer whom he does not consider socially acceptable. Routed at every turn, he decides to retire to his Manzanilla beach house in the North Eastern part of the island only to discover that this property too has been requisitioned for military purposes. This is the final straw for old de Coudray, who becomes convinced that the world he knows is caving in around him. The last hours of his life are disturbed by the sounds of the new progress brought by the Americans as they drill trenches in the road outside his house to put down new telephone cables:

He dreamed of the Americans laying telephone cables. Their machine was digging a trench that entered his yard by the back garden. In a terrible rage he ordered them out. But his voice was so weak they did not hear him. They did not even see him. They were going to attach their telephone cable to his telephone, and he realised with dread and a feeling of impotence that he would not have a shred of privacy or independence any more. The machine was devouring the earth, spewing it out and advancing into the yard as fast as a man could walk. He saw that its operator was the young sentry from Manzanilla. "I'll show you!" he heard the sentry think vindictively. The trench digger came straight at him. He tried to run, but could not, he was too weak. "I'm going to die—going to die!" he cried out. (pp. 106–107)

Before he dies, his last thoughts are of his son André, and he finally admits to himself that he has done wrong in expelling him from the family for his marriage to Elena. Having had a glimpse of what the future could hold for Trinidad under the influence of the Americans and their heightened materialistic values, he comes to admire his son's identification with the working class and opposition to foreign domination: "he has such courage . . . defies us all . . . such high ideals. Yes, that's it . . . high ideals, noble ideals!" (p. 108).

Old de Coudray passes away before he can change his will, and André and Elena are spared the "temptation" which unexpected wealth might have brought with it. André, Elena, Cassie, and Le Maître all reappear in *Rum and Coca-Cola*, but they do not hold the center of the stage as often as they did in *Crown Jewel*. Le Maître, for a start, is in internment for most of the novel. Briefly released, he is again arrested after leading a successful strike of truck drivers in spite of wartime restrictions on political and trade union activities. During her husband's imprisonment Cassie emerges as one of the leaders of the Workers' Welfare which spearheads the protest against the widespread displacement of workers and peasants from their homes by the development of the areas surrounding and connecting the American bases. The association supports or organizes various forms of industrial action against the Americans and the local City Council and exposes the violence and racial discrimination which characterize the Americans' treatment of the host population. Cassie is portrayed as a full-fledged Marxist with a radical understanding of the issues at stake for the workers in the Second World War. While the rank and file of Trinidad's working class are divided between feelings of loyalty to Britain and a vicarious pleasure at seeing their imperial enemy trounced by Germany during the early stages of the war, Cassie reminds them:

In the last war you went to fight to help England win. Well, England win and what she do for you? To-day you haven't a place to lay you' head. Worker must speak to worker—English worker to German worker, West Indian worker to American worker—they must fight for us and we for them, and all against the boss. This country is ours! . . . [T]he English not givin' us anything, the Americans not goin' to give us anything, nor the Germans. It's we who must get together and fight for the right to work, the right to eat every day, the right to sleep with a roof over our heads. Indians, Negroes, Chinese—what difference it makes? We are all sufferin' workers. (p. 35)

André, like Cassie, has also become a fervent Marxist and a valued member of Workers' Welfare. In their political study groups he shares the insights he has gained from his reading of revolutionary literature with the workers. In addition he becomes editor of *People's Age*, a working-class magazine that spreads the opinions of the Workers' Welfare on all current wartime issues to a wider Trinidadian audience. The real test for him comes later in the novel when he is called upon to make political decisions that could affect the welfare of his wife and child. After the truck drivers' strike when almost all of the leaders of Workers' Welfare are interned and *Peo-*

ple's Age is banned, André is left as the only member of the group's leadership free to speak out on behalf of the group in the press. For hours, we are told, he "weighed his duty as member of Workers' Welfare against his desire to preserve his job, his marital happiness and his comforts. Unable to come to a decision, he grew paralysed with fear and shame" (pp. 242–243). Our knowledge of André's earlier ambivalence and the deeply engrained weaknesses of his racial and class origins make it easy for us to appreciate the difficulty of the decision with which he is faced. His wife, Elena, who lacks as full a grasp of the political principles involved as either Cassie or André, reminds him initially that he is not compelled to write something that will put him into prison. Finally, out of a sense of loyalty, she is able to give him the crucial moral support he needs to do what he thinks best. He writes the article, publishes it, and is promptly interned.

Elena's own political development is also recorded. Though she is deeply religious and never reaches the political stature of Cassie, the author allows her to achieve the full potential of her abilities. During her husband's internment she is asked by some of the workers to take his place in their political study group. At first Elena is amazed at their request and frightened by her lack of knowledge of political concepts. She nevertheless agrees to help and soon finds herself "reading with the workers and holding discussions with them." Rather than instructing them, she finds that she is learning from them and finding new ways of dealing with the issues that are of particular importance to her:

Her doubts were many, and [the workers] struggled to clear them up for her. It never occurred to her to forget God or abandon him. On the contrary, what she was now doing seemed fully in accord with her concept of His love for mankind. (p. 246)

One major character in *Crown Jewel* who does not reappear in *Rum and Coca-Cola* is Joe Elias. Asked about this significant omission Ralph de Boissière has explained: "Joe Elias had already disgraced himself by his treachery. He had displayed his great limitations. To bring him in again would have been superfluous."[27] However, Joe Elias's spirit is very much in evidence in the second novel, as a number of new, middle-class politicians of his calibre are introduced. This departure from one typical character to several representative characters may have been an attempt on the author's part to reflect the increasingly dominant role of opportunist middle-class politicians spouting socialist rhetoric during the war years. The consequence of the new political interest within the middle class in the novel is the formation of a "West Indian Socialist Party," which embodies the kind of limited reformist policies which Joe Elias in *Crown Jewel* had envisaged himself fighting for in the Legislative Council. From the description which de Boissière gives us of its members and their aspirations, it is clear that he sees them as a group diametrically opposed to the Workers' Welfare:

Coloured lawyers and doctors, and oppressed owners of petty businesses like Arty Goodman, were its leaders. In their wake followed clerks, who were attracted by the "respectability" of the Party's leadership, and some of the better paid workers. (p. 117)

Arty Goodman, who is mentioned in the above passage, is the father of Indra Goodman, one of the two new characters who are fully developed in *Rum and Coca-Cola*. Mr. Goodman is a small-businessman and a Port of Spain City Councillor. He belongs to the inner circle of the new nationalist party, but is beaten to the winning post for its leadership by the lawyer, La Roche. De Boissière sums up La Roche through the use of a familiar West Indian image in the first description of his physical appearance:

[La Roche] was a tall, stoop-shouldered Negro whose hair had receded from his shining forehead. His jumpy step and his stooped shoulders gave him the appearance of a *corbeau* hop-stepping over a carcase. His enemies referred to him as "King Corbeau." (p. 136)

The image of La Roche as a scavenging bird underlines his attitudes to politics as a source of easy financial pickings and his parasitical attitude in business matters. It is this characteristic of moving in for the feast where others have killed that explains why, having espoused a socialist rhetoric to gain political power, he is among the first of the new nationalist politicians to start "warning of extremists."

He and other politicians were urging that every method be employed to encourage American capital into the island. La Roche had linked his fortunes with those of Arnold Walker. Arnold had invested a great deal of money in an American oil company that was seeking concessions in Trinidad. La Roche was insisting that measures be taken against "subversive elements": the Americans would not invest their money in Trinidad unless they could be assured that our labour forces were not at the mercy of a foreign ideology. (p. 309)

Arnold Walker, an establishment figure who also features in *Crown Jewel*, is only one of a host of minor characters drawn from all walks of life in *Rum and Coca-Cola*: There are old and new members of Workers' Welfare whose development within the party we are allowed to follow. One new member, Charlie, a veteran of the First World War, goes through a series of successively more oppressive personal and economic setbacks which strengthen his political understanding and resolve. Charlie starts off as a poor shoemaker, seemingly secure from the worst effects of the depression at the beginning of the war, until the abandoned wreck of a car in which he lives is bulldozed to make room for the Americans. He then loses one job after another and is cruelly beaten by an American guardsman for distributing left-wing literature on the naval base. Above all, there are the "Invaders," the American soldiers and civilians whose presence places the inhabitants of the island under a state of virtual siege.

Some aspects of the American impact on Trinidad society as presented in the novel have already been noted in this chapter, among them their undermining of the old creole elite class; the political sycophancy they brought out in the new middle-class politicians; and their detrimental effect on certain aspects of the working-class struggle. As the war progresses, the incidence of racially motivated violence increases, and many such incidents are narrated or dramatized in the novel. Even Tom, the fittingly named pro-American worker who acts as a scab during the truck drivers' strike, finds it difficult to justify the way in which a group of Americans punish a Trinidadian man who is working on the roof of one of their houses and is accused of peeping at an American girl: "they tied him by his wrists to a jeep and made him run behind it. When they put on speed he fell, of course. They dragged that man over the earth on his knees. When they cut him loose he was unconscious" (p. 217). The first strike is triggered by the way that the Americans treat Fred Collingwood, one of the new leaders of the Workers' Welfare, who is beaten up, then fired by the Americans because a white Amerian woman in a fit of pique accuses him of having molested her. The strike is organized around the issue of Fred's reinstatement but quickly grows to embrace the issue of differential salary scales for American and native truck drivers. The second strike is also called in response to American brutality, when two Trinidadian fishermen drift too close to some military installations and are shot in cold blood by American soldiers.

De Boissière also shows how the crudeness and violence of American activities and racial discrimination have repercussions in the wider society: In her efforts to make her American lodger comfortable, Arty's wife, Mrs. Goodman, makes her black husband feel like a social outcast in his own home, while even the American lodger is appalled by her treatment of her mother-in-law, Miss Henny, who is abandoned in the servants' quarters of the house and left to do all the heavy, dirty domestic chores. Miss Henny finally meets her death standing in line for the scarce supplies of rationed rice so that the lodger may be given a taste of the local dish *pélau*. The riot for rice in which she is trampled to death is the crowd's spontaneously violent reaction to the sight of a white man blatantly jumping the queue and obtaining his supplies before the doors of the shop have even been opened to the other customers waiting patiently outside. Side by side with the rising levels of racial tension and violence in the community, however,

de Boissière portrays the effect these developments have on increasing the
dedication and militancy of those workers who are politically conscious.

On the other hand, *Rum and Coca-Cola* leaves the reader in no doubt
that a significant proportion of the lower class, unlike the creole elite, were
able to profit financially from the American presence:

There was no one in Trinidad who was not either thankful for, or irritated and
angered by, the presence of the Americans. Those who were thankful were for the
most part workers. Servants ceased working for Madame, or compelled her to double and treble their wages. Clerks out of work for years went to work on the bases,
or got jobs with Trinidadian firms which had lost employees to the Yanks with their
higher wages. In every home there was now more money than before. (p. 93)

Though the sudden prosperity has the effect of making some of the workers
less careful about their industrial rights, the ubiquity of the American dollars and American GIs reduces the local respect for wealth and a white
skin. The colonial awe of the Briton is replaced by scorn for his relative
lack of money and power in comparison with the Americans. On shore
leave, for example, the British soldiers are even snubbed by the city's prostitutes. The pro-American feelings fuel the anti-imperialist sentiments at
all levels of Trinidad society, a state of affairs recognized by the English
business tycoon William Dollard in his relation of the following incident:

While the English Governor was dancing an American officer had tapped him on
the shoulder. "You know the Yankee style," said Dollard. "I tap you on the shoulder, you give up your partner to me. His Excellency ignored the fellow, of course.
The next minute he gets a slap in the face from this tuppeny-ha'penny Yankee
officer. Well, I mean to say! What kind of position are we faced with?" (p. 119)

Dollard's anecdote hints at one possible reply to his question, just as Henri
de Coudray's dream related earlier had hinted at another. While the dream
symbolizes the replacement of feudalism by capitalism, the incident on the
dance floor anticipates the passage from carefully discreet patterns of British cultural imperialism to the more overt forms of American domination
of the Caribbean archipelago through military and economic force. Ironically, Dollard himself is one of the members of the old order who is able
to foresee this economic transformation and align himself with American
capital in time to avoid being edged out of the commercial field.

The working class also shows a healthy respect for the power and industrial organization which make the Americans such formidable opponents.
At the beginning of the novel, when their homes are bulldozed to make
room for the Americans, they are angry and bitter, but they appreciate the
ingenuity of the huge saws and machines which tear down trees and houses

and sense an affinity between themselves and the American workers who man the machines:

Three white Americans drove a jeep on to the land. One was a middle-aged man naked to the waist and wearing a peaked white jockey cap. His companions were youngsters: one wore blue jeans; the other, a tall fair-haired lad, was screwing up his eyes in the sunlight and lazily chewing gum. The tenants were unaccustomed to see white men go half-naked in public. They came to the conclusion that these men were workers, men of their own class, and looked at them with curious but friendly smiles. (pp. 66–67)

From his working-class perspective, Ralph de Boissière makes a clear distinction between the American presence *per se* and the individual, especially the individual working-class American. He emphasizes this distinction by small points in the novel such as the sympathy among some of the American base workers with the truck drivers' strike which is expressed through the frequent arrival of mysterious food supplies when conditions become critical among the striking drivers and their families.

De Boissière does use one individual American figure, however, to epitomize all that he considers ultimately destructive about the American presence in the island. Wal Brown is an American civilian employed at the naval base. During his stay in Trinidad he marries two different Trinidadian women, even though he has a wife back home in America. The two women, Councillor Goodman's dougla daughter, Indra, and the colored prostitute, Mopsy, are the characters who receive the fullest treatment in *Rum and Coca-Cola*. Mopsy's story illustrates the typical uncritical attitude of the average Trinidadian vis-à-vis the American invaders: She sees in them a lucrative source of income and a way of lifting herself out of the dire poverty in which she is depicted at the beginning of the novel. Her function as a prostitute becomes a symbol for the general prostitution that de Boissière perceived at all levels of Trinidadian society in response to the American presence. It is important to note the way in which Mopsy departs from the ethics of the barrack-yard in her dealings with the Americans. Her personal acquisitiveness precedes her encounter with the Americans, as we are shown at the beginning of the novel, when she robs a Swedish captain who picks her up. However, the Mopsy we first meet has all the typical generosity and sense of community spirit that are traditionally associated with the barrack-yard. When at the beginning of the novel the yard in which she, Miss Henny, and Charlie the shoemaker live is threatened by the American bulldozers, she uses her sex appeal to buy time for the yard's inhabitants to clear out their belongings:

Gladys ran into Miss Henny's shack and said to Mopsy:"Speak to him for us, nuh, Miss Mopsy? He goin' to listen to you."

"Yes, yes, she goin' to talk to him!" Miss Henny said. "Go, Mopsy, see what you could do to help us."

"So all of you dependin' on me now, ehn?" Mopsy said. "Uh tell you, if it wasn't for Miss Henny . . . !"

She went out, Miss Henny and Gladys following hopefully.

"Now, listen," Mopsy said harshly to Mat. "If you want to come and see me, give these people a chance to find a shelter. Even if it is only for to-night 'self. Look that ole woman in the rockin' chair—you goin' to kill her! What harm one more night will do?"

"We'll talk about that when yew git back from town, honey."

"No, decide now. If when I come back I find more houses break down, you needn't come near me at all." . . .

Mat stayed his hand. That night the tenants sought and found temporary accommodation at the homes of friends, and even strangers.

Miss Henny was reluctantly taken in by her son, Councillor Goodman. (pp. 73–74)

Once Mopsy goes to live with Mat, the bulldozer driver, she becomes progressively more dehumanized, and in spite of the lavish life Mat provides for her, she becomes greedier and more selfish, unwilling to share even with her housemate, Baby, what she would generously have given to her neighbors in the barrack-yard in leaner years. Eventually Mopsy leaves Mat for an older, less attractive American who can give her twice as much. While living with him she gets one further opportunity of reasserting the positive side of her nature when she becomes friendly with her next-door neighbor Mrs. Henriques, who is Elena de Coudray's mother. The kindly older woman brings out in her some of the warmth and love she had felt for old Miss Henny, the mother figure in the yard she has now left behind. These feelings, however, last only temporarily, and though she continues to see Mrs. Henriques and make use of her help, the author tells us that "Mopsy now counted her favours, expecting one in return for every one performed" (p. 192). Mopsy's financial fortunes continue to rise; she saves enough to open a restaurant and begin to build a house. However, she experiences a tragic reversal when towards the end of the novel she meets Wal Brown, who swindles her out of her money by marrying her and promising to take her to America with him and then leaving her pregnant and penniless when he goes back to America. Faced with the prospect of returning to prostitution, she goes out of her mind. Mopsy's development in the novel illustrates de Boissière's premise that the Americans were giving with one hand and taking away with the other. In particular it points to the relative value of the two sides of the exchange: The Americans give money and excitement, but they take financial control of the island at a personal and industrial level and they corrupt the generosity and community spirit of the lower classes. The crude materialism which their wealth elicits from Trinidadians threatens all feelings of solidarity and community within the working-class movement.

Indra Goodman is a middle-class sympathizer of the Workers' Welfare. At the beginning of the novel she has reached, intellectually and politically, approximately the same level of development as André had achieved at the end of *Crown Jewel*. Like André, she has broken through the racial and social barriers of her class: She is the only member of her family who acknowledges and is proud of her black, lower-class grandmother, Miss Henny, whose role in the barrack-yard had been the traditional one of obeah practitioner and *confidante* to the younger women of the yard. At the beginning of the novel, Indra is engaged to Fred Collingwood, one of the new leaders in the Workers' Welfare. Fred is also a calypsonian and does not come up to the social status which Indra's family wishes to maintain. For Indra, like many of the other politically progressive characters in the novel, working with the Americans marks the beginning of a series of tests, which are crucial to her ideological development. De Boissière utilizes the same strategy of a love triangle which he used with André in *Crown Jewel* to portray the conflicts in which Indra becomes involved. She finds herself vacillating between her commitment to her black fiancé, Fred, and her attraction to the white American, Wal Brown. De Boissière's description of Indra's changing attitude to Fred as her attraction to the American develops is one of the novel's most successful passages. One of their last encounters before Indra breaks off their engagement takes place in Fred's room:

Worn out by his long hours of work, he had only woken when she knocked. He stood before her red-eyed, yawning, in a dirty old dressing-gown. Dismayed by her feelings, she went up and kissed him. "Good Lord! What broad nostrils he has!" flashed through her mind as his bristly cheek rubbed hers. He apologised for oversleeping, and hurried to the bath. She sat on his untidy bed, that smelled of sleep and soiled clothes. She was seized by a feeling of pique at having been forgotten, and by a depressing feeling of dissatisfaction with him, his room and with herself. What was it she had expected? Wasn't he just the same as ever? . . . She took up a book, read a few sentences without understanding them, put it aside. (pp. 170–171)

When Indra leaves Fred for Wal, her association with the Workers' Welfare also ends. Lured into marriage with the American, she only returns to Fred when she discovers Wal's bigamy and is personally disillusioned. Like Mopsy, she also becomes pregnant for the American, but her child is stillborn soon after his departure for America.

The ending of *Rum and Coca-Cola* strikes an optimistic note, but it is a far less happy one than that struck at the end of *Crown Jewel*. The Second World War ends and all the leaders of the Workers' Welfare are released, but a new nationalist party, dominated by opportunist, middle-class leaders, seems on the verge of taking power. The conclusion of *Rum and Coca-Cola* must have posed serious problems for the author, as the objective realities on which the plot is based did not offer the kind of material that could be used to reach the assured climax that the upheavals of 1937 provide in *Crown Jewel*. The author seems loath to end the novel with the emergence of the new nationalist party however, and is forced to go beyond the historical political situation in order to achieve some satisfactory resolution. He chooses to attempt a cultural apotheosis and ends the novel with a description of the celebration of Carnival, which is once more allowed to take place after the war is ended. The atmosphere is one of "wild gaiety in which old scores were forgotten and complete strangers chatted as if they were long-parted friends" (p. 310). With Ben Le Maître and Fred Collingwood, André looks on as the usually unaggressive girl who works for Elena in their home (recalling in her description the placid Mamitz of the barrack-yard stories) knocks a drunk American civilian out of the path of the oncoming bands with uncharacteristic vigor:

"What people, what people!" said Le Maître.

Fred laughed in his own quiet way, but his eyes reflected the admiration he had heard in Ben's tone and that shone in André's smile. They did not need to express the thought. They felt at that moment there were no heights their people could not scale. (p. 314)

This recourse to the celebration of Carnival is in keeping with de Boissière's larger preoccupation with the relationship between progressive politics and the culture of the masses. Here, however, it comes uneasily close to expressing a naive utopian vision of a cultural nationalist solution to Trinidad's problems, a solution which de Boissière's ideological perspective precludes. De Boissière may have sensed this weakness, as he allows an earlier comment from Le Maître to qualify the euphoria. As the autocratic Auditor General allows himself to be embarrassed by the antics of a masquerader, Le Maître remarks with a laugh, "Clever bastards! . . . For two days they slacken the ropes, and for three hundred and sixty-three they pull them in" (p. 312).

This discussion of *Rum and Coca-Cola* is based on the 1956 Australian edition of the novel, and the reader of the 1984 British edition will immediately be struck by several drastic revisions. Although the major thematic thrust of the novel has remained the same, there are numerous alterations in plot and focus in the revised version. For one thing, Mopsy becomes much more of a central character and her fate determines the new ending of the novel. In addition, Fred Collingwood plays a crucial role in the lives of both Mopsy and Indra Goodman. Their mutual American lover of the

1956 edition, Wal Brown, is replaced by two Americans: While the story of Mopsy's liaison with Wal Brown remains similar, Indra Goodman falls for a handsome womanizer called Wilbur Kemp, who leaves her when he discovers she is pregnant. The ease with which the interconnections between characters have been shifted and rearranged in the two versions is itself an indication of the relative episodic nature of *Rum and Coca-Cola* when compared to the inevitability with which relationships unfold in *Crown Jewel*.

De Boissière's third novel, *No Saddles for Kangaroos* (1964), is set in Australia, and though it still demonstrates the novelist's concern with political issues there is nothing Caribbean about its themes or subject matter. It is set in the early 1950s when the Australian labor movement was seriously debilitated by widespread anticommunist hysteria, and tells the story of an Australian working-class family who becomes involved in a series of industrial actions in an American-owned automobile factory, and in the peace movement aimed at ending Australian involvement in the Korean War.

Until the republication of *Crown Jewel* in 1981, Ralph de Boissière and his work were virtually unknown in the Caribbean, England, and the United States. However, judging from the enthusiastic reviews of the new edition of *Crown Jewel* on both sides of the Atlantic, de Boissière's novels seem finally set to receive the critical attention and acclaim which have so far eluded them because of the peculiar circumstances of their publication. Both *Crown Jewel* and its sequel, *Rum and Coca-Cola*, with their dramatic characterization of working-class leaders during the late 1930s, depict the type of cultural heroes whose attitudes and ideology are bound to find new admirers and supporters among today's politically conscious generation of West Indians.

NOTES

1. Ralph de Boissière, unpublished autobiography.
2. Ibid.
3. Ibid.
4. Translations of *Crown Jewel* appeared in Poland, East Germany, Rumania, Czechoslovakia, Bulgaria, Yugoslavia, China, and the Soviet Union. Translations of *Rum and Coca-Cola* appeared in Poland, East Germany, Czechoslovakia, China, and the Soviet Union.
5. De Boissière, unpublished autobiography.
6. Ibid.
7. *Trinidad*, 1, 2 (Easter, 1930), 82–83.
8. Ibid, p. 84.
9. Ibid., p. 100.
10. Clifford Sealy, "*Crown Jewel*: A Note on Ralph de Boissière," *Voices*, 2, 3 March, 1973), 1–3.
11. *Trinidad*, 1, 1 (Christmas, 1929), 9.

12. *The Beacon*, 1, 8 (November, 1931), 5.

13. See Sealy, *"Crown Jewel."*

14. Ibid., p. 3.

15. In this section of the chapter all page references in parentheses are to Ralph de Boissière, *Crown Jewel* (Melbourne: Australasian Book Society, 1952).

16. De Boissière, personal communication, December 12, 1978.

17. Ibid.

18. De Boissière, personal communication, December 12, 1978.

19. See author's note to *Crown Jewel*, p. 432.

20. De Boissière, personal communication, December 15, 1978.

21. See Georg Lukács, *The Meaning of Contemporary Realism* (London: Merlin Press, 1963).

22. De Boissière, personal communication, November 23, 1978.

23. Caribbean critic Vishnudat Singh in his otherwise interesting article on the 1981 edition of the novel, "Ralph de Boissière's *Crown Jewel* and Trinidad Society in the Turbulent Thirties," in *West Indian Literature and Its Social Context*, ed. Mark A. McWatt (Cave Hill, Barbados: U.W.I., Department of English, 1985), pp. 18–32, is unaware of the existence of the NWA and Jim Barrette and therefore sees in Le Maître only a "Butler-type leader."

24. Quoted in Keith Q. Warner, *The Trinidad Calypso: A Study of the Calypso as Oral Literature* (London: Heinemann, 1983), p. 22.

25. In this section of the chapter all page references in parentheses are to Ralph de Boissière, *Rum and Coca-Cola* (Melbourne: Australasian Book Society, 1956).

26. De Boissière, *Crown Jewel*, pp. 422–423.

27. De Boissière, personal communication, January 16, 1979.

CONCLUSION

When in 1972 the University of the West Indies conferred the degree of Doctor of Letters on Alfred H. Mendes, in recognition of his pioneering contribution to West Indian writing, the Trinidad playwright Douglas Archibald wrote a brief appreciation of his work for the pages of *The Trinidadian Guardian*. He reiterated the significance of the two magazines, *Trinidad* and *The Beacon*, in which Mendes's early work had appeared, and the way in which the group of writers around the magazines had "set out to shock the society." In Archibald's opinion, "Trinidad has never been the same since then."[1] This study has set out some of the ways in which the writers and intellectuals connected with the magazines were able to influence the social and political climate of the colony in preparation for the struggle for independence that began in earnest with the upheavals of 1937. The group produced a body of fiction which anticipates in several respects the themes and linguistic features in the work of the writers who followed them in the 1950s and were able to establish the international reputation of the literature of the region. In addition, the early writers set a precedent for successful local publication that must have given subsequent writers the confidence to produce their own work locally.

The precedent of local publication was not solely restricted to the group's publication of the two early literary magazines. Their 1937 anthology broke new ground: Its editor, Albert Gomes, in spite of his earlier success with *The Beacon* (which at the height of its notoriety sold up to 5,000 copies per issue) recalls that he initially doubted whether a collection of local short fiction and poetry could have similar success:

When I was preparing *From Trinidad* for the printer, I asked a prominent Trinidad lawyer what he thought of the proposed publication. "Well, you are a pioneer; you enjoy this sort of thing in Trinidad." That, in so many words, was his reply. The same reply, differently worded, but conveying the same meaning, came from many of my friends. *From Trinidad* was successful in a way that surprised my own fervent optimism. It sold well and was praised by persons whose discernment and sincerity I have never had any reason to doubt.[2]

Albert Gomes went on to publish two of his own poetry collections and his lead was followed by others: In 1939, C. A. Thomasos, a regular contributor to *The Beacon*, published his *Poems*, and A. M. Clarke and R. C. Brown coauthored a short-story collection. Both publishing ventures were favorably reviewed in the revived *Beacon* of November 1939. Gomes began his review of Thomasos's poems by stating: "Another book of poems from a local poet. They will continue to appear. Self-publication is the only solution left to the writer in these parts. Establish your own integrity, write— and be your own publisher."[3]

Poetry in particular seems to have mushroomed in the late 1930s and 1940s, so that by 1943 one of the newer writers, A. M. Clarke, was able to assemble and privately publish the first representative collection of local verse, entitled *Best Poems of Trinidad*. The work of a number of writers who had been connected with the *Beacon* group figured prominently in the anthology, among them Hugh Stollmeyer, Ernest Carr, C. A. Thomasos, Alfred Mendes, Neville Giuseppi, Albert Gomes, Alfred Cruickshank, and Felix Ramon-Fortuné. The anthology also included works by other new writers apart from Clarke himself, such as Harold Telemaque and Edgar Mittelholzer, who after the publication of his first novel, *Corentyne Thunder* (1941), had moved from Guyana to Trinidad. Further publications during the 1940s reinforced the continuity between the new writers and the *Beacon* pioneers: Ernest Carr joined forces with A. M. Clarke to produce *Ma Mamba and Other Stories* which contained six stories by Clarke and eight stories by Carr, including revised versions of "Black Mother" and "The Box" which had originally appeared in *The Beacon*. Clarke undertook a similar venture in poetry with the new poet, Harold Telemaque, and in *Burnt Bush* (1947) published 26 of his own poems and 35 of Telemaque's. The collection deserves special attention as it gives the first intimations that Trinidad poetry was beginning to catch up with Trinidad prose and break with the tradition of Romantic and Victorian imitation. The collection was dedicated to "The New West Indian."

It is the Caribbean . . . that has produced these poems. . . . These Islands have educated us. . . . We have toddled on Caribbean hills and plucked Caribbean flowers. We have listened to the moaning of Caribbean winds by the sea. . . . Art grows as the ideal of self grows, and it is in the midst of this growing that Caribbean art is now produced. It is in its midst that Caribbean effort is happily multiplying and developing a manner of its own.[4]

The new note struck in this collection has since been overshadowed by the appearance of Derek Walcott's epoch-marking *25 Poems* (1948) and *Epitaph for the Young* (1949), the former having been published for the St. Lucian writer by the Guardian Printery in Trinidad. However, *Burnt Bush* was noted and favorably reviewed in the Barbadian magazine *Bim*, which singled out Telemaque's poem "In Our Land" as a fitting epithet for the new spirit of West Indian poetry.[5] The first stanza of the poem reads:

> In our land,
> Poppies do not spring
> From atoms of young blood,
> So gaudily where men have died:
> In our land,
> Stiletto cane blades
> Sink into our hearts
> And drink our blood.[6]

In the poem, Telemaque is able to combine modern themes and an awareness of local color with the sense of separateness from modern European imagery which the poets of the *Beacon* group had felt but were unable to control.

The stress which the authors of *Burnt Bush* placed on the regional nature of the Caribbean experience takes up the concern for a West Indian literary tradition often voiced in the pages of the *Beacon*. The early Trinidad magazine's contacts with writers and intellectuals in other West Indian territories, especially Barbados, has been noted in this study. These links were maintained and developed in the 1940s with the appearance of the new regional magazines, *Bim* (1942–) and *Kyk-over-al* (1945–1961). Contacts between Trinidad writers and *Bim* date from the arrival of George Lamming in Trinidad in 1946. Lamming, who lived and worked in Trinidad from 1946 to 1950, when he left for England, recalls that during this period he "met and started bringing together people to send things [to *Bim*]."[7] The December 1948 issue of *Bim*, in which the review of *Burnt Bush* appeared, in fact marks the beginning of *Bim*'s role as a regional magazine. Its editor, Frank Collymore, states in the foreword: "We take very great pleasure in introducing to our readers a group of five writers from Trinidad. Three of these, Messrs. Telemaque, [Cecil] Herbert and Lamming, have been recently acclaimed as serious poets by Mr. Swanzy, Editor of the popular *Caribbean Voices* programme."[8] Subsequently, the December 1949 issue of the magazine featured a number of old *Beacon* contributors including Stephen Haweis, Alfred Mendes, Ernest Carr, and Albert Gomes, as well as some of the newer names such as Samuel Selvon, E. M. Roach, Douglas Archibald, Barnabas Ramon-Fortuné, and the Trinidad residents Lamming and Mittelholzer. With its appeal to a wider regional audience,

Bim was able to extend the audience for the work of some of the writers of the 1930s who had only published previously in local magazines and collections. It is worth noting that though Barbados and Jamaica are often referred to as the focus of literary activity in the 1940s, Trinidad was able to attract a number of important new writers from other territories. George Lamming, Edgar Mittelholzer and, to a lesser extent through publication, Derek Walcott were all part of the continuing Trinidad-based literary tradition that had begun with the *Beacon* group.

The contact between the newer writers in Trinidad and the *Beacon* pioneers was not merely restricted to casual alliances arising out of their joint appearance in local anthologies and regional magazines. Some of them met in formal and informal literary gatherings similar to those held in the heyday of the 1930s magazines. One of the most important of these seems to have been organized by the English Judge Ernest Hallinan during the latter part of the 1940s. Both George Lamming in *The Pleasures of Exile* and V. S. Naipaul in *A House for Mr. Biswas* have made references to this circle.[9] Though Lamming denies having actually attended meetings of the group he seems to have met with a number of its members more informally and was in close contact with two of them, Ernest Carr and Edgar Mittelholzer. Here again the links between old and new writers become evident, as Ernest Carr seems to have been one of the younger writer's mentors. Lamming has described Carr as someone he "admired and . . . came . . . to regard with deep affection and gratitude. . . . I often went to Carr's house at the edge of some magnificent forest in Belmont, and those conversations were among the best things that happened to me in Trinidad."[10]

Apart from Carr and Mittelholzer, the Judge Hallinan group included former *Beacon* contributors: Giuseppi, Thomasos, and A. C. Farrell; as well as younger writers: Telemaque, Barnabas Ramon-Fortuné, Errol Hill and V. S. Naipaul's father, Seepersad Naipaul. In 1947 the group published an anthology of the work of its members entitled *Papa Bois*, consisting mostly of poetry. Seepersad Naipaul's contribution, however, was a short autobiographical piece, "They Named Him Mohun." V. S. Naipaul was later to "cannibalize" this piece.[11]—to use his own phase—for the beginning of his novel, *A House for Mr. Biswas*, an act which points to one of the most direct forms of continuity between the two generations of Trinidad writers. In the introduction to the enlarged and revised version of the elder Naipaul's short-story collection, *Gurudeva and Other Indian Tales* (1943), V. S. Naipaul has acknowledged his indebtedness to his father's stories and claims that he has come to "see them now as a valuable part of the literature of the region."[12] He goes on to mention two aspects of the local publication of creative writing in Trinidad during his childhood that influenced his own later career as a novelist. For a start, the mechanics of local, self-financed publishing ventures such as those in which his father became involved gave him his first "introduction to book-making."

The printing was done, slowly, by the Guardian Commercial Printery; my father brought the proofs home bit by bit in his jacket pocket; and I shared his hysteria when the linotypists, falling into everyday ways, set—permanently, as it turned out—two of the stories in narrow newspaper-style columns.[13]

The production of *Gurudeva and Other Indian Tales* gave V. S. Naipaul "a way of looking, an example of labour, a knowledge of the literary process, a sense of the order and special reality (at once simpler and sharper than life) that written words could be seen to create."[14]

The second aspect of local publication which influenced Naipaul is related to the "sense of the order and special reality" of fiction which he discovered in his father's publishing efforts. Naipaul points out in an earlier article that he was always very much aware of the discrepancy between the fictional reality of the English novels he read at school and the actual reality of Trinidad life. Initially the English novels offered him by way of mental adaption or transposition a kind of organized structure with which he could bring creative order into what he considered to be chaotic about life in Trinidad. This method of organizing experience, however, imposed severe creative limitations: "I might adapt Dickens to Trinidad; but it seemed impossible that the life I knew in Trinidad could ever be turned into a book."[15] It was at this point that the rudiments of a literary tradition established by the *Beacon* group and maintained in the local publications which continued to appear in the 1940s became important to him as alternative models to the English novelists, as he points out:

Something of more pertinent virtue was needed, and this was provided by some local short stories. These stories, perhaps a dozen in all, never published outside Trinidad, converted what I saw into "writing." It was through them that I began to appreciate the distorting, distilling power of the writer's art. Where I had seen a drab haphazardness they found order; where I would have attempted to romanticize, to render my subject equal with what I had read, they accepted. They provided a starting-point for further observation; they did not trigger off fantasy. Every writer is, in the long run, on his own; but it helps, in the most practical way, to have a tradition. The English language was mine; the tradition was not.[16]

Landeg White in his study *V. S. Naipaul: A Critical Introduction* (1975) has suggested with uncharacteristic inaccuracy that the stories referred to by Naipaul were "no doubt [his father's stories] (together possibly with one or two others by such writers as Mendes, Gomes, and C. L. R. James)"[17]— Gomes after all wrote poetry and articles rather than short stories. In his anxiety to follow through his investigation of the relationship between the work of Seepersad Naipaul and his son, White dismisses other possible influences in a single parenthesis.[18] It falls outside the scope of this study to do more than indicate where direct or indirect links between the *Beacon* group and the later generation of West Indian writers may possibly have occurred, but there seems to be a good case for suggesting that the barrack-yard stories of Mendes and James may have played a much more important part in Naipaul's literary development than White seems here to credit them with. Naipaul was certainly aware of Mendes's stories, which continued to be published in the pages of *The Trinidad Guardian* during the time that his father worked for the newspaper. In the preface to the new edition of *Gurudeva* he even mentions that Mendes was paid "as much as twenty dollars, four guineas, for a story in the *Guardian* Sunday supplement; my father only got five dollars, a guinea."[19] In addition, the features that Naipaul associates with those earlier local short stories—acceptance rather than romanticization, aesthetic distortion and distillation rather than "drab haphazardness"—are most characteristic of the *Beacon* barrack-yard genre. Naipaul's first written book *Miguel Street* (1959), a series of related short stories, is the direct descendant of James's *Minty Alley* and the barrack-yard stories of Mendes.

Mendes's new stories and republications in the pages of *The Trinidad Guardian* after 1940 may also have played some part in the literary education of another Trinidad writer of the 1950s: Samuel Selvon, who edited the literary section of *The Trinidad Guardian Weekly* in the years immediately preceding his departure for England in 1950. Some of Selvon's first stories were published in the columns of the weekly magazine. A short story such as "Wartime Activities," which was included in the collection *Ways of Sunlight* (1957) and describes the brief foray of an Indian cane-cutter into the heady underworld of wartime Port of Spain, has a familiar ring, with its description of Mavis "washing clothes in a tub of nasty water in the yard," and her credulous keeper, Dumboy.[20] Selvon seems to have kept clear of most of the literary groups in Trinidad during the 1940s so that any influence which the earlier writer may have had on his work is unlikely to have come from sources other than the pages of *The Trinidad Guardian*.

Perhaps this study has gone some of the way toward filling one gap in the literary history of the West Indies. In Trinidad the continuous record of local publication throughout the 1930s and 1940s and the singular achievements of the novels published by Mendes and James seem to suggest an organic link between the early work and the emergence of Naipaul and Selvon. From the perspective of the 1980s, there seems also to be a well-defined pattern of development in the changing attitudes of the writers over the years to the themes and settings of their fiction. James's and Mendes's exploration of the barrack-yard in *Black Fauns* and *Minty Alley* are extended in Naipaul's *Miguel Street* to incorporate a whole street and a greater diversity of characters and situations than could formerly have been treated within the scope of the yard. Naipaul's early work approximates the sympathetic treatment of lower-class characters in the earlier barrack-yard novels. His tone changes to satire in *The Mystic Masseur* (1957) and *The Suffrage of Elvira* (1958) and ultimately to the complex mixture of sympathy and ironic detachment that pervades *A House for Mr. Biswas* (1961). Naipaul's sympathetic treatment of the yard in *Miguel Street* is different in origin from that of James and Mendes: Whereas the earlier writers made conscious contact with the barrack-yard because they sensed in it some positive potential lacking in the middle class, Naipaul's sympathy is the reverse face of the profound relief of his developing narrator who sees his escape from the street as the only way through the obstacles to personal ambition or achievement by which its inhabitants are hedged in.

Naipaul was only a very young child when the 1937 upheavals took place in Trinidad, and his impressions of his society are those associated with the war years and the postwar era in which an increasingly philistine middle class had begun to dominate the cultural and political life of the island. His pessimism about Trinidad society as a whole is similar in some respects to Mendes's reaction to the death-bound culture presented in his first novel, *Pitch Lake*, which was written before the optimistic phase of Trinidad writing that accompanied the formation of a militant working-class movement. Of all the Trinidad writers, Ralph de Boissière was most strongly influenced by these developments which transformed him into a committed left-wing writer, able to sustain his optimistic vision of the island's future in spite of the fact that he registered the proliferation of the Joe Eliases and the La Roches of the postwar years in his novels, *Crown Jewel* and *Rum and Coca-Cola*. These figures recur in Naipaul's political novel *The Mystic Masseur* and are mercilessly satirized, but from a perspective that lacks the constructive impulse of de Boissière.

Samuel Selvon's work also picks up the threads of the earlier fiction. His first novel, *A Brighter Sun*, covers similar ground to that of *Rum and Coca-Cola*. His perspective on the war years and the American presence in Trinidad shows certain affinities to Ralph de Boissière's ambivalence about the drastic changes which occurred at all levels of Trinidad society as well as his optimism for the future. However, Selvon's optimism is more politically naive than that of the earlier writer: It is rooted in the belief that a national identity crossing all class and racial lines is being forged, and will eventually bring salvation and true independence to the island. Selvon, like the early barrack-yard writers, has continuously asserted the positive, life-giving potential of the indigenous, lower-class culture. His novels have developed the use of creole introduced in the barrack-yard stories and have extended its use to the narrative voice in several of his works. Even where the narrative voice uses Standard English, both he and Naipaul have, like James and Mendes, been able to suggest a West Indian idiom in their manipulation of the nuances of Trinidad speech.

One final and all-pervasive link between the writers of the 1930s and those of the post–World War II era, which has been touched upon throughout this study, is their mutual indebtedness to the Trinidad calypso. Trinidad writers since the late 1920s have been influenced by such European literary conventions as social realism, naturalism, critical realism, and, more recently, modernism. They have influenced each other's writing and created a distinctive literary tradition, but perhaps it may yet be shown that the form and content of the calypso has had as strong an impact on the form and content of Trinidad fiction as any or all of these factors. Such an investigation, however, would demand a study all of its own.[21]

NOTES

1. Douglas Archibald, "Alfred Mendes: An Appreciation," *The Trinidad Guardian*, January 27, 1972.

2. Albert Gomes, "Preface," in *Best Poems of Trinidad*, ed. A. M. Clarke (Trinidad: Frasers Printerie, 1943), p. 3.

3. *The Beacon*, 4, 1 (November, 1939), 17.

4. H. M. Telemaque and A. M. Clarke, *Burnt Bush* (Trinidad: Frasers Printerie, 1947), p. 8.

5. See *Bim*, 3, 9 (December, 1948), 74–77. This review was written by Gordon O. Bell, editor of *The Forum Quarterly* in the 1930s and *The Forum Magazine* in the 1940s. Bell was a contributor to *The Beacon*.

6. Telemaque and Clarke, *Burnt Bush*, pp. 17–18.

7. "Interview with George Lamming," in *Kas-Kas: Interviews with Three Caribbean Writers in Texas*, ed. Ian Munro and Reinhard Sander (Austin: University of Texas, African and Afro-American Research Institute, 1972), p. 8.

8. *Bim*, 3, 9 (December, 1948), 1.

9. See George Lamming, *The Pleasures of Exile* (London: Michael Joseph, 1960), p. 39; V. S. Naipaul, *A House for Mr. Biswas* (Harmondsworth: Penguin, 1969), pp. 478–479, 484–485.

10. Lamming, *Pleasures*, p. 39.

11. See V. S. Naipaul, "Foreword," in *The Adventures of Gurudeva and Other Stories* by Seepersad Naipaul (London: André Deutsch, 1976), p. 19.

12. Ibid.

13. Ibid., p. 7.

14. Ibid., p. 19.

15. V. S. Naipaul, "Jasmine," in *The Overcrowded Barracoon and Other Articles* (Harmondsworth: Penguin, 1972), p. 26.

16. Ibid., p. 27.

17. Landeg White, *V. S. Naipaul: A Critical Introduction* (London: Macmillan, 1975), p. 41.

18. White's single-mindedness seems to have led him to overlook sources of Trinidad writing outside the pages of *The Trinidad Guardian*, where most of Seepersad Naipaul's work appeared. In consequence he missed the Hallinan group's *Papa Bois* in the Trinidad Central Library, which contained Seepersad Naipaul's "They Named Him Mohun." This story would undoubtedly have provided his study

of the relationship between the work of the two Naipauls with its *pièce de resistance*.

19. Naipaul, "Foreword," p. 9.

20. See Samuel Selvon, "Wartime Activities," in *Ways of Sunlight* (London: Longman, 1973), pp. 82–93.

21. Some groundwork for this type of investigation has been provided in Keith Q. Warner, *The Trinidad Calypso: A Study of the Calypso as Oral Literature* (London: Heinemann, 1983), especially the chapter on "The Calypso in Trinidad Literature," pp. 123–138.

BIBLIOGRAPHY

PRIMARY SOURCES AND CRITICISM

Birbalsingh, F. M. "The Literary Achievement of C. L. R. James." *The Journal of Commonwealth Literature*, 19, 1 (1984), 108–121.

—. "The Novels of Ralph de Boissière." *The Journal of Commonwealth Literature*, 9 (July, 1970), 104–108.

Calder-Marshall, Arthur. *Glory Dead*. London: Michael Joseph, 1939.

Carr, Ernest A., and A. M. Clarke. *Ma Mamba and Other Stories*. Trinidad: n.p., n.d.

Clarke, A. M., ed. *Best Poems of Trinidad*. Trinidad: Frasers Printerie, 1943.

De Boissière, Ralph. *Crown Jewel*. Melbourne: Australasian Book Society, 1952; Leipzig: Paul List, 1956. Rev. ed. London: Allison and Busby; Picador, 1981.

—. *No Saddles for Kangaroos*. Sydney: Australasian Book Society, 1964.

—. "On Writing a Novel." *The Journal of Commonwealth Literature*, 17, 1 (1982), 1–12.

—. *Rum and Coca-Cola*. Melbourne: Australasian Book Society, 1956. Rev. ed. London: Allison and Busby, 1984.

Fullerton, Janet. "Women in Trinidadian Life and Literature." *The New Voices*, 5, 9 (March, 1977), 9–31.

Gomes, Albert M. *All Papa's Children*. Surrey: Cairi Publishing House, 1978.

—. "The Beacon." *Kraus Bibliographical Bulletin*, 21 (August, 1977), 158–159.

—. *First Poems*. Port of Spain: The Author, n.d.

—. *Poems 1939*. Port of Spain: The Author, n.d.

—. *Through a Maze of Colour*. Port of Spain: Key Caribbean Publications, 1974.

—, ed. *The Beacon*. Trinidad, 1931–33, 1939. Repr. Millwood, N.Y.: Kraus Reprint Co., 1977.

————, ed. *From Trinidad: A Selection from the Fiction and Verse of the Island of Trinidad, British West Indies.* Port of Spain: Frasers Printerie, 1937.

Gonzalez, Anson. *Self-Discovery through Literature: Creative Writing in Trinidad and Tobago.* Trinidad: The author, 1972.

————. *Trinidad and Tobago Literature on Air.* Port of Spain: The National Cultural Council, 1974.

Hodge, Merle. "Peeping Tom in the Nigger Yard." *Tapia*, 25 (Sunday, April 2, 1972), 11–12.

James, C. L. R. "The Black Jacobins." In *A Time . . . and a Season: 8 Caribbean Plays.* Ed. Errol Hill. Trinidad: University of the West Indies, Extra-Mural Studies Unit, 1976, pp. 355–420.

————. "Discovering Literature in Trinidad: The Nineteen-Thirties." *Savacou*, 2 (September, 1970), 54–60.

————. *Minty Alley.* London: Secker and Warburg, 1936. Repr. London and Port of Spain: New Beacon Books, 1971.

Mendes, Alfred H. *Black Fauns.* London: Duckworth, 1935. Repr. London and Port of Spain: New Beacon Books, 1984.

————. *Pitch Lake: A Story from Trinidad.* London: Duckworth, 1934. Repr. London and Port of Spain: New Beacon Books, 1980.

————. "Talking about the Thirties." Interview with Clifford Sealy. *Voices*, 1, 5 (December, 1965), 3–7.

————, and C. L. R. James, eds. *Trinidad.* Trinidad, 1929–1930.

Munro, Ian, and Reinhard Sander, eds. *Kas-Kas: Interviews with Three Caribbean Writers in Texas.* Austin: University of Texas, African and Afro-American Research Institute, 1972.

Papa Bois. Port of Spain: n.p., n.d.

Ramchand, Kenneth. "The Alfred Mendes Story." *Tapia*, 7, 22 (Sunday, May 29, 1977), 6–7; 7, 23 (Sunday, June 5, 1977), 6–7, 9; 7, 25 (Sunday, June 19, 1977), 6–7.

Salkey, Andrew, ed. *Stories from the Caribbean.* London: Paul Elek Books, 1965.

Sander, Reinhard, ed. "A Caribbean Writer in Australia: An Interview with Ralph de Boissière." *Komparatistische Hefte*, 5/6 (1982), 195–208.

————, ed. *From Trinidad: An Anthology of Early West Indian Writing.* London: Hodder & Stoughton; New York: Holmes & Meier, 1978.

————, ed. "The Turbulent Thirties in Trinidad: An Interview with Alfred H. Mendes." *World Literature Written in English*, 12, 1 (April, 1973), 66–79.

Sealy, Clifford. "A Backward Glance: *Crown Jewel.*" *Voices*, 2, 4 (April, 1977), 8–11.

————. "*Crown Jewel*: A Note on Ralph de Boissière." *Voices*, 2, 3 (March, 1973), 1–3.

Singh, Vishnudat. "Ralph de Boissière's *Crown Jewel* and Trinidad Society in the Turbulent Thirties." In *West Indian Literature and Its Social Context*, ed. Mark McWatt. Cave Hill, Barbados: U. W.I., Dept. of English, 1985, pp. 18–32.

Telemaque, H. M., and A. M. Clarke, *Burnt Bush.* Trinidad: Frasers Printerie, 1947.

GENERAL SOURCES AND CRITICISM

Baxter, Ivy. *The Arts of an Island: The Development of the Culture and of the Folk and Creative Arts in Jamaica 1494–1962 (Independence).* Metuchen, N.J.: The Scarecrow Press, 1970.

Brown, Lloyd W. *West Indian Poetry.* Boston: Twayne Publishers, 1978.

Cabral, Amilcar. "Identity and Dignity in the Context of the National Liberation Struggle." In *Return to the Source: Selected Speeches of Amilcar Cabral.* Ed. Africa Information Service. New York and London: Monthly Review Press, 1973, pp. 57–69.

Cobham-Sander, Rhonda. *The Creative Writer and West Indian Society: Jamaica 1900–1950.* Ann Arbor: University Microfilms International, 1982.

Corsbie, Ken. *Theatre in the Caribbean.* London: Hodder & Stoughton, 1984.

Cudjoe, Selwyn R. *Resistance and the Caribbean Novel.* Athens, Ohio: University of Ohio Press, 1979.

Dathorne, O. R. *Dark Ancestor: The Literature of the Black Man in the Caribbean.* Baton Rouge and London: Louisiana State University Press, 1981.

Fanon, Frantz. *The Wretched of the Earth.* Harmondsworth: Penguin, 1971.

Gilkes, Michael. *The West Indian Novel.* Boston: Twayne Publishers, 1981.

Hill, Errol, ed. *The Artist in West Indian Society: A Symposium.* Trinidad: University of the West Indies, Department of Extra-Mural Studies, 1963.

James, C. L. R. *At the Rendezvous of Victory: Selected Writings.* London: Allison & Busby, 1984.

———. *Beyond a Boundary.* London: Hutchinson, 1963.

———. *The Future in the Present: Selected Writings.* London: Allison & Busby, 1977.

———. *The Making of the Caribbean Peoples.* London: Bogle L'Ouverture Publications, 1968.

———. *Spheres of Existence: Selected Writings.* London: Allison & Busby, 1980.

James, Louis. *The Islands in Between: Essays on West Indian Literature.* London: Oxford University Press, 1968.

King, Bruce, ed. *West Indian Literature.* London: Macmillan, 1979.

Lamming, George. "Caribbean Politics from 1930s to Tense 70s." *Caribbean Contact*, 5, 11 (March, 1978), 10–11.

———. *The Pleasures of Exile.* London: Michael Joseph, 1960.

Lukács, Georg. *The Meaning of Contemporary Realism.* London: Merlin Press, 1963.

Moore, Gerald. *The Chosen Tongue: English Writing in the Tropical World.* London: Longmans, 1969.

Morris, Mervyn. "The All Jamaica Library." *Jamaica Journal*, 6, 1 (March, 1972), 47–49.

Naipaul, Seepersad. *The Adventures of Gurudeva and Other Stories.* London: André Deutsch, 1976.

Naipaul, V. S. *A House for Mr. Biswas.* London: André Deutsch, 1961.

———. *The Middle Passage.* London: André Deutsch, 1962.

———. *Miguel Street.* London: André Deutsch, 1959.

———. *The Mystic Masseur.* London: André Deutsch, 1957.

———. *The Overcrowded Barracoon and Other Articles.* London: André Deutsch, 1972.

———. *The Suffrage of Elvira.* London: André Deutsch, 1958.

Omotoso, Kole. *The Theatrical into the Theatre: A Study of the Drama and Theatre of the English-Speaking Caribbean.* London and Port of Spain: New Beacon Books, 1982.

Ramchand, Kenneth. *An Introduction to the Study of West Indian Literature.* London: Nelson, 1976.

——. *The West Indian Novel and Its Background.* London: Faber & Faber, 1970.

Rohlehr, Gordon. "The Development of the Calypso: 1900–1940." Unpublished cyclostyled paper, 1972.

Selvon, Samuel. *A Brighter Sun.* London: Alan Wingate, 1952.

——. *An Island Is a World.* London: Alan Wingate, 1956.

——. *The Lonely Londoners.* London: Alan Wingate, 1956.

——. *Turn Again Tiger.* London: MacGibbon and Kee, 1958.

——. *Ways of Sunlight.* London: MacGibbon and Kee, 1957.

Thomas, J. J. *West Indian Fables Explained.* London and Port of Spain: New Beacon Books, 1969.

Warner, Keith Q. *The Trinidad Calypso: A Study of the Calypso as Oral Literature.* London: Heinemann, 1983.

White, Landeg. *V. S. Naipaul: A Critical Introduction.* London: Macmillan, 1975.

BACKGROUND MATERIAL

Baptiste, Fitz A. *The United States and West Indian Unrest: 1918–1939.* Working Paper No. 18. Jamaica: University of the West Indies, Institute of Social and Economic Research, 1978.

Carnegie, James. *Some Aspects of Jamaica's Politics: 1918–1938.* Kingston: Institute of Jamaica, 1973.

Charles, Wendy. *Early Labour Organization in Trinidad and the Colonial Context of the Butler Riots.* Working Papers on Caribbean Society, Series C, No. 1. Trinidad: University of the West Indies, 1978.

De Boissière, Jean. *Trinidad: Land of the Rising Inflexion.* Trinidad: n.p., n.d.

Guérin, Daniel. *The West Indies and Their Future.* London: Dennis Dobson, 1961.

Jacobs, W. Richard, ed. *Butler Versus the King: Riots and Sedition in 1937.* Port of Spain: Key Caribbean Publications, 1976.

James, C. L. R. *The Black Jacobins: Toussaint L'Ouverture and the San Domingo Revolution.* New York: Vintage Books, 1963.

——. *The Case for West Indian Self-Government.* London: Hogarth Press, 1933.

——. *A History of Pan-African Revolt.* Washington, D.C.: Drum and Spear Press, 1969.

——. *The Life of Captain Cipriani: An Account of British Government in the West Indies.* Nelson, Lancs.: The author, 1932.

——. *Modern Politics.* Port of Spain: P. N. M. Publishing Co., 1960.

——. *Party Politics in the West Indies.* Trinidad: The author, 1962.

Joseph, C. L. "The British West Indies Regiment: 1914–1918." *The Journal of Caribbean History,* 2 (May, 1971), 94–124.

Lewis, Gordon K. *The Growth of the Modern West Indies.* New York and London: Monthly Review Press, 1969.

Lewis, W. Arthur. *Labour in the West Indies: The Birth of a Workers' Movement.* London and Port of Spain: New Beacon Books, 1977.

Oilfields Workers' Trade Union: July 1937–July 1977. Trinidad, 1977.

Ottley, C. R. *The Trinidad Callaloo: Life in Trinidad from 1851–1900*. Trinidad: Crusoe Publishing House, 1978.

Rennie, Bukka. *The History of the Working Class in the 20th Century (1919–1956): The Trinidad and Tobago Experience*. Toronto and Trinidad: New Beginning Movement, 1973.

Williams, Eric. *From Columbus to Castro: The History of the Caribbean 1492–1969*. London: André Deutsch, 1970.

———. *History of the People of Trinidad and Tobago*. London: André Deutsch, 1964.

———. *Inward Hunger: The Education of a Prime Minister*. London: André Deutsch, 1969.

INDEX

About the Author

REINHARD W. SANDER is Associate Professor of Comparative Literature at Hampshire College and the Five College Consortium in Amherst, Massachusetts. He is the editor or coeditor of *Studies in Commonwealth Literature, Veronica My Daughter and Other Onitsha Market Plays and Stories by Ogali A. Ogali,* and *From Trinidad: An Anthology of Early West Indian Writing.* His numerous articles on African, Afro-American, and Caribbean literature have appeared in such diverse publications as *Research in African Literatures, World Literature Written in English, Journal of Commonwealth Literature, Ba Shiru, Bim, Caribbean Quarterly,* and *Studies in Black Literature.*